JAMES HIRD
READING THE PLAY

JAMES HIRD

READING THE PLAY

on life and leadership

MACMILLAN
Pan Macmillan Australia

First published 2006 in Macmillan by Pan Macmillan Australia Pty Ltd
1 Market Street, Sydney

National Library of Australia
cataloguing-in-publication data:

Hird, James.
Reading the play: on life and leadership.

ISBN 9781405037648.
ISBN 1 40503764 4.

1. Hird, James. 2. Australian football players – Biography.
3. Australian football players – Anecdotes. I. Title.

796.336092

Cover design by Mark Thacker, Big Cat Design
Set in 11.5/16.5 pt Sabon by Midland Typesetters, Australia
Printed in Australia by McPherson's Printing Group

Papers used by Pan Macmillan Australia Pty Ltd are natural,
recyclable products made from wood grown in sustainable forests.
The manufacturing processes conform to the environmental
regulations of the country of origin.

To Mum, Dad and my sisters . . . Every day I am reminded of the terrific childhood I had. The love and happiness that surrounded my life as a child is something I try to replicate in my adult life.

To Tania . . . You are my best friend, lover and teacher. Together with our three beautiful children, Stephanie, Thomas and Alexander, you inspire me with your love. I hope that one day they will get as much fulfilment from their family as we have from ours.

In particular, Tania, I would like to especially thank you for your enormous help in writing and editing this book.

My one wish is that Steph's, Tom's and Alex's dreams all come true, just as mine have.

Contents

Introduction

The power of a dream should not be underestimated. Dreams have always inspired men and women to great achievements.

This book is about a boy whose dream ended up being his life. The dream had twists and turns, and there were certainly setbacks, including bad injuries and depressingly long recoveries and sometimes heartbreaking attempts to return to the football field. But most of what that boy dreamed as a child growing up in Canberra came true.

When I was young I had dreams about great things, about what would happen in my life. As people get older, they call them goals, objectives or a vision, but when you're seven, you call them dreams. Mine were very specific.

When I was 10, my father asked me what I wanted to do. I looked at him and said, 'I want to captain Essendon to a premiership, marry a blonde girl and live happily ever after.' All of that happened. As time went on, the dream included having children. Again the dream came true. I have three beautiful children – Stephanie, Thomas and Alexander – and they are all different. As long as our family has its strength, and its close bond, anything that happens in our lives will be part of a tremendous journey. This is what faith, love and dreaming can do.

I'm 33 now, and it's frightening sometimes to see how many of the dreams I had as a 10-year-old have come true.

I believe in dreams, and I believe in instinct, in the power of the gut feeling. I do analyse situations, but I usually make up my mind about things very quickly. With a few exceptions, this has worked for me.

Here's one really important example. I was a shy and daggy teenager, and I didn't have many girlfriends. Maybe it was my total obsession with sport and my corresponding lack of experience with girls that led to my having so little confidence with them. Whatever it was, over time, playing football at an elite level boosted my sense of self-worth to a point where I could at least approach a girl and talk to her. One Saturday night in 1993 at the Grand Hotel in Essendon I made a decision to speak to a beautiful and sexy girl working behind the bar. I was operating on pure adrenaline, and possibly a touch of stupidity, but I did it. That turned out to be the biggest and best decision of my life.

I knew within hours of meeting this girl that she was special. My gut said yes, and when instinct takes over like that, it is very hard to stop. Yes, I also did a little analysing. She fitted two of the dreams I'd outlined to my father: she was a woman and she was blonde. Like I said, we now have three beautiful children.

Instinct is also a major part of the way I play football. One of the most common questions I'm asked is: 'How is it that you seem to have so much time when you have the ball and in some ways look as if you're moving in slow motion?' My stock answer is that

I don't know. I don't know because I have never analysed it. I hate analysing my own game. I cannot watch videos of myself playing football, and I'm always trying to dodge the coaches during the weekly one-on-one game reviews.

But I will try now to answer the question as best I can. First, I do not have as many things going for me in terms of football as some journalists and analysts would have you think. I have worked hard in the gym over the past 17 or 18 years, but I lack the raw natural power of a Gary Ablett or a Michael Voss. I am also not quick, and so have spent a lot of time over the past 15 years doing sprint training with my old friends Danny Corcoran and John Quinn. And I have small hands, so I don't have the vice-like grip of a Matthew Lloyd or Tony Lockett.

However, I do have good endurance and a strong work ethic, and I love the game passionately. The most important thing, I think, is my love for the game. I certainly don't love the pre-game meeting, or the nerves – I can't sleep the night before a game. I don't love the marketing, and I don't love the newspaper and television interest in me. What I love is when the ball gets bounced in the middle of the MCG: for the next two hours I get to chase it and try to get it as many times as I can.

It's not even kicking goals or taking speccies that I love – I just love getting the football, knowing that everyone else wants it too. The simple thrill of watching the ball, running after it and jumping on it is as sweet as it gets for me.

But perhaps the most important factor is that when I am on the football ground I don't think about anything; whatever I do just happens. People might say, 'What a load of crap', but it's true: you can't run 50 metres flat out, scoop up the ball with one hand, spin around three players and snap the ball over your shoulder from an impossible angle in six seconds and think about it. You don't train for it with specific drills. It just happens.

I am not going to tell people, after I kicked a freak goal while not looking, that I lined it up, thought about the odds and decided I would go for the one in a million rather than taking the pressure off by handballing it to a bloke 15 metres out. That would be lying. What enables you to do these things is belief, belief in your instincts. I train hard because then I know that I can rely on my instincts to kick in. Winston Churchill was once asked how he made his speeches sound so spontaneous. 'Practice, practice and more practice,' he is said to have replied.

On the other hand, even if I trained harder than anyone in the world, if I wasn't trusting the dream, it would all be for nothing.

They've served me well, my instincts.

Chapter 1

Growing Up

There must have been a time when I didn't have a football in my hand – I just can't remember it.

I was born at Canberra Hospital at 3.40 pm on 4 February 1973, the first child of Allan and Margaret Hird. The hospital doesn't exist anymore; it was demolished in 1999. Tragically, a young girl was killed and others were injured by the flying debris from the explosion after many people had gathered by the lake to watch the event. My birth 25 years earlier was, thank goodness, a lot less dramatic.

My mum, Margaret, was a teacher (she's now the principal of a Melbourne primary school). My dad, Allan, worked in the public service, spending some time in the Commonwealth departments of Defence, Transport and finally Education before moving to the ACT government's Department of Education. Mum and Dad met in Melbourne. They married and moved to Canberra in

1969. Dad, who played four games for Essendon in 1966–67, had initiated the move after his appointment as the playing coach of Eastlake in the ACT football competition.

I remained an only child for nearly three years before my sister, Amilia, was born. Two years later Katherine joined us.

I started my life in a house at Ainslie, then moved to Latham, an outer northern Canberra suburb. Ours was a typical 1970s house: brown brick with a native garden. It was a kilometre from a creek, and my friends and I would ride our bikes down there and go fishing or hunt for yabbies. All the things we liked to do were close, and we'd ride our bikes everywhere. It was a very innocent, carefree time. We didn't worry about cars or strangers, as many people do now.

The only danger I faced on my bike was the magpies. From September to November when they were raising their young they'd swoop at those who encroached into their territory. They were quite vicious. Once they had me in their sights, they wouldn't go away. It was my first lesson in protecting myself.

I liked Canberra, and I think my sisters did too. It wasn't quite the country, but it certainly wasn't the Big Smoke, like Sydney or Melbourne. Both my parents were from Melbourne, and they have never lost their love for it. Melbourne was very much their favourite city; my dad's feelings towards Sydney, in contrast, bordered on hatred. People seemed to have much stronger state allegiances in those days. In Canberra, people were generally more pro Sydney, but that was probably because it was so much closer by road than Melbourne. No one could ever change Dad's view. It's ironic that everyone in the family later left Canberra. Dad is the only one who stayed.

I was a very active child, always running and kicking a ball – soccer as well as footy.

But despite my energy, I was not an outgoing kid. I was

actually quite shy, and anger scared me. I remember my Year 1 teacher calling Mum and Dad in to tell them that every time any teacher shouted I'd cower. The teacher probably wondered whether I became so nervous when voices were raised because my mum and dad shouted at me all the time. They didn't, of course. I still don't like shouting. That aside, I have always had an inner confidence in myself, and even though I was quiet, I never had any problem making friends.

My parents were, naturally, the most important influence on me as a child. There was no doubt that they wanted the best for the three of us, and their thinking on that wasn't locked into traditional gender roles. Mum wanted me to be well rounded, so she insisted I take ballet and piano lessons. She thought ballet would help my football. The piano lessons lasted a couple of years; the ballet lessons lasted much less.

School was fun, but learning was not my main focus. All I wanted to do was play sport and run around with my friends.

The usual game was soccer; the only footy at school was an annual one-day carnival. Fortunately, I had a couple of mates who played footy, so after school we'd kick together.

Some people might find it surprising that I developed good Australian Rules football skills in that environment. But I watched and played Australian Rules whenever I could, and the skills I gained playing soccer and rugby helped my football.

Luckily, I had parents who gave me a level of passion for footy that let me see beyond the lack of football available to me. Positive and passionate parents are essential to happy kids. My father knew his football well; he was great with technical advice. But it was his passion and encouragement that gave me the desire to succeed.

As a parent myself now, I see how easy it is to fall into the trap of parenting by stick and carrot. Sticks to beat your kids when they do something wrong and carrots to entice them to do something right. Children look to their parents as leaders, and as a leader you have a choice: you can force your kids to fill the bucket of knowledge using sticks, entice them to fill it using carrots, or give them a bucket, inspire them, and let them fill the bucket with their own passion. My father certainly disciplined me and rewarded me when I did well, but my inspiration and my true love of the game came from his stories . . . and my exposure to grassroots footy.

We had a huge oval across the road from our house, and that's where I escaped to whenever I'd destroyed too many plants in the backyard with the footy. Eventually the oval became the only place I could play footy: my mum extended the garden beds into the lawn, and as if that wasn't bad enough, my parents put a trampoline on the grass for Amilia and Katherine. Desperate measures, perhaps, but they weren't meant to deter me, and they didn't; they were meant to save the backyard, which they did.

If ever there was a city that had plenty of space for kids to play, it was Canberra. It was a great place to grow up and I always felt that I would only leave to go to university or play footy for Essendon.

Even when I was very young, I was acutely aware that the world of football was in Melbourne, so that would be where I had to be. Melbourne was the football capital. It was where football was lived and breathed. It was where the MCG was. It was where the newspapers were full of footy news and photos of the players and the league leader board and all the player votes – which I would pore over each week. It was where you had to be if you were serious about footy. I distinctly remember, as a seven-year-old, lying in my bunk at night dreaming about running away and going to live at the Essendon Football Club until I was old enough to play in the seniors. I'd wait 10 years at Essendon, I thought, until I was about 17 or 18, then run onto the ground and start my career. I thought that if I could convince my cousin Tom to come with me, we'd be right. At the time, it seemed a perfect plan.

As a family we often drove down to Melbourne to see relatives, and it was always an adventure. Sometimes my dad and my uncle and I would go to the MCG to watch the Bombers play. Melbourne was big, compared with Canberra, and I found it a little intimidating. In Canberra, the streets were all wide, there were great bike paths, and there were no corner shops or delis, no tram tracks, no alley-ways. It was all very clean and structured. Every house in Canberra was on a decent-sized block of land. But in Melbourne there were terrace houses joined to each other. I would look at those little houses and think, *How do people actually live in them?* There were sinister-looking alley-ways which, as a young boy, I was hesitant to walk down. For a young Canberra boy, visits to Melbourne were an eye-opener, but even when I was pretty young I knew that one day I would live there.

Obviously, before my dream could be realised, I had to become good enough at football to play for Essendon. So I spent hours kicking a football or soccer ball around. I remember when I was five or six, spending hour after hour in our large backyard (before it was desecrated by my mother's plantings and my sisters' trampoline), which was the perfect shape for pretending you were a real VFL footballer. I'd kick the ball up in the air, then run and mark it.

I would imagine myself playing for Essendon, kicking goals at Windy Hill or the MCG and, in true sporting tradition, I'd also commentate to myself. I was always Tim Watson or Neale Daniher or Terry Daniher: 'Neale Daniher picks it up, dodges one, dodges two, kicks long . . . Watson marks, gives it over to . . . Terry Daniher, who . . . KICKS A GOAL!' I'd yell with my arms up exultantly. I always kicked 20 or more goals. The last goal, the match-saving goal, would be kicked with only five seconds to go and the team five points down.

When I was young there were a few good reasons why I often kicked the ball to myself. First, after Elliott, my next door neighbour, left, there was really no one else to kick the footy to. And second, as I've mentioned, once I went to school I kicked a soccer ball a thousand times more than I kicked a footy. Both at primary school and high school the three football codes were soccer, rugby league and Australian Rules, in that order. I was the smallest kid in my class in Year 7, so rugby used to knock me around a bit. If I wanted to kick a footy with my mates it was up to me to teach them how to play. As a result, I played soccer.

The shrinking backyard issue at our house in Latham was rendered irrelevant when we moved to a suburb called Reid. Our house was next to a group of four huge ovals, which were in total about a kilometre in circumference. They were beautifully manicured: perfect for me. I just stepped over the road to a rugby field, a soccer field, cricket nets, a couple of cricket pitches, and an Aussie Rules field. It was paradise!

We finished high school at 3.20 pm, and if I managed to convince Mum that I would do my homework later I'd be over at the oval with my mates until our mums told us to come home. It was absolutely sensational. And there were no worries about kids getting into trouble back then in Canberra. In summer I'd ride my bike around Lake Burley Griffin with my mates and then jump in for a swim. The lake was only a five-minute ride away. There really was a lot of freedom after school; now, sadly, I find it hard to give my kids the freedom I had.

It was a very outdoors type of life. The three of us kids didn't watch much television. We were allowed to watch *The Goodies* at 6 o'clock on the ABC, and then *Dr Who*. From 6 until 7 on that one night – that was the only TV we watched during the week.

Mum and Dad were just as enthusiastic about these shows as we kids were. Dad would try to get home in time to see the last 10 minutes of *Dr Who*. If he was held up at work, we'd have to fill him in. Mum would follow the show from the kitchen as she prepared dinner. It was quite a family tradition, and at the end of *Dr Who* Amilia would always call out, 'Dinner time', whether dinner was ready or not.

We were an ABC family, by dictate of Mum and Dad. The only time we were allowed to watch commercial stations was if the footy was on. Most of my school mates watched the news on the commercial stations. I asked my parents why we watched the ABC news, and they told me that it was because it was more likely to be right.

But we didn't watch a lot of football on TV, because we used to go and watch the Australian National University (ANU) team play on a Saturday afternoon. My dad left Eastlake after a couple of years and went on to captain-coach ANU. This was true grassroots footy, played on the university campus.

My sisters and I would work the scoreboard or serve in the canteen, which was fantastic: we each got a free pie and soft drink and some lollies, much to Mum's horror. Mum had strong views about the importance of eating healthy food. She was probably a bit before her time in this area. We had plenty of fruit and homemade treats, but she did not like us having lots of lollies and chocolate.

Mum was part of a health food co-op, and for a while it operated out of our house. Bins of food would be dropped off at our place. They'd be put in the garage and people would come on a Saturday morning and buy what they needed at wholesale prices. The only 'lolly' that we kids were allowed to eat was a chocolate substitute called carob. Carob is, in my opinion, a most disgusting-tasting thing. At the time I ate it because it was better than nothing, but give me chocolate any time. It's interesting that Amilia, Katherine and I are all still keen on lollies. Prohibition didn't work for us.

There was also the offal issue. Mum believed that kidney, lambs fry, brains and tongue were all good for us, but we had other ideas. Even today I can't stand them.

But I also ate lots of great-tasting things because I had a mum who believed in home-produced food and liked cooking: homemade pies and pasties, cakes and biscuits, strawberry ice-cream, jams, roast dinners and lots more. As with everything else, you have to take the good with the bad.

Mum and Dad were quite alternative in other ways, too. They weren't hippies, but they were part of that 1960s and '70s generation that was trying to create a new kind of place in society and was concerned with social issues. They were interested in exploring ideas and different ways of thinking. Dad was a great reader. He'd read a lot about communism and European history.

Ours was a household where ideas were discussed and opinions were voiced. We were encouraged to think for ourselves, to challenge what was presented to us, and to not be constrained by orthodoxy.

Mum and Dad both studied at university for what seemed like years. Mum started at uni a month after I was born and was part of a small group who set up the first co-operative crèche in the ACT, at the Australian National University.

My parents were quite politically aware, and left-of-centre in their politics (although my dad has moved to the right as he's got older). I remember as a kid some strange people coming to the house. I have heard my mum say that it was not unusual for her to be farewelling the Catholic priest at the front door as members of the Spartacus League turned up to sell subscriptions to their magazine. In fact, aged just two and a half, I went to Parliament

House with her to protest about the dismissal of the Whitlam government. It was three days before Amilia was born, but that didn't stop Mum.

While my parents' interests were political and social, what ruled my thoughts and conciousness was football. My favourite players were, as mentioned, Tim Watson, Neale Daniher and Terry Daniher. I couldn't understand what had happened to Neale Daniher. I just thought he was missing for a week or two, but then he dropped right off the radar; his brilliant playing career had been cut short by injury. That left Timmy Watson and Terry Daniher as my two heroes.

I loved reading the Melbourne newspapers, with all the results and the match reports. The *Canberra Times*, our local paper, rarely had any footy news. I remember getting *The Age* when Essendon won the Grand Final in 1984, and again in 1985, and pinning up its huge colour spreads of all the highlights, including photos of the great Bomber players like Paul Van Der Haar, Leon Baker, Simon Madden and Tim Watson. I must have had those spreads pinned up in my room for three or four years; Mum now has the scrapbook I finally put them in.

I loved all the game's paraphernalia, and I loved talking about it, but what I loved most was playing it. I was always at my dad to have a kick. Even when he was watching the football on TV, I'd be waiting for half-time so that we could have a kick. I was like a kid on a car trip, but instead of 'Are we there yet?' it was 'Is it half-time yet?'

It was the same when he came home after work: I would pester him constantly to have a kick. There weren't many times when he refused. Even my mum would get out and have a kick with me now and then.

I used to get told off for kicking socks or a footy indoors. There were certain rules about where I could have a kick – and where I couldn't – and I pushed the boundaries all the time. I read a book about Don Bradman practising throwing a ball against a wall and fielding it. So I'd throw a ball against our wall and try to catch it. I started off using a tennis ball, and that was all right, but then I moved on to a cricket ball, and a couple of times I missed the wall and hit a window. Sorry, Mum.

But I did have a hero far closer to home than the Danihers . . .

There he was, my hero, playing football only metres away from me. I was five, and had been lucky enough to get a position on the fence around the oval. My hero only came on at three-quarter-time; he was old (to a five-year-old anyway), and well past his best.

As the ball came down, with only seconds left, he marked, 45 metres out from goal. He went back, had a shot . . . and missed. His team, ANU, lost. After the game there was no retribution, just tinnies, while my hero talked his mates through that missed shot.

On the way home in the car we were all disappointed that my hero – Dad – had missed. 'Next time, Dad,' I said, 'you should wear boots, not runners.'

We weren't rich by any means, but we never noticed that we weren't, and I think Mum and Dad enjoyed their life a lot. We lived in a nice house in a nice suburb and were always able to do the great things that kids loved – my parents had a group of close friends with kids all the same age, so we spent lots of great times together. As a family we'd go on picnics and trips to the Cotter River, we'd play board games, we'd be read to, we'd visit places like the Australian War Memorial (which was across the road), go to any special event and festivals that were on and go camping, to name just a few things. None of these things cost a lot of money, but we did them as a family, and we had fun.

Our holidays were great. As our relatives lived in Melbourne and Brisbane, Amilia, Katherine and I spent many long hours in the back seat of the car. We had no air-conditioning and would start our trip to Brisbane before dawn or late at night to avoid the heat of the day. If we did have to travel in the heat of the day we'd have bottles of frozen water and wet face washers to keep us cool. We used to play the usual games to pass the time, and every now and then the three of us would have a fight about who was taking up too much room. Of course I always got the blame – but maybe I deserved it.

Once we arrived, we'd have a ball. My cousins in Brisbane had a swimming pool, which we would spend hours playing in, and our grandparents always spoilt us. We'd go to either Brisbane or Melbourne for Christmas, and Mum and Dad were very creative with the stories they spun about why Santa delivered big presents such as bikes early.

The other great holidays we had were at Bright, in north-eastern Victoria. We camped there regularly for several years until Mum decided she'd had enough. Our camping equipment was pretty poor. Also, it seemed that everyone of us would get a stomach upset shortly after arriving and Mum was the one who had to continue to manage. By the time things started to improve, it would be time to pack up.

A few years after we stopped camping at Bright, we found some great flats to rent. They had huge grounds with beautiful big trees, and room for cricket, tennis and footy. And the Ovens River was straight through the back gate. Each morning we'd grab our li-los and our rubber tyres and head down the rapids. Dad and my uncle liked to go on drives, so sometimes we'd all load into the car and drive up to Mt Buffalo or the Keiwa Valley or a local winery. At night we'd wander to the amusement park and play mini golf, jump on the giant trampolines and drive the dodgem cars. We'd finish the night with one of those special ice-creams that have several scoops.

One of my great excitements was going to the football in Melbourne. This was a fantastic experience, which would involve a long road trip with my family; a couple of times my Uncle John and my cousin Tom came. The first game I saw was in the late 1970s: Fitzroy and Essendon at the old St Kilda Junction Oval. I was six. Tom was three years older than me and I looked up to him. He was great to go to games with.

Often, though, it was just our family driving from Canberra to Melbourne on a Friday night to go to the footy. These trips were a pretty big adventure, and I loved them. We'd stay at my grandparents' house in Romsey, an hour north-west of Melbourne. Their house was on a few hectares, and it seemed massive to me.

It was always special to be with my grandparents. My grandmother, Joan, could not have loved us more. She always made time for us and always had an endless supply of lollies and treats. This did not quite fit the healthy food model Mum was pushing, but she seemed to understand. She and Joan were special friends: the mother-in-law stereotype didn't apply to them. Also, the treats never affected my appetite for Joan's roast dinners.

My grandfather – who's now 86 – is also special to me. He could be quite gruff at times, but we never took that seriously. When we would come down for the football late on a Friday night he would have a big open fire going. It was very welcoming.

On one of our trips we parked up near one of the hospitals and then walked through the parklands which surround the MCG. I really wanted to wear my Essendon jumper that day, but Dad wouldn't let me. We were going to a Carlton and Richmond game, and as my grandfather was an AFL Life Member and a member of the Melbourne Cricket Club, I had to dress appropriately – and that wasn't an Essendon football jumper.

My most memorable trips to Melbourne were when Essendon were in the Grand Final, which they were in 1983, 1984 and 1985. In 1983, when I was 10, I went to my first Grand Final. It was the first of three consecutive Grand Final clashes between Essendon and Hawthorn.

An epic rivalry had developed between these two teams. Hawthorn beat Essendon in the 1983 Grand Final. In 1984, Hawthorn led by four goals at three-quarter-time and again looked likely to win, but Kevin Sheedy made some key positional moves and the Bombers won the game by four goals. The following year, Essendon won again. It was a great time to be a young Essendon supporter.

During that period there was a fantastic Bomber side, with players like Paul Van Der Haar, Simon Madden and dashing centreman Leon Baker. They were the powerhouse years of the first 'Baby Bombers', a great young team that Sheeds took to the heights.

Hawthorn had a great side, too, with Leigh Matthews, Dermott Brereton, Gary Ayres, Gary Buckenara and Chris Langford. They were coached by Allan 'Yabbie' Jeans, a man of the old school. He had shaped a ruthless, uncompromising unit in his own image. Not that they were automatons; no team which included the wild colonial boy from Frankston, Dermott Brereton, could be accused of lacking flair or charisma. I hated Dermott then, though. I didn't see the flair or the spectacular football nous he used as a bone-crunching centre-half-forward. I just saw the precociously talented smart-alec who famously ran through the

Essendon huddle, kissed Billy Duckworth and broke Bomber hearts. There wasn't much to love there.

Having Dermott as the guy in the black hat only increased my excitement during the lead-up to the 1984 Grand Final. I lay in bed the night before the match, with the rain pouring down, knowing that the next day we were going to watch Essendon play in a Grand Final in which they were favourites to win. For a 10-year-old boy, how much better does life get?

In the morning my dad, my grandfather and I hopped into the car and headed south on the Hume Highway towards the MCG. It was a boys' day: just the three of us.

After the match, walking out of the MCG was like floating on air, being pushed along by a sea of jubilant Bomber supporters. I felt part of that big club, full of happy people in red and black scarves and jackets, everyone buzzing with excitement.

We drove back to Canberra on the Sunday, talking in the car about the great victory, going through each play, each great goal, the moment when we knew the game was won, little vignettes made heroic by the context.

Great deeds on Grand Final day are of course more significant than great deeds in any other game. Players make their names in Grand Finals. Gary Ablett did when he kicked nine goals for a losing Geelong side in 1989. Dermott Brereton always shone in finals, including his very first game – a final in which, as a stick-legged teenager, he kicked five goals. Everyone knows about Harm's punch, Gabelich's run and, after the 2005 Grand Final, Leo Barry's game-saving mark just moments before the final siren. On Grand Final day, history is made, and even as a young kid I appreciated that.

But my joy wasn't shared by my mates when I saw them back in Canberra. On the Monday I told my friends at school all about what had happened. 'What are you talking about?' they'd say.

They didn't care. THEY DID NOT CARE THAT ESSENDON HAD WON A GRAND FINAL! All they cared about was rugby league. In Melbourne footy was huge. In Canberra, it hardly registered.

The next year, Essendon and Hawthorn again played in the Grand Final.

Like the previous year, we drove down from Canberra the night before, picking up one of Mum and Dad's friends on the way. This turned into quite a memorable trip. We had a Holden Premier which I think was about 20 years old. It had a big bench seat in the front and back, so three of us could sit in the front. On this night it started to rain, sheets of water, and the windscreen wipers broke. Mum kept driving while Dad leaned out of the window, wiping the windscreen with a rag. He did this for what seemed like forever, until the rain eventually eased.

Again, Essendon won. Again, Bomber delirium. Again, indifference from the schoolmates. Again, they'd ignored the greatest show on Earth.

My interest in school was not great. Academically I turned out all right, which is something of a surprise because I often just didn't want to go. I found sitting in a classroom boring. Mum would work with me at home after school and try to make sure I understood what I was being taught. I would tell her I didn't have any homework. That didn't seem to worry her; she was more interested in my understanding maths than on working through some book.

I learned at an early age that understanding the fundamentals of a subject was what was important. I also learned two things that are not important. First, repeating something over and over just for the sake of it. Second, something my dad has an expression for when I'm playing badly: 'Son, you're bloody sheepdogging again.'

Loosely translated, this means running around the outside of the pack instead of going in and getting the ball. I have met many people who have fallen into both these traps. Those obsessed with doing the exercise without understanding why they're doing it and those who go round and round the issue without getting to the heart of it. Football clubs are notorious for being full of people who require the exercise to be completed but don't understand the reason behind it. When Matthew Lloyd practises his goal-kicking he does not have 50 shots for the sake of it; he has 20 and learns something new every time.

Mum always read to all of us, and she bought us books she thought would interest us or that were popular. She still gives me a couple of books for my birthday and for Christmas. When Dad bought me some George Orwell books – *1984* and *Down and Out in Paris and London* – I was hooked. When I was 15 they gave me *The Count of Monte Cristo*, by Alexandre Dumas, which is still one of my favourite books. I came to really enjoy reading, but only books that captured my imagination. Even now I have a hard time reading things at work if they don't interest me, and it takes me longer than I believe it should.

I lacked dedication and enthusiasm at school for anything except sport. The piano lessons didn't have much of an impact either – after all those lessons I can now only play a couple of scales. Not even a tune. I'm tone-deaf, too, which didn't help my musical career. I love a song as much as the next bloke, but I'm told I should approach karaoke nights with extreme caution.

Sport was my passion, and the thing I succeeded at. I don't think I was substantially better at football than my contemporaries, though. When you're young you don't care whether you are any good or not; you just enjoy running around. My club team was pretty ordinary. Ainslie struggled to get numbers, and we didn't win any games for three years. My position on the field was wherever the ball was. I'd just run around and get the ball. That probably had something to do with the way I play footy today.

When I was 14 I started to put a bit of pressure on myself. Dad decided that if I was going to become good at the game I had to show a bit of commitment, so he'd get me out of bed three mornings a week and we'd go to the oval across the road and run laps. We'd run four laps of the oval, which was 3 or 4 kilometres in total. Then we'd do some footy skills for about 20 minutes. And remember, this was in the middle of winter. It was freezing cold. I would wear two tracksuits and I was still cold. I enjoyed it to start with, but after a couple of weeks it was hard. I didn't like getting out of bed. All my mates were in bed, so why wasn't I?

I began to understand that if I wanted to be a footballer I had to do things that were difficult, like getting up early on cold winter mornings. Until that point I was merely a better than average player; this helped me develop the capacity to work hard. I had to learn how to train hard, by myself. I had to learn to be self-motivated. That was probably one of the most important things I learned. And knowing that my mum and dad believed in my potential definitely helped me believe in myself. Sometimes the whole family, including Amilia and Katherine, would get out there and do the run with me. Looking back on it, it was a great bonding experience.

I think that the way my mum and dad brought me up had a lot to do with my success at football. They taught me self-discipline, that I was responsible for myself, and that getting somewhere was not always going to be easy or fun; sometimes it was going to be hard work.

As I've said, I don't think I had exceptional skills as a kid. I wasn't a sensational kick. I was reasonably well skilled and I could read the play and know where to go. I had enough ability, more than enough passion and desire, and the capacity to work hard.

I also had a desire to take my football to another level. All of this made me the player I have become.

The self-discipline I learned back then will be with me for life. It is one of the building blocks I will always be able to fall back on. It's like a safety net. The knowledge that you can fight through tough times is one of life's greatest strengths.

I have Essendon genes; there's no doubt about it. My grandfather, Allan Hird, played 102 games (without a break) with the Bombers from 1940. He started with Hawthorn in 1938, after being recruited from Williamstown. He was regarded as a speedy half-forward, half-back and occasional ruckman. He played on the back flank in the 1942 Essendon premiership side. He went on to captain-coach St Kilda from 1946 to 1947, and then returned to Essendon as the captain-coach of the seconds. He was on the committee in a variety of roles before becoming club president. The Allan T. Hird Stand at Windy Hill is named after him.

Despite this, I knew that getting drafted by Essendon was far from a certainty. My dad only played four games with Essendon, in 1966 and 1967, so I did not qualify under the father–son rule. I just had to cross my fingers and pray that the Bombers would grab me.

In the early 1990s, Sydney, as well as the fledging West Coast and Brisbane clubs, had two priority zone selections. Canberra was in Sydney's zone, which meant they could take two players of their choice before the official draft. The Sydney Swans had some interest in me and came down to watch me play a couple of games for Ainslie. I was suffering with shin splints when they came so my performance was pretty ordinary. Hawthorn also came down to have a chat with me around that time. They were semi-interested. Fifteen years on, Hawthorn drafted my cousin Matt Little.

I'm not sure whether this is true, but the story goes that Essendon rang Sydney to enquire if they were going to draft me. Sydney said that if Essendon took me, they (Sydney) would take another two Canberra players they thought were as good or better. Sydney had in fact spoken with me. I had said that I couldn't go to Sydney because the university course I wanted to do was in Melbourne. They were obviously not terribly interested in me. Essendon drafted me as their seventh choice overall, at number 79.

I was ready to go and play for Essendon.

MARGARET HIRD
ON JAMES

'Sunday's child is full of grace'

Sunday, 4 February 1973 is memorable for two reasons. It was the day on which the long hot summer finally broke in Canberra, and more importantly for me, it was the day my first child, James, was born. He had delayed his entry into the world and was certainly in no hurry to arrive. He was late, and having started his journey, he still took his time. With the help of the doctor and his trusty pair of forceps James arrived safely. He was exhausted, and so was I. James was a beautiful baby, round-faced, with blond hair, long, dark lashes and stunning big blue eyes that stole everyone's heart. He would melt even the hardest heart when he cried ever so gently, and let big tears gently roll down his face.

James had loads of energy as a toddler and would run every-where. As he gained his balance he would run around the yard kicking a football. One of my precious memories is of this little blond bombshell running around the backyard, his hair bouncing up and down, wearing yellow gumboots (his football boots) and an Essendon football jumper, marking and kicking the football. He would play by himself, or with Allan or me or Elliott, his friend from next door. He didn't care, as long as he could run and kick a ball.

It was not all footy for him. He loved stories – Toucan, The Three Billy Goats Gruff and his Richard Scarry books, to mention a few. He was always happy to paint at his easel or draw on his blackboard and fashion shapes out of playdough. He would spend hours playing in his sandpit with his Tonka truck, buckets and spades, and an assortment of wooden toys my dad had made for him – and which his own children now play with. Riding his bike, painting, cooking and our evening walks along the creek or to the park were also on his list of favourite activities. He never walked; he ran everywhere, and covered twice the distance we did.

I was studying during James's early years and at two and a half he would sit on my bed doing his 'ooniversity work' as I did my assignments. Before long James had a sister, Amilia, to share his life with. She was 'okay', but did not compete with his love of playing footy, and certainly was useless as far as a playing companion was concerned.

Soon it was time for James to start school. My only concern about his move into schooling was whether he would be happy and not feel alone in this new environment. I don't know why I felt concerned – he had always had lots of friends to play with before he went to school. Each day as I would talk to him about his day I would ask him who he played with. It didn't take long for him to realise from my reaction that the right answer for an anxious mother was 'No one.' Not wanting to panic, I decided to take a look for myself, from a distance, one lunchtime. James was certainly not on his own, and he looked anything but unhappy. That night I asked the usual question and got the same hang-dog reply – 'Nobody.' I never asked again.

Shortly after James started school, Katherine was born. He was five, old enough to be very proud and protective of his new sister.

It was during his early years at school that James learned never to trust 'the Magpies'. They were his natural enemies, and they certainly never played fair. James walked home from school at an early age, as most kids in Canberra did in those days. During the magpie season I would hear his cries for help as he came up the hill and I'd have to race out to rescue him. He would be with other children, but the magpies always singled him out. They knew that one day he would cause them serious problems, so they took the chance, while he was young, to inflict some serious blows to his head. James finally took to wearing a solid blue Batman helmet to and from school for protection during the magpie season.

I believed that James should have cultural and sporting opportunities – hence the piano, ballet, acting and French lessons. His early French lessons are probably most memorable for the trouble he got into when he dropped his marbles on the floor, the piano lessons for his 'wooden style', and the ballet lessons for the ribbing they have brought him in later life. But his acting brought him acclamation for a wonderful performance as Pharaoh, when he was 11, in the school production of Joseph and His Amazing Technicolor Dreamcoat.

James's sights were always firmly set on playing football for Essendon. Allan and I tried to delay his entry into competition football, but he was determined to play. He had an early dalliance with soccer, but after that he never wavered. We moved house when he was eight and he joined the Ainslie Australian Rules team. Many a Saturday he would play two games of football, one with his team and one with the grade above. It was in his early teens that he briefly played with Nathan Buckley – when he was playing up a grade. James had a shelf full of trophies at an early age. From the start he was an honest, hardworking player who wanted the ball desperately, got it often and used it for his team.

James loved all sport and was good at most. He played school rugby, was in the ACT Primary Schools' cricket team, represented the school and district at athletics, cross-country and soccer, and represented the ACT in Australian Rules football from the age of 11. When he was fully involved in training, his schoolwork improved rather than suffered. Like so many mums, my contribution to his football life was very much behind the scenes: the words of encouragement; the ferrying around to training and games; the washing of shorts, socks and towels (if I was lucky enough to have them brought home); the selling of raffle tickets and chocolates and the other things that made it possible for him to play.

James was a quiet, unassuming kid who was popular with his peers. He was school captain at the primary school he attended. Although quite good at his schoolwork he was not noted for his dedication and study habits. When he reached Year 11 and embarked on two units of higher-level mathematics, I decided to keep him company. I spent many evenings sitting around the dining-room table with him and his friends trying to bring some light to bear on a seemingly unfathomable problem. I always felt a great sense of achievement as together we reached a solution, but for them it was more just a task to be done, a problem to be solved.

James has two sisters, Amilia and Katherine. The three siblings are very close. One of my special memories of his bond with his sisters was when he was about 11 and Katherine was six. Katherine had finally been given her own room, which she had longed for. It was at the other end of the house, but she was happy with that. Each evening when we'd all gone to bed and Katherine had been asleep for a couple of hours, we would hear a familiar creaking in James's room. It was the trundle bed being pulled out from under his bed and Katherine quietly settling down for the night next to her big brother. Nothing was ever said. Next

27

morning she would slide the bed back and return to her room. James was happy to share with her while she needed his company.

Family has always been important to James. He grew up in a loving family with Allan and me and his two sisters. He also had doting grandparents, aunties, uncles and cousins in both Melbourne and Brisbane. Added to these he had his de facto family in Canberra – our close friends and their children, with whom he shared birthdays, outings, day-to-day play, friendship and watching football. From the time they were born, Emily, Disa, James and Gavin and their siblings braved the cold to watch their dads play with the Australian National University Australian Rules team or, in the early days, to play their own games while ANU played theirs. As the children got older they would serve in the canteen. At that point the canteen profits suffered, as they did more than their fair share of sampling. James loved being in the change rooms with the players and being in the thick of things with the footballers, just as his own two boys do now. He was awarded a supporter's award as a teenager because he was so involved. Football was his passion, and Terry Daniher was the subject of a couple of school assignments. As we lived in Canberra, James did not go to many Melbourne games as a young boy, but he did go to the 1983 Grand Final – and shed a tear or two when Essendon lost.

James was a great kid as a teenager. His football kept him focused and out of harm's way. He lost what may have been his first love because he wouldn't go out the night before he was to play in a football match and probably was so exhausted after the match that he would not have been the life of the party.

During James's last year in Canberra he played with the Ainslie seconds. He was 17 and aspiring to the firsts. At this time James was plagued with shin splints – he had missed games as a result. As the season progressed and the draft edged closer, it was important for him to impress the scouts and recruitment staff from the various clubs as they came to Canberra, but he was sidelined by injury. He had been selected, for the second year running, as a member of the ACT TEAL Cup squad, which was to play in Brisbane, but he never made it onto the field. His shin splints were now a stress fracture.

Through the coincidence of talent and good fortune, James did play in the ACT Grand Final with Ainslie seniors, and they won. This was a game for men with mature bodies. James was a skinny youth, but what he lacked in strength of body he made up for in talent and determination. He kicked two goals and was named among the best players. Ainslie won and he fell asleep on the stage of the club as he waited to be presented to the supporters after the game. Needless to say, he celebrated long and hard . . . and missed a day or two at school. This was the first of many occasions on which injury seemed poised to deprive him of a longed-for opportunity, but his determination – mixed with a dash of luck – has usually provided the opportunity and he has grabbed it with both hands.

James was Essendon's number 79 draft pick in 1990. There were no bells and whistles. In Canberra it was hardly noteworthy, but for him it was the chance to live his dream. For me it was what I wanted, but at the same time I felt a sense of impending loss – he was so young, my first-born. Each of my children is special, and saying goodbye to them is not easy, particularly the first time. Yet it was what I wanted for him. Early in January 1991, Allan and I took James to Essendon and finally farewelled him at the club. We did not make it far along the road back before Allan stopped the car and we had to comfort and reassure each other that this was what was best for him.

Fifteen years ago telephone calls were not so easily made, flights were not so cheap, and Amilia and Katherine were young

and needed our time. When James first went to Melbourne I
would write to him each night and send the letter after I had
completed a few days' worth of writing. After the first month or
so very few letters arrived from the other direction. Maybe that
had something to do with the post rather than James's lack of
penmanship. It didn't matter. I wrote because I wanted him to still
feel connected to his family. I have always written to James when
he has been faced with adversity. I do this to remind him of the
journey he has made so far and what he has gained from it. James
has taken the skills and talents he has been given and used them;
he has always pushed himself to be the best he can be. He has
faced many challenges, and has grown in strength of character
and self-knowledge as a result.

Mum is special. She was always there for me, and she still is. When I fell off my bike for the first time, 28 years ago, she picked me up; when I tore my calf in March 2006, she was there. Without her, I might still have been a footballer, but I would have lacked education and culture. She drove me because she loved me. She has supported me unquestioningly, and she knows my faults and forgives them. That's why I love her. It's fair to say that, through her love and dedication, I was moulded into the person I am today.

Chapter 2

The Early Years

I was getting ready for school one morning in November 1990 when the phone rang. It was Dad.

'You've been drafted by Essendon.'

In one sentence, Dad had told me what I would do for the next 16 years of my life, and beyond.

I was excited, I was overwhelmed, but mainly I was relieved. I had been passed over by Hawthorn and Sydney, but taken by Essendon. I couldn't believe my luck. I hadn't particularly wanted to go and live in Sydney, and the idea of playing for Hawthorn was my version of hell – the images of Dermott Brereton winning games against Essendon in the 1980s, with Dad and me watching and hating him as he pranced around after a goal doing that cocky 'chicken walk', were still too fresh.

No, Essendon was where I wanted to play. It's where I'd dreamed of playing. The dreams had been so strong and certain, and now they had come true.

When I put down the phone I was so happy that I jumped straight on my bike and rode down the driveway towards the main road we lived on. My dream had been realised and I was invincible.

That's when the semi-trailer hit me. Wham! The truck whizzed past and clipped my wheels. I fell off my bike and landed unceremoniously on the nature strip. Luckily, everything seemed to be in place and unbroken; I only received a few scratches. So I went from being drafted to nearly dead in the space of two minutes. I don't think the semi-trailer driver even knew he'd hit me, because he just drove on. Those scratches might lay claim to being the first of many injuries I have sustained as a player at the Essendon Football Club.

That night Mum, Dad, Amilia and Katherine and I went out for dinner and had a bit of a celebration. I wanted to jump straight onto a plane and go to Melbourne, but I had to finish Year 12. It was early November, and I had a few exams still to do. The club didn't want to see me until January anyway.

I spent Christmas with the family and a few days at our usual summer holiday spot, Bright. All I could think about was getting down to the club. The days felt like months, but finally the day came for Mum and Dad to drive me to Melbourne.

We arrived early at Windy Hill and I blithely waved them goodbye. It was a pretty emotional time for them, but I just wanted to get started. Later I found out that almost as soon as they were out of sight they stopped the car to console each other. It must have been a long trip back to Bright.

It was a defining moment in many ways: the start of my football career and the start of my independence. But the break from my parents was hard. I can now look back at their tears as I farewelled them and completely understand their feelings. Back then I just wanted to throw myself into my new world of football, and the big city I'd moved to. I also wanted to look cool while I was doing it.

About two hours before my first training session I was already sitting in the change rooms. The only people there were Ken Betts, the property steward, and me. Ken walked over and gave me a jumper with my dad's old number on it, plus a pair of socks and a pair of shorts. That was huge for me. In Canberra, no one had ever given me a jumper and a pair of shorts and socks to keep – except Mum and Dad, that is. So there I was, dressed and ready to go two hours early. I even had my footy boots on. Little did I realise that you don't wear footy boots for the first couple of weeks of pre-season. Here was I ready to run the Tan in my footy boots.

I sat there, looking around at the rooms where all the great Essendon players had changed into the red and black, revved themselves up, listened to the coach, tended to injuries and received rub-downs. This was hallowed ground. I was overcome by the realisation that this was it – my football career was really beginning. Some of the things I used to dream about were actually happening. I hadn't had to run away and live at the Essendon Football Club. They had chosen me to and asked me to join them; the rest was up to me. Wow!

My knowledge of Essendon history probably only went as far back as the 1984 premiership, which meant that I was anxiously awaiting the arrival of the two players who had been my heroes since that time: Tim Watson and Terry Daniher. Finally Tim and Terry metamorphosed from the bedroom wall of a Canberra teenager into two big men walking past me. They were flesh and blood, as real as my mind would allow them to be, but they still lived in the world of myth, where all heroes live. I don't think I said an intelligible or audible word to Tim or Terry for two years.

When you've dreamed of something for almost all of your 17 years of life and then it happens, it's hard to deal with. I had wanted this so much, but how was I to act, what was I to say and do? When all the other players started to file in and I had to meet them, I was almost cowering in the corner. I didn't want to shake anyone's hand. I was too awe-struck. I remember I did a lot of mumbling. The players – people like Tim, Terry, Mark 'Bomber' Thompson and Simon Madden – were all very close friends. They'd played a lot of footy together over a long time. Simon was approaching the end of his great career as a ruckman when I was starting. It felt like an extraordinary moment to be at the Essendon Football Club.

I trod gingerly. First, I was shy, and second, I felt it was best to edge slowly into the group. All the older players greeted me, but that was it for the moment. Gavin Wanganeen was a new boy, too, having come across from Adelaide, and we became mates pretty quickly.

It didn't take long for me to feel a part of the club once we all started playing practice games together. Eight weeks after I started we played a practice match in Bendigo. I came off a mark, landed badly and hurt my knee. It wiped out the season for me. I missed the next 16 or 17 weeks, which was very hard in itself. And on top of that, I was on crutches. I couldn't drive, I couldn't catch a tram . . . and I was trying to study civil engineering at the Royal Melbourne Institute of Technology (RMIT). It took forever to get anywhere with all my uni books on my back. I'd be late for lectures because I couldn't get from one place to another quickly enough, and not every lecturer was sympathic, even though it was quite obvious why I was late.

It was a difficult time. I was away from home, and so had no mum to drive me around, my football was not going as I had envisioned, and I was struggling just to get around. I had to catch taxis from uni back to training and then back 'home' to Keilor Park, where I was living with the Colemans.

Every player who was drafted from outside Melbourne was placed with a family. I lived with Grace and Reg Coleman, a family who had a strong connection with the footy club (although they weren't related to the great Essendon player John Coleman). Grace and Reg were terrific people. They had two sons, one of whom was away in Perth, so I used his room. Their other son, Russell, really looked after me. Initially I became closer to his group of mates than to the guys at the footy club, because I wasn't training much or playing. So during 1991, I hung out with Russell's crowd. All the kids in Eliza Street, Keilor Park, were really close. I was fortunate to be placed in that sort of environment. Fellow Bomber Mark Harvey's parents lived next door to the Colemans, so every now and then I would get a lift home with him. It was a good family environment and it certainly made life with a knee injury easier.

The disappointment of being injured right at the start of my dream lasted a few days after I got out of hospital. Apparently, I was very lucky to even stay on the players' list: I survived a majority decision against me. As the story is now told, at the end-of-season review, six people got to vote on who would get the last place on the Essendon list for 1992. Four voted to de-list one J. Hird, and two voted to keep him. Luckily, the two who voted for me were Kevin Sheedy and Brian Donohue, the two most influential people at Essendon in the last 25 years.

At the time I was sure I belonged, and I trusted my instincts. I was very frustrated by the injury, but I wasn't going to give up. My passion for the game hadn't faltered. Without realising it, I was setting small goals along the way: walk without crutches; walk without a limp; jog slowly; jog quickly; start training; train harder; and finally, play a game. I had figured out that when I worked hard, I stopped feeling sorry for myself.

Even when I was injured, I went to every match with my Auntie Susan and her family. We stood under the Showers Stand at Windy Hill and hurled abuse at the opposition like everyone else. I got so used to the routine of being a spectator that for the first few games after I returned and played in the reserves, I would look for my auntie in the crowd. At the end of the reserves game I'd have a quick shower then join my auntie and get back to hurling abuse at the opposition.

In my first year I established the Hird tradition of wearing a long-sleeved jumper. If you've ever been to Canberra in the middle of winter and played a football match at 8 o'clock in the morning, you'll understand it. The simple fact is that no one in the juniors in Canberra wore short-sleeved jumpers in winter. It was just unheard of. Even when I started playing senior footy in Canberra, half the team wore long-sleeved jumpers. It's not like a winter in Melbourne, where the coldest it gets is 6°C. In Canberra it's often 0°C or below in the morning. So when I started wearing short sleeves it just didn't feel right. I reverted to what I felt comfortable in, a long-sleeved jumper. Now I always wear a short-sleeved jumper for the first couple of rounds – and in the finals if it's hot – but come the cooler weather I whack on my old favourite, the long-sleeved jumper.

There were some fantastic senior footballers playing in 1991. Terry Daniher was in his second-last year. Terry was part of a great family of footballers that included Neale, Chris and Anthony (I played with Anthony and Chris in the mid 1990s). Neale's brilliant career as a half-forward had already been cruelly cut short by injury; he'd retired by the time I arrived at Essendon.

Terry was a matter-of-fact man, completely unpretentious. He was almost a caricature of an outback Aussie bloke, with his broad accent, she'll-be-right-mate attitude and great generosity of spirit. He approached his nights out with the view that he'd drink tonight and train as hard as he could tomorrow. 'She'll be right.' He would train for hours and hours. It was amazing to watch how hard he trained. Even the Thursday before the reserves Grand Final he did weights until 9.30 at night. The weights weren't likely to help him two days out from a Grand Final, but he did everything as hard as he could until he couldn't do it anymore.

This attitude even applied to his window-cleaning business. You'd hear incredible stories about the three brothers, Terry, Chris and Anthony, and their daring feats and great work from their customers. The stories were probably grossly exaggerated, but there is no doubt they took on many tough challenges in their work. Some of the stories about Terry's climbing antics are pretty scary.

The great ruckman Simon Madden was close to retirement when I joined the club. As a kid I'd watched Simon dominating ruck duels and taking screamers over packs.

Because I was injured for most of my first year, I got to know many of these players as people first, and teammates and players the next year. It was a slightly different way to start a relationship with a group of footballers from what I was used to, but there were definite advantages in this. The main one was that by the time I played with them, I could understand their behaviour on the field pretty well. In those early years, I gained greater respect for those men who I saw were genuinely caring people who had families like mine. More recently, as captain, it has been a great help to know the people I am playing with. I know who can be relied on when the going gets tough, who is selfish, who can handle direct criticism and who needs to be treated with kid gloves. I also know how to cajole individuals into a common direction. The other benefit – perhaps an unexpected one – of getting to know some of these players well is that it has made me a more insightful and better person.

Playing alongside Mark Thompson, for instance, was a fantastic experience. He's the best leader, as a captain, of any team I've been a part of. It was his sincerity that stood out. He was passionate about the club, and about the success of the team. He inspired players, and drove them to succeed as a group, rather than as individuals, but he also made every player feel that he was known and valued as an individual. He didn't talk much, but when he did, everyone listened, because we knew he had something important to say. Many people in footy just berate players, and when they do that, any other message they want to send is lost. He had high expectations of every player and he never gave up on his goal of getting us to work together as a team. I learned a lot from Mark about the way to speak to people, and I tried to follow his approach seven years later when it was my turn to captain the club.

In 1991, I had a lot to learn. That year was the beginning of my long friendship with Tim Watson, who had been a hero of mine since I was a kid. He became a great mentor and a major influence on me. He retired at the end of the 1991 season, but was lured back by Kevin Sheedy in 1993 for one final year, which meant we were able to play football together.

The 1991 team was a young group, and he was like a father figure to four or five of us. He'd take us shopping, make sure we knew our way around – and crucially, he broke down the mystique surrounding Kevin Sheedy. Tim showed great leadership in being a conduit between the coach and the younger players, who were in awe of, even scared of, Sheeds. We all began to see Sheeds more as a person, and not just as the coach, someone remote from us.

In the 1992 pre-season, the first Foster's Cup game was played in Albury, but I wasn't picked. We lost the game and therefore were out of the competition, so we went to Maroochydore in Queensland for a practice game against Brisbane. It was not seen as a serious game. Sheeds took up a young side. I was picked, and played really well. I played on John Worsfold's younger brother and kicked a couple of goals. From then on I pretty much went from playing in the seconds to playing in the seniors. I thought, *This is good. How long is it going to last?*

The next week we played another practice game, this time against Hawthorn at Skinner Reserve in Sunshine. The ground was horribly dry and windy but it treated me well. I chalked up 38 possessions playing on John Platten, Andy Collins and Andrew Jarman – all of them gun midfielders. They might collectively have accumulated 100 possessions, I have no idea, but I'd never got the ball 38 times in my life in one match. Things were definitely on track.

The next week we played Collingwood in a practice game and I didn't do as well, but I did kick two or three goals. The week after was Round 1. My form was good, and I believed I had a chance to be selected.

Round 1, 1992, was against St Kilda at Waverley Park, and I *was* picked in the team – but as an emergency. I would play only if someone pulled out because of injury.

I was at home when the phone rang. A voice at the other end of the phone said, 'You're in.' Terry Daniher had a hamstring injury. I rang Mum and Dad, who jumped on the first flight down to Melbourne. This was a huge moment for me. All that kicking the ball to myself in the garden and mucking around with a football, all the early mornings at the oval and the hours of training were about to pay off. A dream was about to come true. I was unbelievably excited. I was 18 years old.

My first game was on Sunday, 21 March 1992. The game would begin at 2 pm. I drove out to Waverley with Mum, Dad and my grandfather. We left very early, to avoid any traffic hold-ups . . . and arrived very early.

I ran out, through the paper banner made by the Bomber cheer squad, onto the huge arena. The oval seemed to go forever. I was glad I'd only been told I was playing the night before; otherwise I would probably have expended all my energy on the build-up and anticipation. It was nerve-racking enough as it was. Here I was, about to play against guys I'd watched on TV. As it turned out, I played on Russell Morris and a couple of others, and kicked two goals. I did just okay.

Most of us like to put some people on pedestals. Some people worship movie stars and expect them to be perfect. Unfortunately, when worshippers meet the worshipped they are likely to be disappointed. In the workplace, most of us put those who are the best at their job on a higher plane; when we get a chance to work with them, we are immediately at a disadvantage because of our perception of their power, wisdom and strength. My first game was like that. It was like a first date with someone you've wanted to date for 18 years. I'd been staring at these people all my life, building them up to superman status. So when it came to this first 'date', I froze. In my case, the date happened to be with Russell Morris, aka 'the Fly'. I had wanted this so badly that I'd built it up to be something more than just a game: I was one little human out there among 35 superhuman robots. What hope did I have?

The next week Terry Daniher came back from injury so I was dropped. In the reserves game against Fitzroy the following week I tore my medial ligament – six weeks out. I returned to the seconds.

One cold, wet winter day when I was finally back on the field, we were playing Sydney at the MCG. I turned around to receive a handball and didn't see Ben Doolan coming. He put his knee straight into me and broke three ribs, one of which went through my lung. There was a burning pain in my back from the broken ribs, but worse than that, I couldn't get my breath. My lung was slowly going down like a punctured balloon. With every breath I took, the air escaped through the hole in my lung into the cavity between my lung and my ribs, which meant my lung couldn't expand. I was in a lot of pain, but it was also pretty frightening not being able to breathe.

At the hospital, the doctors soon realised that I had a punctured lung, so they grabbed a pen-sized tube of metal, punched a hole between two ribs and inserted the tube: this allowed the air to escape from the cavity. I could see and feel it all happening – I'm sure they forgot to give me a painkiller.

I was in hospital for four days and missed another two weeks. I didn't know Ben Doolan then, but he later became a teammate and a close friend. It was ironic that the guy who broke my rib and punctured my lung would be there to console me the day after I re-injured my foot in 1999.

I came back to play a few more games with the reserves, then I was picked in the seniors for the last three games of the year. In the game against Melbourne I played at full-forward and kicked four goals. Against North Melbourne I got a heap of the ball. Then I played against Geelong at Waverley, the last game of the year, and the final game for Simon Madden and Terry Daniher. Tim Watson had already retired, but he joined them for a lap of honour. It was a big day for the club, and being able to play that day was very special for me.

I had played only four games with the firsts in the 1992 season, which meant I qualified to play in the finals in Essendon's reserves side. We won the flag with Denis Pagan coaching. I might not remember too much about that game, but it would be difficult to ever forget some of Denis's addresses. They were always spirited, sometimes fearsome, often inspirational. There are messages and images he used that are still with me today. The most memorable one was: 'Don't get carried away with yourself, because someone will bring you back to earth very quickly.'

It had been a good start to my football career. Sure, I had played only a handful of senior games, and I'd suffered serious injury, but I had also proved to myself that I had what it took to play with the big boys. It had taken me 18 years to get my first date with AFL football. Granted, I wasn't choosing the restaurant, but I was ordering my own food and holding hands at dinner. You could reflect on 1992 in two ways. Four games of AFL football, a punctured lung, a Grade 2 tear of a medial knee ligament and a Grade 2 tear of a medial ankle ligament could make it look like a tough year. James Hird thought it was the greatest year of his life so far.

Chapter 3

1993: The First Grand Final

By the end of 1992, Tim Watson, Simon Madden and Terry Daniher were all gone; it was the end of an era for Essendon. A crop of new young players was about to grasp the opportunity to shape the future of the club. David Calthorpe, Joe Misiti, Mark Mercuri, Steve Alessio and I all made our senior debuts in 1992. I'd played some pretty good football with this group, who'd been part of a terrific under-19 side. It wasn't long before we became known as 'the Baby Bombers'. There had been a team called that back in 1983, when Tim Watson was a young player. Luckily for us, Tim was lured out of retirement by Sheeds for the 1993 season. He took on the role of Baby Bomber adviser, mentor, protector and, on Grand Final day, calmer of nerves.

But all that was seven months away.

We were the exemplars of the youth policy that Kevin Sheedy was so determined to pursue, a group of talented 20-year-olds all beginning to mature as footballers at the same time. Combine our talents with those of the senior guys and something special could happen. Sheeds always thought it was smart to give kids games early, so that when they were needed, they'd be ready. They were like an investment that could mature at the right time. He didn't expect miracles from the inexperienced; he expected growth. Years later, when I was captain, he would often select a young player when he picked a team, a tactic I sometimes questioned. I'd ask, 'How are we going to win with six young kids in the team?' His answer was: 'We might not win this game, but we might win a Grand Final a year later because we've blooded them.'

In 1993, the investment he was making in the future paid off much sooner than anyone imagined. I was about to become part of a young team that would win a premiership.

They were great days with a fantastic group of people. We were under the eye of a group of older guys who looked after us really well. As well as Tim, there was Mark Thompson, Paul Salmon, Darren Bewick, David Grenvold, Gary O'Donnell and Michael Long. Longy guided us well, demanding a lot and making sure we didn't get too cocky. Gary O'Donnell was also a strong influence on us, and Mark Thompson was an outstanding captain of the 1993 side. His personality lent itself perfectly to the job.

Among the young guys, I was particularly close mates with Joey (Misiti), Mercs (Mark Mercuri), Sess (Stephen Alessio), Stumpy (Dave Calthorpe) and Ola (Rick Olarenshaw). When I arrived in Melbourne, aged 17, suave Ricky looked after me. He introduced me to all his mates and took me surfing with him. Rick used to chase the girls like there was no tomorrow. It was great to be around someone who was so smooth and confident. I was not at all confident with women. Rick was the ideal friend to have.

We might have been young, but we had a lot of respect for each other. David Calthorpe was the loud one of the group. He'd tell great jokes and had an outgoing personality. He even had the front to take the mickey out of the senior blokes. And Steve Alessio was one of the funniest men I've ever met; any situation was fair game.

One such situation involved David Wheadon, a very serious footy tactician whom we called 'the Professor'. David turned footy into a science. He would break it down into bits and talk us through every detail. The whole process was very analytical. On Wednesdays he would hold a meeting at which he'd throw up scenarios and talk through tactics and stats. The atmosphere was deadly serious. We certainly didn't laugh at those meetings; we didn't even look sideways. All eyes were on the board. If they weren't, David would crack it.

At one of these meetings David asked us a question. 'Now these are tactics we're going to use – what are the things that would happen to make these tactics not work?'

Sess put up his hand. 'An earthquake?' Not quite the expected answer, but it gave us a bit of comic relief.

People like Sess and Longy are essential around a footy club, because you were never quite sure whether or not they were serious. When we'd lose two or three games in a row and the mood was pretty flat, these were the guys who would distract us with a few jokes and get us on track again.

Fifteen years later I've played over 230 games, and close to 200 of them with most of these guys. It has been wonderful to share my career with such people. We have all developed – not just as footballers, but also as people – and grown in all aspects of our lives.

Playing football with a group for such a long time is similar to any long-term relationship: its success is based on mutual respect. Whether it's a marriage or a business relationship, you cannot expect to like or agree with every decision your partner makes.

But you must be able to respect what the person stands for and why they made the decision they did.

The respect I have for the guys I've played with derives from all the hours of training we put in together. Each of us has seen the emotional rollercoasters the others have gone through, battling injury and personal drama, and we have still always tried to achieve the most we could as a group. It is a bond that will never be broken.

Essendon started the 1993 season well, winning the Ansett Cup Grand Final against Richmond. I kicked five goals that game, which was huge for me.

I played pretty good football for the first 11 rounds of that year, but there was one match, against Hawthorn at Waverley in June, that stood out for me. I came to think of it as my break-through game. The Hawks were a fantastic team, just on the way down at that stage. Essendon and Hawthorn had had a great rivalry over the years, of course. As an Essendon supporter, I'd grown up hating Hawthorn, especially after they'd beaten Essendon in the 1983 Grand Final. In 1993 they still had good players. There was the great back-pocket player, Gary 'Conan the Barbarian' Ayres, the man with football's most famous mullet hair-style, and the supremely skilled and immovable Chris Langford.

Having my breakthrough game against a team I'd hated my whole life was very satisfying. It was the first time I was able to get back at every one of those dirty rotten Hawks players who had made my life a misery as a kid.

It also had a lot to do with the fact that I'd trained for this my whole life: when I was given the opportunity, I was ready to step up. Sheeds often says that you don't know when the moment will come, but when it does, you can only grasp it with both hands and make the most out of it if you have prepared for it. I'll go further: luck can play a big part in success in any area of life, but so does preparation. When you are presented with the moment, don't let it slip by because instead of preparing for it you have wasted valuable time worrying whether it would come.

My total for that day was five goals and 30-odd possessions. I felt I could do whatever I wanted to do on the field. Radio station 3AW gave me the Man of the Match award. After the game, Sheeds drew favourable comparisons between my childhood hero, Terry Daniher, and me. That capped off my day.

Unfortunately, 1993 turned out to be another year marred by injury. I tore my hamstring badly in a match against Melbourne. I had been moved around a bit and just couldn't get into the game, and when I jumped up to take a mark I felt my hamstring go *bang*. It was a pretty decent tear. I missed four games. Then, playing the Eagles a few weeks later, I did it again. I missed eight weeks altogether, which was both annoying and frustrating. I had to do a huge amount of rehab work to get back onto the field.

The second hamstring injury, in Round 12, was really frustrating because I knew that I was finally playing at the standard needed to be in the side. I was playing pretty good football, we were on top of the ladder, and I wanted to be part of it.

The problem with a hamstring injury is that it makes you lose confidence, and it changes the way you play. You worry about tearing it again, which makes you a bit tentative. Those two hamstring injuries continue to affect me. I'm never confident that I won't tear them. Thirteen years later, the scar tissue from that injury remains a problem for me, which says something about the size of the tear. I still have a hole the size of a 20-cent piece in my left hamstring tendon.

The right level of confidence is essential to a happy life. Too much and people see you as arrogant, which leads to all sorts of problems; too little and you will never achieve your goals. My left hamstring has taught me a lot about what is the right level to have. Whenever I worked hard and did the right training, I would be confident that my leg would get me through a game, but when I didn't think I had done all the work or the right type of training, I would lack confidence in my leg and play accordingly, lacking run and approaching the ball in a timid way. To balance the argument, when I got too cocky and didn't respect my hamstring, it would trouble me.

The lesson I took from this was that without confidence you will never reach the heights you aspire to, but you must always respect the elements and people around you too, because arrogance can lead to blindness.

Another important factor I identified early on in my senior career was the need to feel inspired before a game. Only then can you do something truly inspiring once you're on the ground. The truth is that sometimes football can feel almost sterile. You jump in your car, you park it underneath the ground, and you walk up to the rooms. You don't see anyone, so you don't pick up the sense of occasion that comes with the game. You can also become too nervous and think too much about the game. Your focus becomes too narrow, and you forget why you're playing in the first place.

Back in Round 8 of 1993 I decided that I'd think of myself as an Essendon supporter, but one who also runs out onto the ground and plays. This was my fifteenth game in the seniors, and my career was beginning to go really well, yet I felt I needed something more . . . Perhaps thinking and feeling the way a supporter does would inject some extra passion into me. As a supporter you yell, your heart's on your sleeve, you bleed for your club.

We were playing a night game against Fitzroy. I didn't live far from Essendon station, so I caught the train to Flinders Street and in the dusk walked to the MCG. I was wearing my Essendon uniform – a black suit with a little emblem – but no one knew who I was. I felt like a supporter going to the game, and picked up on the excitement of the other supporters on my way. I carried that anticipation and excitement onto the ground with me.

I always felt that if I could play the way I supported, I would play well. A supporter is never flat. A player might come off the ground and say, 'I was flat today, I had no energy', but I've never seen supporters who are flat and lack passion. They're always up. Being around them, thinking like them, created added atmosphere for me; I struggle in sterile environments.

Even today, if we're playing at the MCG, I'll park in East Melbourne and walk across the car park to the game – because it gets my adrenaline flowing.

In the build-up to the Grand Final, against Carlton, I was still anxious about my hamstring. Even more importantly, I was afraid I might not be picked for the match, especially because I'd played poorly in the preliminary final the week before. On the Monday before the big game, Tim Watson saw I was concerned and asked what was worrying me. I told him I was worried that I would not be picked because I felt I hadn't done well in the two previous games. Tim reassured me: 'I promise you, you won't be dropped. Get that off your shoulders and think about the footy.'

Now, Tim wasn't on the selection panel, and he didn't have any inside knowledge, but it was fantastic for me as a young, inexperienced player to be offered that certainty. I believed Tim: how could he be wrong? I thought I was going to play, so I relaxed and concentrated on training and the game ahead instead of wasting my energy worrying about whether or not I would be selected.

It was an emotional and exciting week in other ways, too, because Gavin Wanganeen won the Brownlow Medal. There were some celebrations, but we had to play in a Grand Final five days later so we didn't go wild. I felt for Gav. He was 20 years old, and after the Brownlow win there was a ton of pressure on him. Maybe it's easier being young when these things happen: at least you don't know what to expect. He had the media turn up on his doorstep at 6.30 the next morning, for instance, when he'd probably only had four or five hours' sleep. In spite of all the pressure, he played a good game in the Grand Final.

The dramas of the week hadn't finished. On the Thursday night, Sheeds read out the 18 players in the team and then named six for the interchange bench. Only three of these interchange players would get a game. Those six blokes were shattered; they probably all thought they deserved a game. Sheeds was leaving it until the Saturday morning to tell them who would play.

One of the six was Derek Kickett, who had played every game that year. Sheeds leaving Derek out of the team was a bombshell – and it was all over the papers, of course. I know there was outrage in some Essendon quarters over the decision. And Derek found out on the radio, which was hardly ideal.

I think the decision has affected Derek's life. It certainly would have affected mine. I don't think he has spoken to Sheeds since, and I don't think he has ever forgiven him. I've spoken to Derek a number of times but we've never broached that subject.

As soon as my name was read out on the half-full-flank (or wherever it was!) I switched off. I thought, *Thank God for that!* and walked out and got into my car and drove home.

We all felt for Derek, but that didn't change anything. I was relieved I was going to play and focused on the Grand Final. We would go out there and do our best to win. I felt extremely lucky to have been given the opportunity.

Carlton went into the game as favourites. They had experience, whereas we were young and inexperienced. The big question was whether a group of talented kids could stand up to the pressure of a Grand Final.

The Blues were a good unit, with some outstanding senior people: giraffe-like Justin Madden in the ruck, uncompromising defenders Brett Ratten and Andrew McKay, relentless runner Craig Bradley, full-back Stephen Silvagni and, up forward, the great goal-kicker and captain Stephen 'Sticks' Kernahan.

During the build-up in the rooms, everyone was nervous. As a young kid, when I'd run in an athletics carnival, I'd be so nervous my legs would shake like jelly. I was also a pretty good cricketer when I was young, but one of the reasons I gave it up was that going out to bat made me too nervous. I just couldn't handle that type of pressure. In footy, if you miss a mark, you get another chance. In cricket, if you miss a shot, that's it. When I was 15 I'd represented the state in cricket, and in my first game I was opening bat. I was out first ball. It was then that I figured out that footy was a better path for me.

As the time approached for us to run out on the ground I became more and more anxious. My stomach had knots in it. I was trying to be calm and relaxed, but it was hard. I could hear the crowd outside. I knew that there would be the banner and then the national anthem . . . and the eyes of the world on us. It wasn't a great idea to think too much about what was about to happen.

It was time to go. We had received our instructions from Sheeds: we knew what to do, we knew the game plan, we'd warmed up. There was nothing more to do.

Except tell a joke. And that's where Tim Watson came in.

Tim was very good at reading people's emotions. He noticed that a few of us were really nervous, just like young kids, and as we walked up the race, Tim grabbed three of us and started telling us a joke. I looked at him and thought, *We are walking out onto the MCG to play a Grand Final and you're telling me a* joke? *You must be kidding!* But he kept right on going, all the way down the race as the crowd noise became louder and louder, and even as we moved onto the ground.

I can't remember the joke. All I remember is that it really relaxed me for a couple of minutes before the game started. It was another example of Tim's guardianship of us, and his leadership. He had been one of the youngest VFL/AFL players: he played his first game when he was just 15. He'd had a magnificent career at Essendon, and was loved and admired for what one writer called his 'barnstorming grace' on the field and for his moral and physical support on and off the field. On this Grand Final day, which he knew could mark the end of his career, he still took the time to help us young ones and make it a great day for everyone.

The first strong memory I have of the game itself was Michael Long's unbelievable goal in the first quarter, where he dodged and wove around the Carlton guys before drilling it through from centre-half-forward. That goal was inspirational for us, and has stayed in the memory of many because of its sheer grace and audacity. It was the first goal kicked that day, and it sent the message that Essendon were not going to be intimidated.

We felt we had the game under control early. At quarter-time we were five goals up and we sensed that we were in a really strong position. Gary O'Donnell was shutting down Carlton's rovers Adrian Gleeson and Brent Heaver, and Mark 'Bomber' Thompson played the first half on Fraser Brown and took him out of the game. Sean Denham kept Greg Williams relatively quiet. Joe Misiti dominated across half-back. Mark Mercuri starred across half-forward, and Mark Harvey was rock-solid at centre-half-back. I played a reasonable game. Michael Long was outstanding, with 33 possessions, and was a clear winner of the Norm Smith Medal for best player in a Grand Final.

Grand Finals are hard to get into and harder to win, so the game is never over until the siren sounds. But due to my lack of experience, halfway through the last quarter I thought the game was iced. I ran out to take a mark, took it a bit casually, and Ang Christou got his fist onto the ball.

The runner came out. 'Sheeds is not happy.' The coach's instruction was quite clear: 'Play it to the siren: if you don't play it to the siren you'll come off.'

I thought, *Hang on. We're six goals up, it's late in the last quarter and we're almost certain to win.*

His message was a big reminder. Our coach was a perfectionist, which meant that even at that late stage of the match he was going to demand that we keep doing everything properly and not let the game slip away.

We won the game 20.13.133 to 13.11.89. A comprehensive victory.

When the siren sounded, it was an extraordinary feeling. I remember watching Gary O'Donnell fall to the ground in a heap. Gary had missed out on the 1984 and 1985 premierships, but now he'd finally been part of a premiership team. The year after our victory I told the *Herald Sun*: 'He was so happy and so relieved that it was all over, that he'd finally achieved what he'd probably been after for the whole of his life. He was like a little kid afterwards. And to think I'd been there for 20 games. It makes you realise how lucky you are.' It was a prophetic quote. It was to be seven years before I played in another Grand Final.

As Kevin Sheedy said: 'It's a year that Essendon Football Club stole a premiership.' Our leap from finishing 8th the year before to the premiership was the biggest jump up the ladder by any club since 1980, when Richmond too came from 8th to win the flag. The victory gave Sheeds his third Grand Final from five attempts.

It had been a great year for Essendon. We won the Foster's Cup, Gavin Wanganeen won the Brownlow Medal and Michael Long won the Norm Smith Medal – all in the Year of Indigenous People.

The game had been an average one for me. I'd kicked a couple of goals and certainly earned my spot. But I was only 20 years old, and I remember thinking that it had all happened very early.

In the reports on the Grand Final match the next day, the newspapers spoke of 'the miracle of youth'. There were headlines like 'Baby Bombers forget about respect for Blues'.

Were there dangers in winning the flag so early in our careers? Could experiencing premiership glory too young lead to complacency? I've certainly heard players who've won a flag a couple of years into their career saying they'd thought it would always be easy . . . but had then had to wait another decade before they even played in another Grand Final, let alone won another flag. If players haven't got the right influences and environment around them and don't have that inner drive and self-discipline, I believe there can be problems.

In 1993 I was 20 and a lot of the guys I played with were around the same age. It's possible that it took a few of the players some time to get back on track. They'd lost the hunger, and thus the ability to really push forward and give it everything.

Sheeds was asked about the dangers of early success. He did not subscribe to the view that a young team that won the flag could 'become blinded by the afterglow' of the win. He was quoted in the *Herald Sun* as saying, 'Early success didn't affect the players I played with, like Hart, Bartlett, Bourke, Clay and Green. I can't see why these guys are any different.'

There were major celebrations after the 1993 Grand Final win. We went to the Hilton Hotel for the 'big dinner'. I might have achieved premiership glory just hours earlier, but to me another triumph lay ahead: I was about to be interviewed on *Hey Hey It's Saturday!* This was a show that Mum, Dad, Amilia, Katherine and I used to sit at home and watch on a Saturday night when I lived in Canberra. It was a really surreal experience now to be on it myself. It was as good a sign as any that I was beginning to make a name for myself as a footy player, and secretly I hoped that my mates back in Canberra were watching the show.

Chapter 4

The Hangover

It's dawn in early 1994. From my flat in Moonee Ponds, I can hear the traffic building up on Mt Alexander Road; the commuter crawl is about to start, people are going to their jobs. I'm already at my job. Well, I'm training for it. I've kicked a football against a brick wall and it's flying back at me. I catch it going up, going down, whizzing off in different directions. Sometimes I'm surprised I manage to catch it; other times it seems perfectly reasonable that it lands neatly and cleanly in my hands. Why do footballers live to have a footy in their hands? I'm exposed to the endless mathematical equations that exist when an egg-shaped leather ball hits an immovable object and returns. It's the variables I'm interested in, the not-quite-knowing where it will go, the crazy angles it veers off at, the whole imponderable of a football.

I'd always been taught by Dad and my footy coaches – or even through hearing stories about Don Bradman hitting a ball against a water tank with a stump – that a lot of footy is about touch. If you have good touch and good hands and you don't fumble, you'll be competitive. Former St Kilda coach Stan Alves once came to speak to the Essendon players and spoke about touch: you should always have a football in your hand, he said, because the guy with the best touch will always have an advantage. I worked out that if there is no one to kick to – and often there isn't – I should throw the ball against the wall. I still do it now. It gets my hands and my reflexes going.

I went through a few footies, mind you. They'd be grazed by the wall until they were virtually furry, the redness of the Sherrin reduced to brown through overuse. (The property steward at the club hated me because I asked for a new footy every four or five weeks).

What this exercise means is that when a ball comes to you in a game you won't fumble. A fumble means a lost possession. The less you fumble, the more effective you are. It's about playing the percentages. Possessions are precious, and not to be wasted. If you get the ball and handball it within a second, not many people can stop you.

In life, when opportunities come your way, do you have the confidence or 'touch' gained through practice to seize the opportunity?

In 1994, I think we let ourselves down. Sure, David Calthorpe and Mark Mercuri played state footy for Victoria and I won the best and fairest at Essendon, but it did take the team too long to get back to where we were in 1993. We missed the finals. We should have done better.

On the other hand, we'd been relatively lucky to win the 1993 Grand Final. We were the best team that year, but the standard wasn't exceptional. We weren't the classic premiership team we would be in 2000, or that the Brisbane Lions became from 2001 onwards or that North Melbourne had been in the 1990s. In 1993 there had been no standout team.

I think we crept up on teams that year. We definitely deserved to win the Grand Final, but if we'd been put up against a truly great team, I don't think we would have come out as well. Sheeds's remark about us having stolen the flag was probably right.

There were reasons for our mini-decline. We lost some influential senior players. Mark Thompson barely played anymore, and the 1993 Grand Final had indeed been Tim's swan song. A lot of the older guys who'd been the backbone of the team were close to retiring also: David Grenvold, Darren Bewick, Peter Somerville, Paul Salmon, Gary O'Donnell and Michael Long (who seriously injured his knee a year later). We couldn't get a full team back in time to consolidate our 1993 success.

The young kids were the cream, but we hadn't yet become the backbone. In hindsight it is easy to see the lessons: young people need to surround themselves with the more experienced and make sure they learn from wise heads, and older people need to let that vital youthful exuberance rub off on them.

In 1994 we started well, beating Adelaide in the Ansett Cup Grand Final. We were going all right, but then we were hammered by injuries. A few of the guys probably thought they were travelling a bit better than they were. We lost our way and we lost focus. It's amazing how quickly things change when the focus is gone.

For me personally it was a pretty good year. I played all but two games and won my first club best and fairest, which I was proud of. I missed those two games because of a punctured lung – this was the second time I'd sustained one from a current or future teammate. The first was courtesy of Ben Doolan in 1992, and the second was from Michael Symons, who kneed me in the back when we were playing Fitzroy: friendly fire.

In 1994 a lot of the senior players were injured, so it was up to the young ones to stand up to some of the tactics being used on us. One day I found myself in the unlikely role of the tough guy. It was not something I was terribly successful at.

In a game against Sydney (the club Derek Kickett went to after being left out of the 1993 Grand Final side) it became a physical contest, which we were losing.

I went to Sheeds and told him: 'We're getting knocked around out there. A lot of the younger guys are getting hammered. What should we do?'

'If one of their players gets one of ours,' Sheeds advised, 'don't go out and hit him. Go and hit the bloke next to him, and say, "For each one of ours you hit, we're going to knock down one of yours."' That was his theory.

So I tried it.

Derek Kickett knocked a couple of ours over, so I went and knocked over one of the Sydney players. Then I went up to Derek and said, 'If you keep knocking over our blokes, I'll keep knocking over yours!'

Derek looked at me as if to say: 'Are you serious?'

Then he went and knocked three more over. I realised at that point that this was not a competition I would win.

I said to Sheeds: 'You'd better get someone else to do it, because it's not working that well for me.'

In 1994 I began to emerge as a leader, though not officially. Gary O'Donnell was out there, but most of our natural leaders were injured. Sheeds was throwing a lot of players into the mix. This had worked really well in 1993, but it wasn't working in 1994.

The ones he threw into the fray that season just weren't up to it. I wouldn't call 1994 a building year; I would call it a year where we wasted time with a few guys.

I was starting to hit my straps as a player, although it was probably in 1995 that I really began to become dominant. In 1994 I'd only played about 35 games in total. Even though I was starting to build a reputation, people weren't too worried about me, so I was still getting under the opposition's guard.

I played a few positions that year: a lot of centre-half forward, a bit of full-back, a bit of centre-half back. (I played a lot of centre-half back and full-back when Dustin Fletcher wasn't there, or when Mark Harvey was injured.)

I took my football very seriously, but managed to combine it with my civil engineering studies. I always thought a lot about how I would play the team we were meeting, and which player I would probably get. I still do this, which might explain why I don't sleep well during the football season, and sometimes have to take a sleeping pill on the night before a game. I'm always right on the day of the game and I sleep sensationally when there's no footy on, but around footy games I become anxious the night before and find it hard to sleep.

Part of my sleep problem might also stem from a car accident I had in 1994 before a game. I used to do shopping-centre appearances with a man called Mike Williamson, a delightful rascal who in the 1970s had been a football commentator on television and famous for his excitable calls – well before Rex Hunt began going over the top. Mike's main claim to fame was when, in the thrilling Grand Final between Collingwood and St Kilda in 1966, with just minutes left on the clock and suggestions that the match would be a draw, Mike yelled: 'I tipped this!' At one point Mike's co-caller,

Alan 'Butch' Gale, said: 'I think I'm going to have a heart attack!' to which Mike replied, 'I've had three already!' It was wonderfully raw commentary, well before the days when commentators were slick, with stats at their fingertips.

Mike organised us to do appearances where we would run handball clinics and talk to kids. A few AFL players were involved, including Paul 'Fish' Salmon and Collingwood's Tony Shaw. Mike and I got on really well, the appearances were good fun, you earned a little pocket money, and it gave me valuable experience in appearing in public and talking on a microphone in front of a live audience (which could often be quite big). I did these appearances for him for a couple of years and it certainly increased my confidence in dealing with the media.

One day Fish couldn't make it and he asked me if I could do him a favour and go to Cranbourne Shopping Centre at 8 o'clock on a Friday – for something like $15. I think Fish was pocketing the rest of the money. But at age 20, $15 is $15. So I said, 'No worries.'

The Cranbourne Shopping Centre gig went well, and I agreed to do one at Werribee Plaza before a game one night. At one traffic light on the way to the shopping centre I thought I had the green, but I didn't. I went through and a car hit me. It was my fault, but although we hit pretty hard, the passenger in the other car was fine and I was fine.

That night I couldn't sleep, and ever since then I've struggled to sleep before games; I've sometimes stayed awake until 3 in the morning. Luckily, it doesn't cause me to play badly – the adrenaline lets me play through it. And having children means I'm continually a bit tired, so these days sleep comes faster. If I need to, I'll take a sleeping tablet the night before a game. Otherwise, a vicious circle can develop: the less I sleep, the more anxious I get. Then I start punching the pillow, or have a go at my wife because she's breathing a little bit heavily – due, of course, to the fact that she's sleeping and I'm not. It's best to step away from that kind of cycle.

When I was studying for my civil engineering degree at RMIT, I would sometimes study for an exam all week, getting only four hours' sleep each night, and then go out and play footy, and play well. It's amazing what a fit 20-year-old body will let you do, and I guess if you don't do it regularly you're okay.

In the middle of winter in 1995 I played what I call a 'milestone' game.

It was against Richmond on a Friday night at the MCG: the result was a draw. But in that match I felt my game changed into something new. I dominated that night. I did things I'd never done before. I kicked five goals, had the ball on a string, did some really special things, turned possessions into goals. I felt I took my game to another level.

During that game I remember thinking that I could get the ball at will. I knew that when it came to a contest I would win it. I knew when I was lining up for goals that the ball would go through. This had never happened to me before, and it gave me the confidence to try anything. I have often wondered if this is how Wayne Carey felt week in week out, or if Tiger Woods knows every time he hits the ball that it will end up down the middle of the fairway, or if Pelé felt like this during his great World Cup campaigns. For me it was the first time it had happened. Unfortunately, it was a rare occurrence, but the 1995 season is the one I will always remember as the first time I had that feeling. As I got older and listened to more experts I realised that this is what is known as 'being in the zone'.

At the end of the 1995 season the club agreed that I could have five weeks off. I had been studying pretty hard, and had finished my exams in the middle of November, and football-wise, it had been a bruising, long and sometimes frustrating year. I needed a break. Tania, my girlfriend and wife-to-be, and I went to Europe.

It was an eye-opening trip backpacking through Europe, and it really cleared my head. When I returned, I was fresh in body and mind, ready to train and ready to play. It was fantastic to get away and not think about football for a while.

Not that I ignored training. I think I'm psychologically and physically programmed to train all the time, even when I'm with my girlfriend somewhere like the beautiful Belgian town of Bruges, north-west of Brussels. I wrote in *The Sunday Age* about the memorable training sessions I did:

> I had thermal underwear underneath a tracksuit, a balaclava over my head and still the icy wind went straight through me, returning bad memories of Windy Hill on a cold August night . . . Finding gyms was a bit tricky. Even though Europeans on the whole are very friendly and have good English (much better than my French, German, Spanish and Italian), I still ran into difficulties. I turned up at a German gymnasium expecting rows of dumbbells and buckets of sweat only to be greeted by a very refined school of German students practising music. Gymnasium, or 'gimnazioom' as it is pronounced in German, means a school of learning, and differentiates schools as we know them from trade schools.

At the end of 1992 I probably hadn't been ready for senior football, for the reason that I didn't have the fitness I needed. I knew I had to work on that, so Danny Corcoran (who was the club's fitness adviser before he became football manager) and I organised a program that pushed me through to a new level of fitness. Without the work Danny and I did, I wouldn't have had the motor to keep going for a long season, and to play at the level I wanted.

So, body and soul were ready in 1996. I broke my finger in one match and missed a game, but other than that, there were no injuries, which was a rarity in my career. I was performing consistently.

The 1996 season went according to plan in almost every way, in fact. I was virtually injury-free, I played good football – and sometimes dominated – and my studies were going well. It was a pretty heady time for a 23-year-old.

That year, one game stands out for me, though it was probably not the most glamorous or memorable to watch. It was the match against Sydney, mid-year, on a boggy SCG – horrible conditions. I was playing on Paul Kelly, a rugged and hugely competitive player who'd won the Brownlow Medal the year before. We had a great contest. He's a terrific guy to play against because he's very physical and very tough. He's always going to give you everything. I had a fantastic game that day and I think he played pretty well too. The game was a draw. That was disappointing, but I knew I had given everything and had dominated. When you know you're in a contest and you come out of it having given everything you had, it's pretty special.

This was a match that now makes me think about how one moment can determine whether you are considered a failure or a success. Is it right that one rushed behind or missed kick can decide a person's fate?

Throughout my career I have followed the 'winning is the only thing that is important' line. Now this seems harsh: judging a sportsperson or team on one roll of the green or bounce of the ball shows a lack of empathy, and an ignorance of the part that luck plays in life and sport. The greatest example of this is Greg Norman, the Shark. Some say he is a choker; others declare him a champ. What a difference one fluked chip off the green can make to the legacy of a sporting icon.

That night in Sydney I believe we were all winners. We had worked our butts off to draw that game. We didn't bring home the bacon, but we did, like the Shark, play as hard and tough as we could, and walked away with our heads held high.

In the second qualifying final against Brisbane I had a very good game, kicking two goals and being named among the best.

A week later we played West Coast in the second semi-final. Coming into that game I felt exhilarated – I was going to have a great day as a footballer. All I could think about as I walked down the race to the ground was my dad's comment: 'Make yourself a player.' And as I stepped on the ground I started smiling. I looked around at 80,000 ready to watch me play footy and knew I would never be in better form; I was in the best shape of my life and there was nothing that could stop me. How happy was I? I was there to do a job and I was as fit and good as I was ever going to be.

I got the ball 31 times and kicked three goals in the second quarter. We won the game by 77 points. My instincts had been right.

Garry Lyon in *The Age* wrote: 'I challenge anyone to walk away from Saturday's game between West Coast and Essendon and talk about anything other than James Hird . . . As a fellow forward who also fancies the odd run on the ball, Hird's perform-ance was a joy.' He went on:

It was the first time I had observed Hird from the grandstand, and maybe for the first time I'm starting to appreciate his special qualities: deceptive speed, great lateral movement, quick and creative hands and hard running. When you start out in the AFL, you tend to pick out players as role models for your specific game. I remember paying particular attention to the way Terry Daniher, Tony Morwood and Dermott Brereton went about their footy, and unashamedly trying to apply some of the things I learned from them. You are never too old to learn, and the injury gods willing, I would not mind trying to add a little bit of Hird's style to my game as well.

Eagles coach Mick Malthouse also praised my performance, making a prophetic prediction: 'I think they have probably got the Brownlow medallist playing out there at centre-half-forward, half-forward flank or wherever he chooses to play. He is one of the best players I have seen running around for a long time.'

I'd felt fantastic going into that game. Running out onto the ground, I couldn't help smiling and laughing. I felt so good about playing footy in front of a big crowd, knowing I would play well.

Later the players watched a highlights package of the game in the TV review, and they saw me laughing as I walked out. My good mate Rick Olarenshaw said, 'I know why you're laughing – because you know you're going to thrash anyone you play on.'

He knew how I felt.

By winning, we'd booked a place in one of the two preliminary finals. We were to play the Swans at the SCG. Not one of us knew how the result of that game would haunt us.

The ball flashed up and down the SCG. The play was at a frenetic pace, given what was at stake: a place in the Grand Final. It was a tight encounter all night, but it was in the last 30 minutes that the extraordinary drama unfolded.

I put one through two minutes into the last quarter, which put us in front. Michael Symons kicked a beautiful banana snap to give us a two-goal break – there were four minutes left. Then wingman Stuart Maxfield delivered the ball to Dale Lewis in the goal square, reducing the gap to one goal.

And then, for us, it all went horribly wrong. Swans centreman Darryn Creswell goaled to level the scores. There were 90 seconds left . . . The Swans' Wade Chapman then passed to the big man, Tony Lockett, who marked – 18 seconds before the final siren. Our chances went up in flames when one of my teammates (I've forgotten who) didn't go back to the ball as hard as he should have and Plugger took that mark. Lockett used that 18 seconds to prepare for his kick.

It was the classic finish schoolboys dream about: the kick after the siren to put your team in the Grand Final. Everyone knew the game was over when the siren sounded. Tony Lockett is, of course, one of the very great full-forwards of our time, the holder of the goal-kicking record (1357) and an awesome physical presence on the field. If anyone was going to kick a score from 45 metres out, it was him. We didn't know he'd been struggling with injury, and had had trouble kicking over 40 metres in a private session during the week with coach Rodney Eade.

The big man settled over the ball, as he'd done hundreds of times before, and came in for the kick with every eye in the SCG on him, never mind the football-loving nation watching on TV. He lumbered in and kicked. It started straight, then veered left. The kick sailed through for a point, but it may as well have been 10 goals. It put Sydney into the Grand Final, to play North Melbourne, and left us shattered.

As the goal umpire signalled the most valuable behind Plugger ever kicked, the Swans players leapt onto him and formed a human pyramid. It was devastating for us, and lucky for Plugger that he had the strength of three horses – he now had his whole team sitting on him.

We'd thrown the game away. We had been four goals up at one stage in the last quarter, and you don't lose a game from there. Plugger's point served us right. We had given them a chance to come back and they had taken it.

We had taken our foot off the pedal. However, we would have been beaten by 50 goals the next week anyway, because Wanganeen was out, Lloydy had a lacerated kidney and Darren Bewick and Michael Long were injured. We would barely have had a team for the Grand Final, and North would have decimated us.

In the unlikely venue of the romantic old cricketers' rooms at the SCG afterwards, Sheeds lost it. He was furious. I've never seen him so angry at a group of players before or since. He's on record as saying he regrets some of the things he said that day.

He smashed the wall, put a hole in it, yelled some obscenities, ripped into Rick Olarenshaw and Justin Blumfield, before ripping into the rest of us.

I'm not convinced about the method of communication he used, but I understood why he was angry. We threw that game away. It was pretty shattering to walk away knowing that we'd let a chance to get in the Grand Final slip. That's a terrible reality to face, because you never know if you'll get another chance to play in a Grand Final.

But life went on.

Two days later, we had to attend another big event: the Brownlow Medal count on the Monday night. The newspapers had started mentioning my Brownlow chances as the season came to an end. I was playing good, consistent football in the final weeks of the season. The last four home and away games of 1996 were some of the best footy I'd ever played. We played Adelaide,

Collingwood, Sydney and the Western Bulldogs, and in those games I was awarded 11 Brownlow votes.

I had never dreamt of winning a Brownlow – it was too much of an individual honour. My dreams were more about *team* success. Still, even as a kid I had been very aware of its significance. I'd heard all the stories about someone having to go around to Bob Skilton's house in 1959 to tell him he'd won; about the great players who'd never won one: Leigh Matthews, Kevin Bartlett, Gary Ablett. Brownlow night was always a good one. There were the match-by-match highlights, the television close-ups of favourites taking nervous gulps of beer as the night came to a climax, not to mention the bold fashion choices (Swans player Graham Teasdale's brown velvet suit stands out in my memory).

And here I was, late in the 1996 season, one of the favourites for football's highest honour.

The build-up to Brownlow night is always intriguing – players firming in the betting, the possibility of a roughie bolting. When you're part of the speculation (and I was one of the strong favourites, along with Michael Voss) it becomes both exciting and a bit of a distraction.

I didn't feel too much pressure on me though. I'd think about it more now, at 33, than back then. I was only 23, and I just got on with playing. Also, footy wasn't as big in the media then as it is now. It wasn't the back six pages of the paper; it might have been one or two. And there weren't three channels covering it – Foxtel didn't even exist. So although it was big, you could still get away from it. It's not the same now.

The count was held at Melbourne's World Trade Centre, the home of the Crown Casino before it opened over the river. I was living with a guy from Canberra at that stage who played for the Uni Blues football team, and they'd just played in a Grand Final. He said, 'Come up at 1 o'clock. We're having a drink at Jimmy

Watson's.' We lived nearby, in Parkville, so I walked up and had a couple of beers with him before the count, to settle my nerves.

We took our seats at the Essendon table alongside Steve Alessio, Gavin Wanganeen, Joe Misiti and Gary O'Donnell and their partners. I knew I had a fair chance of winning. The votes were going all right. And then, about halfway through the count, I went to the toilet. I'd had enough of sitting there chewing my fingernails, which is a bad habit of mine. I needed a moment to myself, away from the cameras panning onto me every now and then, away from the tension. Plus I was still in a foul mood about the loss to the Swans.

By Round 17 I thought I should head back to the table – and then it started to get tense. With two rounds to go I was three votes behind Michael Voss. In the last round, Vossy's game was before mine. He got a couple of votes and that put him three in front of me, so he couldn't lose. And then I got my three, and it was a three-way tie between me, Vossy and Corey McKernan.

The three of us scored 21 votes each, but Corey was ineligible because he'd had a one-match suspension in Round 6 for deliberately kneeing Geelong's John Barnes in the back. He was the first man in VFL/AFL history to lose the award this way. However, Corey was playing in the Grand Final, so I didn't feel too sorry for him. He'd be where we all wanted to be on Saturday.

So Michael Voss and I were joint winners. It was amazing. You don't think you're ever going to win something like that, and you definitely don't play for it. In the years since, I've never thought, *Oh, I could do that again.* Putting together 20-odd good games is pretty hard. You can't plan it or have it as a goal – you'd burn yourself out. And there are so many variables. The umpires have to see you play well. There are plenty of games where you think you should have got votes and you don't, or you shouldn't have got votes and you did. And it's easy to understand how the umpires can get it wrong. When I go to the footy I can't tell who was the best player on the ground. It's very hard to get it right every time.

But not everyone appreciated the significance of the medal. Later that night Gary O'Donnell grabbed me. 'Come on,' he said, 'we'll go out and have a few beers.'

We went out to Bobby McGee's, on the corner of Exhibition and LaTrobe, in the city, but they wouldn't let us in.

'Come on, mate,' said Gary. 'He's James Hird. He just won the Brownlow!'

The guy was immovable. 'I don't care who he is. I don't care what he's won. You're not coming in!'

So we went home.

All that week Michael Voss and I went everywhere together – signings and lunches and appearances at the Royal Melbourne Show and photo shoots. The last of these almost never-ending commitments was a lap of honour at the MCG. And then at the Grand Final we were sitting next to each other again. Michael wanted to jump on a plane back to Brisbane and I just wanted to go to bed. I estimate I'd had about five hours' sleep the whole week. Everyone expects you to have a beer with them. It's a great week, but by the end of it I think Michael and I were both well and truly sick of the sight of each other.

Vossy's a terrific guy. I haven't really spoken to him in depth for a few years now, but back then he was very relaxed. He's a champion player with an intense desire to be good at what he's doing, but he also obviously enjoys life. He's gone on to an amazing career, captaining the Brisbane side to three premierships. He's tough and hard and uncompromising – and very skilful. He is as good a player as you'll ever see. I think he's been able to keep a very level head and a good perspective on life. He has a wife and kids, and I think he respects a good family life, which gains him points from me.

On the eve of my 200th game, he wrote an article about me which was very complimentary:

> I had a very public first meeting with James Hird. It was the 1996 Brownlow Medal dinner, in front of 1500 people, and with a few hundred thousand watching on television. We'd just shared the game's highest honour. We were just a pair of kids living a football dream. He was 23 and I was 21. It was the beginning of an extraordinary week and of a lifelong admiration for one of football's genuine greats.

He described our incredibly busy week:

> Hirdy was my chaperone. He'd pick me up from my hotel in the morning and deliver me back there afterwards, and we sat together during the North Melbourne–Sydney Grand Final . . . Getting to know Hirdy was fantastic. It gave me a real insight because, for all the public pressure I copped, his was much, much heavier. I've always said I'd love to experience football life in Melbourne, but I know there'd be parts I wouldn't particularly enjoy. That smothering attention is one of them.

They were kind words. One day when we're both retired we may have a beer and reminisce about that mad week in 1996.

That year I won my third club best and fairest in a row. I didn't realise then how special that was. I didn't go out and celebrate hugely after any of those awards. I thought playing hard and playing fair was just what you were meant to do: you were given a job and you did it.

After 1996, when the injuries started piling up, I realised that it isn't so easy to win a best and fairest after all. It took me until 2003 – seven years – to win another one.

I look back on 1994, 1995 and 1996 as years when I was maturing. I didn't feel as much in control of the game then as I did sometimes in 2000 or 2003, or even recently. I felt I still had a lot to learn, but that I was getting better all the time. It's a strange feeling to win best-and-fairests when you really don't think you yet have command of the game.

Winning the Brownlow did change my life, but not all parts of it. The way I was regarded inside the football industry didn't change. People know who the good players are, and you get respect as a good player. But outside the inner sanctum I definitely received more recognition. I would walk down the street and even people who are not footy heads would come up to me and say, 'Are you James Hird? I heard you won the Brownlow Medal.' I received better endorsement deals, more money. So there are certainly advantages. It was a pretty fine cap to a mostly fantastic year for me.

But I would have gladly swapped it for a Grand Final win.

Chapter 5

Family

The Grand Hotel in Essendon was a local pub where the 1993 Bomber players went every Saturday night. It has now been turned into apartments, so like the hospital I was born in, it exists only in history and memory. But the Grand will always hold a special place in my heart, because it's where I met Tania Poynton.

Tania was studying law and working part-time as a barmaid at the Grand. I was 20 years old, shy with girls and unsure about the best way to approach them. Not only that, but things hadn't always gone according to plan in the past.

Just a few years before this particular night at the Grand, I'd asked a girl to go to my Year 12 formal with me. That was a big enough deal in itself – I had no idea how to ask. I was so embarrassed, I sort of mumbled an invitation. Not a Hugh Grant sort of mumble, more an awkward teenager sort of mumble. Still, she said yes, and I was rapt. But a couple of days before the big night, I came down with a really bad cold; I couldn't breathe through my nose and I sounded shocking. Now, back then, whenever I had a bad cold before a footy game I'd use smelling salts. So I decided to give them a go just before I picked her up.

Feeling more confident with an unblocked nose, I picked up my date from her place, and off we went to the formal. When I arrived, I took off my jacket, put it on a chair and went over to talk to my mates. (You know how it is – all the boys on one side, all the girls on the other.) Halfway through the night, it was time to put my jacket back on for a special dance. But my jacket stank. I couldn't work out what it was, and I could see my partner thinking, *What's that smell?*

The smelling salts bottle had broken. Now, smelling salts are really strong, so soon everyone was asking what the smell was – and I was asking too. I was holding my partner quite close as we danced, and there was nothing else for it: I had to lose that jacket. It was never seen again, that coat. Unfortunately it was a hired jacket, so I lost my deposit.

To this day I can remember that smell. I believe my date knew exactly where it was coming from.

So, fast forwarding to 1993 . . . I saw Tania working on the bar and asked our group if anyone knew her. Stephanie, Gavin Wanganeen's girlfriend, said she did, and we went across to say hello. In Tania's break, we had a drink together and I asked her out to dinner. I'd been best on ground the previous week and had won a dinner for two at the Melbourne Oyster Bar. That became our first date. At the time I thought it was pretty cool, but I look back now and cringe.

I didn't say very much that night, but luckily, she is a good talker and kept the conversation going. I was as nervous as I would have been before playing in a Grand Final. I used to watch my mates and wonder how they did it. How were they so smooth? I definitely wasn't smooth.

I don't think she was terribly impressed – it took me a long time to get another date with her. Weeks later, I invited her to the 1993 Brownlow Medal count. We were sitting with Gavin Wanganeen and Stephanie on the Essendon table, and we watched as Gavin won the medal. This second date worked out a bit better, probably because there were hundreds of other people in the room and you couldn't talk much while the count was going on. We had fun together and we were both thrilled for Gavin. Five days later Tania and I – and again, thousands of other people – celebrated once more when Essendon won the premiership.

Tania and I were married four years later, on 11 October 1997, in a traditional wedding at St John's Church in Toorak. Our reception, with 170 close friends and relatives, was at Ripponlea, in Elsternwick. It was a fantastic day which, as the old saying goes, 'went too quickly'.

The next day we left for Paris, an exciting place to begin our new life together. Paris became then and remains my favourite travel destination. I love going there and experiencing the food, the wine, the people, the clothes. Just walking around Paris and looking at the people can occupy you for hours. The architecture is beautiful, and history and culture are part of the air you breathe.

We spent two weeks travelling around France, including the Loire Valley, the wine areas around Burgundy and Bordeaux, and Avignon, Nice and Monte Carlo. In Monte Carlo we ran into umpire Scott McLaren, who I would have an interesting time with a few years later. Scott and his wife were also on their honeymoon. Eight years later, in 2005, when I was trying to make up with him after the spray I'd given him on *The Footy Show*, he brought up that meeting in Monte Carlo, saying that when we met on their honeymoon, we'd had a good chat and had seemed to get on really well . . . and then I went and did this to him! It's a very small world.

Tania and I first fell in love with Europe in 1995 when we went backpacking there. That was the first time Tania and I went away together. The five weeks off that the club had given me was an extraordinary break for a footballer, and I made sure I didn't waste the opportunity. We booked a big trip – to Egypt, Israel, Italy, England, Spain, Austria, Germany and Belgium.

Possibly my favourite place on that trip was Bruges, in Belgium. We had intended to stay there for one day and ended up staying four. It was a cobblestoned village with chocolatiers on every second corner and beer halls on every other. They like their beer in Bruges – there are something like 760 varieties available. It was also the first time I'd experienced snow in a town. We were walking around in that medieval village when suddenly the first snow of the season began to fall. There was magic in that.

The fact that Bruges is also the starting destination for Flanders and the battlefields of World War I was not lost on us either. You get a feeling for the enormity of what the soldiers experienced when you visit bunkers in $-3°$ Celsius temperatures and pass row upon row of white crosses in the cemeteries, when you look at the trenches and you read about the conditions the soldiers endured. They didn't have the right equipment, and many of them froze to death. There were more deaths in the winter from freezing than from gunfire. We were there in the middle of December – which is not the coldest time in Europe – and I had on all the jumpers and coats I'd brought. How someone could live through that, in the mud, is quite astonishing. It's living history there: even now an average of five people lose limbs to undetonated mines each year in the fields of Flanders.

I was 22 and it was a big education for me. I had never been overseas, except with the footy club (where you stay in your own little world and rarely see anything of the history or culture of wherever you are), so it was a fantastic experience.

We bought Eurail passes and travelled by train between stopovers. I felt fitter than ever before because I was walking everywhere and training here and there. Lugging a backpack for five weeks is pretty hard work.

Sometimes we stayed on the train, and sometimes we stayed in crappy places. Other times we got lucky. One of the most amazing rooms we stayed in was the attic of a Viennese woman's house, which you accessed up some windy stairs. When we reached the top we were met by a vaulted ceiling, feather eiderdowns, Tyrolean hand-carved furniture and a view of snow falling outside. It was picture perfect.

Tania is a huge bargain hunter. Within reason, she'll bargain anyone down, and she often takes great pride in it. In Florence, for instance, we got off the train at 11 o'clock at night and had nowhere to stay. I could just see us looking for somewhere for the next two hours. A guy approached us and asked if we were looking for somewhere to stay. I said, 'Yes', and he said, '100,000 lire.' Tania immediately said we weren't interested at that price and offered him 30,000 lire. She got him down to 50,000 lire, with breakfast included. I was rapt. It turned out to be a great room, too, with full-length shuttered windows, a huge parquetry floor and terrific furniture. It had a lovely homely feel. He even personally brought us breakfast in the morning. I think if you're an attractive blonde girl, haggling works. I would just stand in the background and wait for the price to be agreed on.

It was all part of the fun of being a long way from home and experiencing a different world. It was a good way to live, but we haven't done it like that since. It would certainly be a lot harder with children in tow. Also, footballers today don't have the freedom we had then. There is too much at stake financially, for a start. We went skiing in St Moritz. Today, if you were injured doing that, it would nullify your contract. I was careful – and I wasn't ridiculously ambitious with my skiing, but I was in my early twenties, had a great opportunity in front of me and a long time to get over an injury if it happened.

The trip was a terrific experience in terms of culture and history – we both learned a huge amount. One of my regrets is that while footy has let me see parts of the world, it hasn't let me spend as much time as I would like overseas. There is so much to learn and experience.

I will encourage my kids to do as much travelling as they can while they are young. It is easier then, because you don't care as much about the standard of your accommodation, you're hungry for adventure, and you're not too committed financially and professionally at home. It is an invaluable experience. People who have a year off between school and uni are doing a smart thing, in my view.

Football doesn't allow this sort of personal development time. It does make you mature in many ways long before you are ready: social responsibility and the ability to handle success are things most footballers develop before their peers. What footy doesn't leave room for is the development of a worldly perspective. For most footballers, including me, the centre of the world is the football ground they are playing on and the newspapers they are described in. This can insulate young men from the realities of life, but it is understandable. People say we need more perspective, but the passion we footballers have for our game, which is one of our most important tools, brings with it a kind of narrowness.

I would love to find a way to bring a greater understanding of other views to footballers – and to people in general. Can anyone say they truly understand someone else's view of the world, or someone else's culture? How many wars or arguments could have been prevented if people didn't get trapped in their own small world? When negotiating a deal in business, wouldn't we achieve more successful outcomes for both sides if we truly understood the other side's wants and background?

My trips overseas and my relationship with Tania have given me a broader outlook on life. I am the person I am to a large extent because of Mum, Dad, Amilia and Katherine, all of whom I love very much. They gave me – and still give me – a great sense of perspective. Fortunately, when I met Tania Poynton I met another family who broadened my view of the world.

When I met Tania, back in the winter of 1993, I was spellbound by her natural beauty and the ease with which she talked and entertained those listening to her. What I didn't realise was the extended clan that came as part of the package. Tania comes from a family very similar to my own: very tight, very friendly, and very principled.

Her family extends from Melbourne to the western districts, where her grandfather, Tag, and Grandmother Ivy made a huge impact on the social, and the physical, landscape. Tag was a successful developer, farmer and architect in the city of Warrnambool, and many of the town's buildings and parks bear his stamp. One of the more famous is the Fletcher Jones Gardens, which still hold pride of place as you drive into Warrnambool on the Melbourne road.

As a footballer you travel the country a bit, and many a time down Warrnambool way I have been stopped by a resident of the town who either knew Tania's grandparents, or went to school with her mother, or was a lifesaver at the local surf lifesaving club with Tania or her brother Greg, or is directly related to the Walter family.

Tania's family are a friendly, talkative bunch, and they welcomed me into their home from the start. Robin (Tania's mother) and Bill (her partner) had a house first in East Keilor and later Toorak which was a welcome sanctuary – and a pleasant change to living with my mate Alistair Carr in a two-bedroom flat next door to the local funeral home.

It took me a while to convince Tania that she should see me regularly; remember, I was a shy young kid from Canberra with not much to say. But her brother Greg was well and truly in my corner. After my first dinner at her house he said to Tania, who was at that stage quite unsure about me, that he thought I was a good person and she should give me a chance and not judge me too hastily.

After Greg's recommendation our relationship grew. As time went on I was further and further embraced by the family. Many a night I would stay after dinner to talk with Robin, Bill, Greg, Cathy and Chris while Tania was upstairs studying. We would discuss many topics, from football to politics, religion to music, usually sampling one of Bill's first-growth 20-year-old French wines.

These were fun times. Tania would pop her head out of the office now and then, and listen as Robin would treat me as one of her own, not wanting to take over from my own mother but realising that the young man in front of her needed a bit of guidance. In hindsight, I see how important this was to me. I was a long way from home, with only my mates as role models, so occasionally I did need a wise head or a piece of stern advice.

During this time I spent a lot of time with Tania's younger siblings, Cathy and Chris. At the time Cathy was going through her last two years of school. She would often grab me for 'a quick chat' . . . which would go on for two or three hours. The chats would encompass boyfriends, studies and life in general.

Cathy is an extremely gifted and attractive girl with the world at her feet. She has married a great guy (another James) and they now have their own family: Charlotte was born in August 2005.

Tania and I were very excited for her and James, but nowhere near as excited as our kids, who finally had their first cousin.

With both Greg – a successful businessman and a former member of *Young Talent Time* – and Chris, I had brothers. They're both good people (and lots of fun), but I didn't always have the nicest things to say about Chris. Chris has always been a great kid, and until we had our own children, he was someone I spent a lot of time with. Most of these excursions were fun, and we both had a laugh along the way. I met Chris when he was five, so we did some very cool things together. We went to the circus, the zoo, the footy and always had a great time.

Tania is a great person, and she is made better by her family. They are terrific, and when Greg finally asks Danielle to marry him they will be even better. The Poynton family I know is a credit to themselves and to Robin. She is the matriach of the family in a good way, making sure they all feel loved and treat each other with respect, and always having an open ear.

Spending time with them has made me a better person, and luckily, my family and Tania's family get on like a house on fire. We regularly spend Christmas Day together as a large group and now all holiday together in Queensland over the Christmas break. And it is a large group: all Tania's siblings and their partners, her mum and Bill; plus my mum, Amilia and her husband Cale, and Katherine and her fiancé Doug.

This is great for our kids also – because if it's not Tania and I taking them for a swim, it's Greg and Danielle going bikeriding with them, Chris playing with them at their level, Cale and Amilia playing tennis with them, Katherine and Doug doing creative things with them, or Cathy and James helping them to be responsible with baby Charlotte. I am sure it increases their self-confidence to know they are loved unconditionally by so many.

My family means everything to me. The best moments of my life involve my family, whether it's seven-year-old Stephanie in her mermaid costume telling me about her day, five-year-old Thomas begging for a kick fully dressed in his Essendon uniform (complete with number 5 on his back) or Alexander, who's three, wanting a cuddle.

Having three children is a delight, and hard work, especially for the first two years of the third child. But Alex is getting easier now and Tania and I are regaining a bit of a life together. When Alex was just born, Stephanie was four and Tommy was two, and you would sometimes just throw your hands in the air and hope the chaos would pass.

There is nothing I look forward to more than spending time at home with my family. What I like most about it is that it's completely unstructured. I organise my work commitments for the day into their pigeonholes, but I won't 'squeeze' my kids into a schedule. I don't believe in so-called quality time. What you need is *quantity*. You need a substantial amount of time to get to know them, and they need time to get to know you. Sometimes that means just being around.

It's interesting to look at previous generations and the way family roles have changed. Our grandfathers didn't have nearly the time to spend with our parents (their kids) that I have to spend with my children. I am lucky, too, because I work flexible hours and can have more time with my family than many parents can. But I notice that even so, when I go away on a training camp it takes some time to regain that ease; young kids especially gravitate towards those who give them time. It's pretty simple, really – if you give kids time, they love you.

I get to be a normal dad at Stephanie's school. In Year 1 a number of students tried to get her to have me sign things, but her teachers were fantastic. Given that there are a number of children with well-known parents at the school, the entire staff discussed the issue and decided on what is appropriate behaviour across the board (with no names mentioned). We have had little trouble since. I think it helps that in Melbourne there's so much footy that kids see a lot of footballers around; this reduces the issue somewhat.

My friends sometimes get annoyed with me when I won't go out with them because I want to hang out with my family at home. Whenever I have a choice about what to do, it is always that: stay at home with my family. Yes, kids are hard work at times, and sometimes they won't do what you've asked them and they are completely frustrating, but the joy you get from them is very special. We take lots of photos of them but not enough video. Tania asks me to take more footage, but I'm always afraid that if I'm shooting video, I'm actually missing the moment.

I will be really sad when my kids have grown up. I have no interest in them becoming 'easier'. Sure, at 4 am when one is vomiting and one won't go to bed you want to fast-track their growth, but if I could pick a Groundhog Day, a day around right now would be great.

Some parents say that when you have children you leave your ego at the door, and totally devote yourself to them. I haven't done that. You do need some ego to play footy. In some ways I consider myself reasonably selfish; there are times when I just say, 'I have to go and play footy' and I leave. And that's that. From February through to September I get a bit pedantic about things, and demand a bit more of my wife and kids. Playing footy is a high-pressure job, as are most jobs. But with footy, it's pressure to be good physically. One of the results of this is that in footy season you spend a bit more time on the couch than most people would. There's a reason you're sleeping a bit longer, but it still means your partner has a more demanding role than they might otherwise have. I am eternally grateful to Tania for picking up the slack.

I have a busy life now. If I'm not at the footy club, I'm at the office or at home. I do have a strategy for when things get too much: I turn my phone off and hide for the day. I ring the club and say I'm sick or ring work and say, 'Training's full-on.' On those days I sit at home, take Stephanie to school or have a kick with Tom. It doesn't happen often, but there are odd times when you literally can't find me, and I need to do that.

Taking your daughter to school might sound routine, but it's rewarding for me. I ensure that it happens routinely, at least once a week. When I hang out with my kids, I stumble across some precious moments. Stephanie is seven now, and tells me what she wants to listen to in the car on the way. At the moment it's a program called 'Battle of the Sexes' on FOX-FM that one of her friends at school listens to. We have a laugh and competition – it's a dad–daughter thing.

Tommy loves kicking the footy with me, just as my dad did with me. My mum has said Tommy reminds her of me at the same age. She told *The Australian* a story about Tommy in the back garden shouting, 'I'll be Matty Lloyd, Daddy. Who are you? You can be Dean Solomon, Daddy!'

A short word about each of my children . . .

Stephanie. My first child. My princess, my organiser, my achiever, the girl who always strives to please. Sometimes my inexperience makes me a hard taskmaster, but one who loves her. She has stolen my heart and she knows it. Her birth was a realisation of the love between Tania and me. I look at my angel and wonder how I'll be able to cope with the time when I'm no longer the most important man in her life.

Tom. He calls me his best mate. I'm sure he doesn't know what it means. But I do, and it gives me the strength to take on the world. He isn't petty, he isn't judgmental, he has a great inner strength, and he loves me because I'm his dad. His love is unconditional and he's always brimming with cuddles. Tom's love is honest, it's beautiful, and it's why I will do anything to protect my little number 5.

Alex. This boy, he's tough. I'm his daddy shark and he's my baby shark. Together we eat his older siblings, who we call 'the fishermen'. Next to the word 'stubborn' in the Macquarie Dictionary is a picture of Alex. But what can you expect with parents like Tania and me? Without his dimpled smile, warm cuddles and personality, our world would be a sadder place. This boy will change the world, and the rest of us will be better because of it.

Tania has been a huge support for my career. There's an old line used in many speeches: 'I couldn't have done it without her.' Well, I can assure you that is true with Tania. We have been through so much together, good times and bad. She has always been there, and is always rock solid with advice. She has shared my frustrations with the way football clubs are run. Sometimes they can be so small-minded – do players really need to be reprimanded if they don't have the right socks on at training? When people get caught up in stupid little things like that they lose sight of what is important. How can you have a vision about leading people and being successful and winning Grand Finals and living out your dreams when you're worried about what sort of socks someone's wearing at training? That stuff stops you being as good as you can be. Tania believes that it is my frustration with the small-mindedness of the club that will end my career, rather than injuries.

As happy as my family life is, I do have one great sadness, and that is my relationship with my father.

Growing up, Dad was my hero. He was the person I most wanted to be. He and my mother inspired me to be the footballer and the person I am. They formed me as a person. It wasn't a complicated formula. It was based on respect for people, a good work ethic and enjoyment of life.

My parents split up in 1994–95. My sisters lived through it; my middle sister, Amilia, bore the brunt because she was the oldest kid living at home. I'm not sure when the divorce papers were finalised, but it has actually hurt me more as time has gone on. My relationship with Dad was good until he and Mum separated. Unfortunately, when there's fracture with your parents, you're almost forced to take sides, and that's the way it's panned out. Whatever it was that happened between them, I didn't like the way it came about and the way my father treated those who loved him. The effect of that split on my relationship with Dad is the greatest regret in my life. It is as much my fault as it is his; I take half the blame. But I don't know how to solve it. I don't know how to make it better. Our relationship can never be the way it was.

When Dad came to visit me while I was in hospital in Perth, I was surprised but also pleased, and we talked again for the first time in years. We still do have a bond, and I do think he's a terrific person, but it is a difficult relationship because we haven't fully talked through and resolved what happened between my parents. It is strange to reflect that for the first 16 years of my life there was no greater influence on me than Dad (except maybe Mum) but for the second 16 years he has had no steady influence at all. It is sad for him, sad for me, and sad for my children, who don't see their grandfather. They have terrific grandparents on Tania's side and in Mum, but it's not the optimum outcome. I hope one day our relationship will be better than it is now.

I am not naturally a confrontational person, but the lesson I have learned from my relationship with my father is that not laying all your cards on the table, not being totally honest, leads to more hurt and pain. I have never been totally honest with my dad about the hurt I felt, and that has set up a permanent barrier between us. Fear of hurting someone or ruining a relationship makes most of us let things slide, and I believe this is a mistake.

TANIA HIRD ON JAMES

My purpose in writing this isn't to focus on James Hird the footballer; so many can do that and with much greater knowledge of football than me. My expertise, if you can call it that, lies with James Hird the person, the husband and father, and the way football has affected and continues to affect our life.

First, James Hird the person. The four adjectives I believe best describe James are 1) motivated 2) hardworking 3) strong in character and 4) good, and not necessarily in that order.

James is a typical first-born in many ways. He is sure of himself, although rarely arrogant; he is very principled; and although a natural leader, he's largely a conformer. Like many first-borns and high achievers he is highly critical of himself – often to a ridiculous extent. A job taken on must be done exceptionally; if it isn't, he blames only himself. (In footy, I have known him to play with broken fingers, concussion and many other injuries, and not once has he used these as excuses for a less than exceptional performance.) Pressure and stress result, both in footy, and (to a lesser degree) in home life, but perhaps they're necessary in order for him to achieve his ambitions.

In my opinion there are two main reasons James has excelled in footy and will continue to succeed in life and business. The first *is his hardworking ethic, and the second is his ability to listen, retain and implement.*

James has an untouchable belief that a person who works harder and smarter than everyone else will be as good as or better than the competition. Beginning as Essendon's 79th draft pick, this philosophy has worked for him. It has also given him the confidence to undertake new challenges in life and business, in areas where he initially has little knowledge; he knows that if he works hard and smart he will do well in that area. He is now a partner in a seafood café, and in a sports and advertising consultancy, and is on the board of a publicly listed company.

James is by nature reserved, very much a listener rather than a talker, and he remembers and thinks about what he is told. The extent to which he does this is exceptional. When I met him in 1993, he was a shy, quiet, young 20-year-old, vastly different from my family, who all speak simultaneously at the dinner table. But within a week of meeting my stepfather, he was discussing wines with sommeliers, reading further about them and developing the information he received from my stepfather at the dinner table. His passion and knowledge of wines continues to grow to this day.

Great friends and advisers are of course a big factor in his life, and James is happy to seek opinions. He recognises where he lacks expertise and ensures that he obtains it. But it is James who knows which questions to ask and who makes the most of the information given to him – whether it's from my legal background, Danny Corcoran's training expertise or his myriad friends in business.

James is a very private person who shares his feelings only with his closest family and friends. He is extraordinarily principled and strong, and while I hesitate to use such an unromantic adjective, he is solid! Living in Victoria, where footballers are admired to the point of adulation and where sports journalists number one to every four footballers, this has largely protected us as a couple and a family. I have never been left wondering where he is or is going to be, I have never been placed in an embarrassing situation by him, and I have never been given any reason to question his whereabouts or lack trust in his word. This respect is of course essential in any relationship, on both the female's and the male's part, but it becomes even more important in the 'public' life of a footballer, where stories can be and are concocted by fans, and where players can and do get themselves into trouble.

The fact that life is busy and there are unavoidable nights apart doesn't help. I feel incredibly angry at the footballers who for some reason believe that their god-given talent (and, yes, I will concede, their hard work as well) means that they can act without consideration or respect for their partner. It also taints the image of the large number of footballers to whom this doesn't apply. The public following that footballers attract exacerbates the already impossible task of dealing with a husband's infidelities. Relationships, which all have difficult times, must be unworkable where there is a lack of respect and trust.

I am often asked (and often by the partners of players) whether I 'let' or will let James go on a footy trip. First, there is no question of 'letting' him go; he is a grown man and can make the decision for himself, but second, unless there is a good reason not to go, it can be a great opportunity to see overseas places and enjoy mates. (Cleverly, James always suggests that we meet overseas at the end of it, which softens the question.) I do understand some partners' hesitations, but I know James will not compromise himself or succumb to peer group pressure in any substantial way. I could not be married to anyone who did. He respects himself too much and knows where the boundaries of the acceptable are. But some (not many) don't respect themselves or their partner enough. This is not peculiar to footy trips, of course. Footy trips can also be dangerous – I remember one year when

James's bottle of water was spiked when he left it on the bar (luckily the smell gave it away before he drank it). The death threats he received when captaining the All Australian team in Ireland were also scary. You only have to look at what happened to Ricky Dyson and David Hookes to see that in these times, being careful and taking precautions is necessary everywhere.

James is a great person and I love him greatly. He is principled, caring and fair. He tries to do the right thing and help those in need, and he is fun to be around. That is not to say he is without fault (but who is?). Like all footballers, he can be moody, stressed and self-absorbed. These are what I call 'footballer traits', idiosyncrasies that all players share to some degree. The nature of football as a profession requires their personal life to be affected. It stems from the fact that they are required to be self-obsessed. They are drilled on what to eat, when to sleep, what they can do during the day and how they must regulate their social life. They are told how to prepare for a game (and believe me, it does not include vacuuming the floor or looking after children), and how to recover – to mention just a few things. These traits are further enhanced by the attention they receive from the public and the fact that most people they talk to want to talk about them. On a scale of 1 to 10, I would rate him a 6 or 7 in this regard.

This should not be confused with unthoughtfulness. One only has to look at our last family holiday at the snow and the fact that footballers are expressly prohibited from skiing to realise that he didn't suggest that destination for his own enjoyment.

A tribute to James the person can't be complete without a short paragraph on James the father – in one word, he is sensational. His family and its wellbeing is by far the most important thing in his life, and this is evidenced by the time he ensures that he spends with us. When at home he is always involved with the family and believe me, a game of soccer, footy or cricket, a swim in the pool and even trips to the park are greatly improved when he is around. He ensures that he invests time in each of our children individually and addresses their needs. Because of this he will always be their friend as well as their dad.

How does footy affect our lives? It is apparent from the questions I am continually asked that people are interested in the way footballers and their families live – sorry to quash expectations, but we live very normally most of the time.

Yes, there are definite timetable implications – our social life is governed by when James plays, as is the amount of time he will spend with us as a family. The best-case scenario is when he plays a game on Friday night; that way, after recovery on Saturday morning, he is free to join us. The worst is when he plays on Saturday night (and has recovery Sunday morning) or plays a Sunday game. On these weekends I am largely a one-parent family and we don't catch up with friends. This is also the case during training camps, community camps, leadership camps, end-of-year footy trips and All Australian trips. On the other hand, and unlike many professional husbands and fathers, James is home most nights at 6 and has dinner with the family. This enables him to be a consistent and very prominent figure in our children's lives and is an incredible benefit. We probably won't be this lucky when he finishes football and makes his consultancy full-time.

As I mentioned above, footballers do have certain dietary requirements and restrictions on their day-to-day activities. For example, we would never go for a walk the day before a match or play tennis – a not too stringent restriction. However, the night before a game is greatly affected. The same routine is always followed (as footballers are also superstitious): pasta for dinner, children to bed by 7.30 and a video which must be watched with NO talking. (It is apparently imperative that I am there, but I am not allowed to talk.) A little overboard, perhaps? But easy enough to comply with, especially when you realise the extent to which some footballers go – I know of one who requires his wife and children to stay at his mother-in-law's house on the night before a game.

We do control footy's effects on our children. Yes, they are dragged week in, week out to watch James play, even though Stephanie, our eldest, would rather be anywhere else. I do believe that the lesson in family support which results is a good one and our boys absolutely love it – there is no holding them back. We restrict our children's appearance in the media and play down the occasions when James is recognised on the street. This has become more difficult since Stephanie began school. The fact that she is 'recognised' as James Hird's daughter and that her daddy is 'famous' has left her slightly bewildered and unsure. I tell her that she is known because she is such a lovely person, and try to impress on her that being 'famous' is not desirable nor commendable; it's the achievement of excellence in any pursuit that one should be proud of. I hope she understands the message. Only time will tell.

We don't talk much about football at home. First, because James breathes footy most days, and when he gets home, he needs time out. Second, there are too many other things to talk about. A third possible reason is that while I enjoy watching James play, I have never developed an overwhelming passion for the game and am quite happy not to discuss it too often. My interests in music (I play the violin and piano) and sport as a child (I was a Victorian state swimmer) left little time for football following, and I had only seen two football games prior to meeting James. That and the fact that he was not then well known were terrific for the beginning of our relationship. We were able to learn about and experience each other as individuals without footy playing a major part.

We do of course attend the sensational events footballing life is renowned for. We have been to some outstanding sporting, theatrical and business events and have met and spoken with many extraordinary people. My favourite, without a doubt, was during the 2000 Olympics in Sydney, when we stayed, thanks to Channel 7, on an ocean liner on Sydney Harbour and travelled to the Games each day. That was an incredible experience.

The places we cannot attend as a family are minimal: places with confined areas and large crowds, like the Melbourne Show and shopping centres, for instance. But most people who ask for autographs and photos are courteous and it is no inconvenience.

Balance is a continuing battle in football households. It's a common problem for footballers and, for different reasons, for their partners. In terms of the players themselves, a remarkably small number of them study, take apprenticeships or invest in a career outside footy. This is an astonishing fact given that the average footballer's career is over by the age of 26, and the money they earn from the game, while giving them a good start, is only that – a start – and then only if invested wisely. At 26 (or 30 if you play that long), it is difficult to begin building a career, particularly when it means starting at the bottom. Financially there are usually mortgages, partners and children to support by then, and psychologically it can be difficult because for 10 to 14 years they have been proud and satisfied in their jobs and admired by those around them. The clubs and the AFL encourage and support continuing education for the players, but often there is neither the will nor the understanding of its importance, so it is not pursued. Also, the time requirements of the football club are almost prohibitive.

As I said, balance is also a problem for the partners of players. Given that attention is so heavily weighted towards the footballer and football, it can be difficult for the partner to retain their indi-viduality and their sense of self. Not only is this problematic for the partner, but long term it cannot be good for their relationship. It is impossible to have a meaningful relationship with a person who lacks individuality, interests and opinions, and on the partner's side, it is easy to become resentful if you are not satisfied with your lot. This is compounded in football by the fact that many players and their partners are from interstate and do not have close family and friends living near them. The difficulties can be accentuated further as the partner of the footballer normally takes on the care of the children and the organisation of the home. It is incredibly important for footballers' partners to retain (or take up) interests of their own.

Football has greatly affected our life together, and has affected and continues to affect the person James is, and to a lesser extent who I am. Financially it has enabled us to invest in property and business and to travel regularly, opening our minds and lives to different cultures, ways of life and languages. Through footy we have met an enormous range of people, many of whom have become lifelong friends, and all of whom have taught us some-thing about human nature, about life, about ourselves. We have experienced incredible highs (such as being part of a team winning a premiership) and also lows, frustration and fear. James's head injuries in Perth and other concussions were the most difficult. Footy has seen me leave the law for the time being, to be there for our children, but this would have been my choice whatever his career. This has also meant that I've had time to engage in other pursuits, such as renovating, painting and learning French, all of which have given me a lot of joy and satisfaction. To our everyday life, football adds another dimension and makes our already hectic schedule busier. It is incredibly important to James, so we embrace it.

Chapter 6

Plagues and Pestilences

I recall little details clearly, but only vaguely remember the actual coming together. The impact of my head hitting my teammate Mark McVeigh's knee at force sounded, according to one journalist, 'like a stockwhip being cracked in the late afternoon air'. It is a graphic but probably appropriate description. And thinking about it still chills my blood.

I've had my fair share of injuries – plagues and pestilences, in Sheed's words – but what happened on Saturday, 4 May 2002, in Perth was the one that made me seriously question whether or not I should keep playing football. It was the one after which I came closest to giving up the game.

It was a hot day in Perth – probably more difficult for us than for the Docker players, who were used to it – and I was playing on Fremantle's Matthew Pavlich, who is a rising champion, a tall, athletic centre-half-forward who has become one of the stars of the competition. Pavlich was definitely starring on this day. In the first half he kept running off me down the ground, getting away, and setting up opportunities. At half-time Sheeds strongly instructed me to go out and beat him. It was a fair request – Pavlich had been giving me, in the language of footy, an old-fashioned towelling. And I didn't like it.

I felt something was missing that day. I didn't feel fresh. I felt that my body wasn't getting into the game. I wasn't injured, I just felt a bit tired. The other guys must have felt the same way. We were playing ordinary football, which was a huge worry, because we were expected to and needed to beat the Dockers.

I think Pavlich's tactic was to expose me to his running, which would help take me out of the contest. He was in super-fit form and I wasn't as good as I should have been. So there came a time in the match when I was playing for pride. I was not going to continue to allow this guy to beat me.

About 10 minutes into the third quarter, the ball was in flight, Pavlich was charging down the ground and I thought, *I'm not going to let this happen!* So I stayed right on him, keeping up. My main thought was to make sure that if I didn't get it, neither did he. I was going to put my body between the ball and Pavlich. The ball went over both of our heads. In the seconds after the ball flew past us I lost my bearings for a moment. I think Pavlich might have given me a push – nothing deliberate. I dived for the ball and hit something. It was the heaviest, worst blow I'd ever felt on a football field, and I knew I was in trouble. My face had smashed into Mark's knee.

The trainer, Gary Miller, came over. I felt as if all my teeth had been knocked out (which I was later told was due to nerve damage). I said to Gary: 'Mate, where are my teeth?'

'No, no,' he said, 'your teeth are fine.'

'What about my nose?'

'No, your nose is fine.'

'Well, what's wrong?'

'Well, you've got a hole in your cheek. Your eye is just about popping out of your head and you've got blood going everywhere.'

At this stage the pain was pretty bad, but I was in shock, which probably reduced it a bit. Reidy, our club doctor, came over, looked at me and said, 'Get off the ground, we need to get you to hospital.'

By the time we got to the changing rooms I was experiencing unbelievable pain. It was a level of pain I'd never experienced before. I grabbed Reidy by the shirt and said, 'Give me some painkillers – this is killing me.'

'I can't.'

'Why not?'

Reidy explained that I had a depressed fracture of the skull, which meant my skull might be pressing on my brain, and also that I could have eye damage. He summarised: 'We don't know whether your brain's working, so we need to ensure that all tests are conducted with you alert and able to describe the pain.'

It wasn't the cheeriest of prognoses. All I knew was that my brain was working sufficiently for me to know that I needed pain relief.

'Give me the phone, I've got to ring Tania.' I could just imagine her sitting at home watching the footy and seeing this. Reidy rang her and said, 'He's all right, don't worry about him.' Which was an absolute lie.

Though he was trying to reassure Tania, Reidy was also concerned that there might be bleeding in the brain and into my eye, and that I might lose the eye or incur brain damage. I was still in absolute agony, swearing at Reidy, demanding painkillers that he couldn't give me. I asked him to stay with me until I was all right. He stayed with me all through that night and the next day. He didn't have to do that and I'll always be grateful.

By the time we got to the hospital I was allowed some morphine, as it was now a couple of hours after the accident. While it did help, the pain was still almost intolerable. It was as though someone had a knife and was moving it around my face and into my brain. I cried.

My appointed surgeon, Sean Hamilton, arrived. Luckily, I found out later, he is one of Australia's best car-accident plastic surgeons. He explained to me that the damage to my face was similar to what used to happen before the advent of airbags when a person's face would smash into the steering wheel and fracture.

'How're you feeling?' he asked.

My reply must have put him in the picture. 'I'm not sure who you are, but if I ever want to play that stupid game again – you tell me not to. I want nothing to do with it.'

After some CAT scans and other tests, it seemed I had seven fractures of the face and a depressed fracture of the skull. The surgeon told me that he would open my head from ear to ear, peel back my skin to my chin and re-make my face with metal plates. For some reason (I realised later it was probably the morphine), I burst out laughing and couldn't stop. The morphine was also causing constant vomiting. I didn't have much to laugh about, but I'm grateful to the drugs for taking me to another place, even for a moment.

At 11 o'clock that night I had the operation. It was the night of the FA Cup final, and I was really keen to watch it. When I woke, sometime in the middle of the night, it was on TV, just finishing, which disappointed me. My priorities were, a bit like my face and head, slightly out of whack.

I was told the operation went well. The following day most of the Essendon people had gone back to Melbourne, but a few came in to see me: Paul Barnard, Sean Wellman, Barry Young and Sheeds.

Tania had jumped on the first plane the morning after the injury and arrived in Perth at about 10 o'clock. She brought our daughter Stephanie with her. Stephanie was three and Tom, our son, was one. Tom stayed in Melbourne with Tania's mum and my mum. At that stage we didn't know how long I was going to be in hospital, and Tania didn't think Tom would be happy at the hospital day in, day out. Luckily, her mum, Robin, was able to take some time off work to look after him. Mum wanted to come over but I asked her to help with Tom. My manager, Ben Crowe, flew over, as did my close friend Rod Law.

Tania was scared, but once eye and brain damage were ruled out, Reidy was very good at easing her fears. Tania's dad was a doctor, so she's pragmatic about medical stuff. In fact she is always the last person to go to the doctor, and our kids have to be dying before they get there. The fact that Tania was concerned about me showed how bad the injuries were, but she dealt with it very well in her own way, and was very strong about it. When she walked in and saw me with cuts everywhere and my face badly bruised, she was obviously a little freaked out. It was a bit confronting for Stephanie too, but the cuddle she gave me after her initial reservations wore off made me feel like a million bucks. It was fantastic to see them both.

My dad flew over from Canberra. Our relationship hadn't been good for a while, which meant this was the first time I'd seen him in a couple of years. I appreciated him coming to see me and was pleased to have Stephanie spend some time with him. Stephanie actually loved her time in Perth – she was taken out to breakfast every morning, got to swim in the hotel pool, went to the park all the time and coloured in and played at the hospital. She was accepting and grown-up as she told each new visitor, 'Daddy's got a sore face but he's going to be fine.'

It wasn't until a week later that I fully comprehended what had happened. Before that the morphine and pethidine had relaxed me so much that I couldn't think properly or react properly. Conversations with visitors were interesting because I'd sometimes fall asleep mid-sentence. This happened when the former North Melbourne champion Barry Cable came in to see me. I later felt very embarrassed about that. After three days I asked to be taken off the drugs. The result was not great, but it was preferable – I couldn't sleep properly and I was having really weird dreams about footy, and life.

There was a big issue I had to address: the strong feeling that I didn't want to play football again. I'd had enough, and I didn't want to feel such pain ever again. I was conflicted about it, because deep down I still loved the game that had been such a huge part of my life. But I also had a young family, and I wanted to be there for them. And I wondered what I would do as a career if I let footy go, and how that would affect us financially. The pain and discomfort, and the hangover from the drugs, didn't leave me in the clearest state of mind for making such a momentous decision.

I rang Tania at her hotel at about 1 am the second night, and told her, 'I think I'm going to give footy away.'

She said, 'Don't be too hasty. It's a really emotional time and the most important thing for you to concentrate on at the moment is getting better. The issue of whether you play again or not can be dealt with later and I'll be 100 per cent behind whatever you decide. If you still believe there are things you want to achieve in footy, then you'll need to consider that; obviously, overcoming your fears will be a really big issue as well. Don't worry about the financial side of things – we will manage – just concentrate on getting better. You've got my support either way.'

I was grateful to Tania for her strength and support. She was right: it wasn't a great time to be making decisions. Everything needed to be done slowly. Getting better was the first priority. The surgeon who I'd asked to make sure I never played again came in one day and repeated to me what I'd said. He said, 'I think you should go and see a psychologist.' I never did, of course. Footy players are too manly for that!

I was in hospital for five days. Several Dockers and Eagles players came in to see me, including Docker captain Peter Bell, Freo's footy manager Stephen Icke, former Essendon teammates Michael Prior and Judd Lalich, and Glen Jakovich from the Eagles.

Matthew Pavlich came in too. I said to him, 'Mate, this is all your fault. If you hadn't kept running down the ground it wouldn't have happened.' The Eagles and Dockers guys were fantastic. John Worsfold, the Eagles' coach, sent me a nice letter, and Trent Croad, of the Dockers, offered us his house for a week while we were in Perth. It was a good feeling to have the footy world supporting us.

There were some really great people in the hospital, some amazingly efficient, calm and compassionate nurses to whom I will always be grateful. They routinely had to perform the most revolting tasks – like four times a day cleaning out a pus-and-blood-encrusted tube that ran through the scar across the top of my head. They always did it cheerfully. I was hugely impressed by the way they worked and have enormous respect for what they do and how they do it. Their selflessness left me humbled.

And there are other sorts of memories as well. Every night from about midnight till 4 in the morning an Italian lady who had a bit of dementia would yell out, 'Roma! Roma! Roma!' As a result my sleep was always interrupted; I didn't complain, though, because she was obviously in a worse way than me.

When they let me move to the hotel to recuperate (I wasn't allowed to fly for at least 10 days), I was shown an article Sheeds had written in *The Australian*. 'James, your coaches, your teammates and your fans all wish you a thorough recovery, not just a quick one,' he wrote. 'In your enforced absence, we recognise you for what you are: a great footballer and a great friend. The long-sleeved number 5 is washed, cleaned and ironed, waiting for you to put it on when you're ready. Look after yourself, son.'

I cried when I read it.

When I got back to Melbourne, I would have a different head from the one I'd left with. The bone is supposed to integrate and grow around the metal plates which had been inserted.

But first I had to get there, and given the media interest, the trip was interesting. Tania and Rod acted as decoys while I was escorted through the bowels of the hotel to a waiting car and whisked to the cargo entrance of the airport. We experienced the staff quarters of many buildings that day, and I am forever grateful for the extra precautions taken by those in charge to minimise my exposure to the media. It didn't end when we arrived in Melbourne either, and I recall racing to my front door past a large number of reporters held in check by Tania, Rod and Ben. All I wanted was time to recover, rest and think about my footy future. Most importantly, I wanted to cuddle my son, whom I hadn't seen in 10 days.

The Footy Show wanted me to come on exclusively on the Thursday night, but the AFL wanted me to do a press conference. I decided on a compromise: I'd do a five-minute press conference to all the media and then expand on it that night on *The Footy Show*, because of the contract I had with Nine. It still caused grief among the media, though: they thought I had 'saved' talk of my possible retirement for *The Footy Show*. Tim Lane gave me a slamming, but in truth it had nothing to do with me 'saving' information for Nine. I still wasn't completely lucid, or thinking clearly, and I certainly wasn't dealing with the media in a strategic way. I think context was left behind in Tim's attack.

My recovery was clearly going to take weeks, and Tania and I decided to take it slowly and see where my thinking went about a return.

My face gradually felt better, and seven weeks later I felt ready to return. I was referred to Ian Carlisle, who took over my treatment from Sean Hamilton. He ran his finger along my face and took about 30 seconds to decide I was okay to play.

People asked me how I could play after what had happened to my face. Well, eight weeks had passed and the brain is very good at removing memories of pain.

Coming back was natural for me. The doctors had told me that my face was actually stronger now, with the plates in, and that the headgear would disperse any force across my forehead. Also, at training the week before I returned, I copped a couple of whacks on it, which was good for my confidence. I did not want to go onto the field and look timid. I didn't want people to be wondering whether I was fearful or had lost my nerve. I probably over-compensated. Whenever there was a contest I tried to stick my head in and say, 'Here it is! I'm not timid, I'm ready to go again.' There was feedback in the newspapers and TV that this was courageous. But it was a pragmatic, conscious decision – if I was going to come back and play footy, it was important for me mentally to get past these things early on.

The first game was on a Saturday night against the Bulldogs at Telstra Dome. The headgear I had to wear was uncomfortable and looked stupid. It was well made, and it was as good as you can get, but it made me sweat because it allowed no airflow.

Still, it didn't stop me doing anything. The umpires were really supportive. One made a point of stopping me before the game and telling me that while they wouldn't protect me or give me free kicks that weren't there, they would pay a free if someone went for my head or helmet maliciously. Luckily, that didn't happen. The closest it came to happening was in a later match against Brisbane, when I had a bit of a wrestle with both of the Scott brothers and they tried to rip it off my head. They were just playing hard footy, though, which I admire; I didn't take it personally.

My first game back went pretty well. I moved around the ground, at times playing as a loose man, picking up Chris Grant at centre-half-back, moving up forward. I finished with 25 disposals and eight marks, and was named best on the ground. In fact, in both the next two games (in Subiaco, the scene of the accident, and at Colonial) I was again considered best on ground, with 24 and 26 disposals. I felt reassured that I could play on as if the accident had not happened. I was back playing good footy, and the decision to continue playing had been the right one.

What happened in Perth was probably the granddaddy of them all, but my career had, sadly, been peppered with injuries. My poor run started before my professional football career did, and as they mounted up, they played havoc with my career.

Let's recap. First, at 16, playing for Ainslie, I developed a hip ailment which made running painful. I then suffered shin splints in my right leg, which developed into a stress fracture. At 17, during my second practice match against North Melbourne, I fell on my knee, broke my kneecap and tore a tendon from the bone. I had an operation, spent six weeks on crutches and missed 16 weeks. At age 19, in 1992, I experienced one of my more scary injuries when Ben Doolan, a Swans player at that time (later a teammate), crashed into me on the MCG. I broke three ribs and punctured a lung. That time, after a week in hospital and two weeks of rest I was able to play in the 1992 reserves premiership.

In 1993 the injury clouds broke a little, though I did a

hamstring and missed four matches. I was developing, out of necessity, the ability to come back from adversity.

In 1997, Cross Keys Oval, just half a kilometre from Windy Hill, was Essendon's summer training ground. It now has a gruesome reputation as the place where Jason Moran was killed in a gangland shooting while watching his son play Auskick. The only reputation it had when we trained there was for potholes. It was like training on a paddock.

It was Friday night on the Grand Prix weekend in March and I was doing a simple marking drill. I went for a mark against David Grenvold and rolled my ankle in a pothole, causing an ankle sprain. (Incidentally, it was also the end of Cross Keys. We never trained there again.) The injury probably needed six weeks to get right, but I took only three weeks before playing again. Sure enough, the ankle got worse and worse, and in my third game I strained my right calf because it wasn't bending: all the force was going through my foot and calf. After a couple more games I couldn't run on it anymore. An MRI scan showed a stress fracture. I was in plaster for seven weeks and the season was over for me.

When the plaster came off, I spent a lot of time doing weights in the gym, mainly out of boredom. By the 1998 pre-season, I had bulked up from 89 to 100 kilograms, and this caused a problem I hadn't anticipated: I started tearing hamstrings as a result of the extra weight. In Round 2, I tore my hamstring and missed four games, and I missed another five games from Round 10 when I repeated the injury. It was a circle of injury – one causing the next.

In 1998, Dermott Brereton launched into me in an article in which I found both hurtful and wrong. 'Having played only half his club's games this year because of injury, Essendon hasn't had value for money since '96,' Brereton wrote. 'When a club enters into a long-term contract, with a figure attached to it the likes of which the club has never seen before, the club should factor into the contract the player's ability to physically cope with the stresses of league football, that is injuries and how easy the player finds them.'

Two days after that article, we played West Coast. Determined to prove Dermott wrong, I went out hard. Two minutes into the game I tore my hamstring. Then, in the second-last round, against the Bulldogs, I went to kick a goal in the goal square and my foot got caught underneath a Bulldog player's foot and broke. I felt it crack and thought, *Here we go again.* I played the next three weeks, till the end of our season, knowing that my foot was broken and would be sore. When we lost the final I spoke to Julian Feller, an orthopaedic surgeon, who said he would operate on my foot the following week.

In 1999, I got what was coming to me as all these injuries piled up on top of each other.

The pre-season had gone pretty well. On the way to a practice game against Hawthorn four weeks before the start of the season, I dropped into a hospital in Heidelberg to get a scan before I played. The scan revealed that the crack in my foot had grown bigger. Stunned, I got back into the car. I thought this could be the end of my career – this was the third time my foot had been broken.

Still, I decided to play the practice game and see how it went.

I played terribly . . . but surprise surprise, my foot didn't hurt. I thought maybe the scan results were wrong. I didn't tell the club doctor that the crack had grown bigger.

I played the first week of the real season, against Carlton, on Steve Silvagni. I always enjoyed playing on him because he was a terrific footballer. I played okay, kicked a couple of goals, and though the foot was a little bit sore, it wasn't too bad. However, during that week it got worse and worse at training.

When I went into the next game against the Kangaroos, I thought I might struggle with it. Sure enough, in the second quarter I put up my hand to come off. I was shattered. Against the Kangaroos, too. I've always had a good rivalry with them and I wanted to do well against them.

I sat on the bench and literally stared at the possibility that the rest of my life would be one without footy in it. I didn't know what to think. I'd broken my foot three times in two years. I knew I wouldn't play again that year, and that I would be facing a huge amount of rehabilitation work, and the isolation that goes with it, if I wanted to even attempt the following year. It was a terrible, empty feeling.

I don't think there would have been many around the club who thought I would be able to come back from that. But I wasn't ready to give in. I still had football in me. There would be some very dark days before I ran onto a field again, though, and they started the day after the injury.

Within 24 hours I felt shocking. I was frustrated and needed to occupy myself, so I decided to plant some hedges at our newly renovated home. There I was, holding plants in one hand and hobbling around on crutches, when my teammate Ben Doolan came round at 9 am. He was kind enough to give me a hand, but more importantly he made smalltalk and tried to console me about the possible end to my career. He'll never know how much his support meant to me.

Sean Wellman phoned me at 2 o'clock that day to invite me to an Easter barbecue, and though I didn't want to talk to people, I really appreciated him ringing.

Instead I stayed home, sat in the garden and listened to talkback radio. Not a good idea – they just took me apart. They said I was finished, gone, would never play again. Some said that while I'd had some great games, I hadn't turned into the champion they thought I would become. It was devastating to hear . . . almost worse than the injury. I don't know why I kept listening. It was almost like watching yourself about to be hit by a train: you keep watching and watching, and sure enough, you finally get hit.

My mind was full of dark thoughts: *Is my career going nowhere? What am I doing to myself? What am I doing to my family and also the Essendon footy club?* I was being paid a lot of money, and was beginning to think that perhaps Dermott was right.

The only good news came from Julian Feller, the surgeon. He was optimistic about another operation using a new growth protein that had been tested in the United States.

Tania was also very positive and supportive. She realised how much I wanted to keep playing. Provided there was hope, and I wanted to do it, she supported me in trying to get back.

It seems a lot of wives and partners go the other way, and want their men to finish with football – they want more time with their husband/partner and more help from them. I think Tania's more realistic, and I think it's because of the legal world she comes from. She looks at the footy life and sees it as the greatest career of all time. We're passionate about what we do. We get to keep fit. We get to be outside. We get paid to do what we love. Yes, there are injuries, the media knock us, and we get bagged by the public . . . But professionals in offices work twice as hard, twice as many hours, and get paid half the money, and are not necessarily following their dream. As long as I could play and wanted to play, according to her, I should play.

I agreed. I would try to come back – however long it took. I had the operation, and the growth protein was put into the fracture in my foot. As I write now, it has held for seven years without a problem.

The rest of 1999 was an incredibly frustrating time for me. I sat on the sidelines and watched the team, feeling left out and a tiny bit jealous as they kept on winning games and looking as if they could go all the way. Certainly, the other 99 per cent of me was ecstatic for them, for the coaches, the supporters and my mates in the team, but I can't deny that there were moments of self-pity.

In August I asked the club whether they would mind if I took a week off. I believed that the escape would be beneficial. A good friend, Frank Truccolo, and his family were going to Italy for two weeks and invited Tania and me to join them. I needed to clear my head; luckily, the club thought it was a good idea.

We flew out on the Saturday after a game and returned before the next game. It was a magical week. We went to Florence for three days and Portofino for two days. I'd been to Italy twice before, but both times had been in winter, so I had mostly visited buildings – monuments, museums and galleries. Now I discovered how superb Italy is in summer.

We stayed in a beautiful place outside Florence – Villa San Miguel, an old abbey designed by Michelangelo. One night Tania and I were sitting on the verandah overlooking Florence, having dinner with my friend's family, and I have to say that if I hadn't been extremely dedicated and if it hadn't been my dream to play footy again, I could have stayed there for the rest of my life. The view was exquisite, we tasted caviar for the first time and drank French champagne as we discussed the tours our friend had organised through the wine regions of Italy for the next day. Foot injuries seemed a long way away that night.

It was a relaxing break, but the injury never quite left my mind. I knew that the rest of my career as a footballer was going to be on the line in the next six months.

When I got back in August I believed that I had a chance at playing again in the 1999 season. I thought the boys would go all the way and I wanted to help them achieve that. Essendon's fitness adviser, John Quinn, had worked out a fitness regime to keep me in shape while I wasn't playing, and he and I had been working pretty hard. I said to him, 'Mate, if I don't have a crack at coming back this year I'm going to regret it for the rest of my life. I want to be part of this premiership.'

'All right,' Quinny said. 'We'll have a crack – to a point. We're not going to break your foot again, but we will try some things. If it gets sore, you tell me, and we'll pull the pin. If it doesn't get sore, we'll keep going.'

I didn't realise then the implications of that decision.

Quinny and I began the next day, on Windy Hill oval. We got through the first couple of weeks, slowly increasing my running, doing a bit off-line – little swerves – and increasing the pace of routines. Quinny was guiding, advising, and continually asking me how the foot felt. The foot didn't get sore. I was rapt. We did the sessions after everyone else had left, because we didn't want anyone to see what we were doing. I knew that if I came back I wouldn't be the best I could be, but I also knew I'd be as good as the 18th-best player and able to cope with that.

One day I was keen to know how the foot was going, so Quinny and I went down to a paddock at Royal Park and he asked me to do 10 sprints flat out. I got through the first five or six without pain, but on the seventh the foot felt a bit sore. By the ninth sprint I said, 'Mate, I'm feeling pretty sore here.' He pushed my foot around a bit and said, 'You can go on, but if you do you're probably going to break your foot again and that will be it. What do you want to do?'

'I want to keep going,' I said. So the next week I did a little more running . . . and I got sorer.

After the second-last round of the season I was in the rooms with the players when Bruce Connor (the physio) and Reidy (the doctor) asked me about my foot. I wasn't sure whether or not Bruce and Reidy knew I'd been running, but I soon gathered that Quinny had enlightened them. They told me that they knew I was running and that my foot was getting painful. They said, 'We are not going to let you play from now on, and we've told Sheeds that even if you get yourself fit, you're not playing for the rest of the year.'

What they were doing was protecting me, and making sure that I would be right for the next year, but when I walked out of the MCG to go home I was as dirty with people I'd thought were my friends as I had ever been, and as distraught as I'd ever been. I felt betrayed, and was angry at Bruce Connor and Reidy because I thought they had just ruined my chances of playing in a premiership. In hindsight, of course, I can see that they did exactly the right thing.

A few days later Reidy, Quinny and Bruce came over to my place and we had a few red wines and some pretty aggressive discussion. In essence, they told me that if I kept running, I would break down, and they couldn't let that happen – for my own good and for the good of the club. They needed me fit for next year.

This was a perfect example of how much we all need wise heads as advisers. In life, most of us think we know it all, but without trusted advisers to guide us and challenge us we can all make the wrong decisions. What happened that night took a lot of courage from Reidy, Bruce and Quinny. They put a friendship on the line for the greater good. They showed me the value of friends and advisers who truly care, not sycophants. They were not to know that 12 months later we would win the premiership, or that their decision that night would enable me to achieve my greatest moment as a footballer.

That was that. Essendon played Carlton in the preliminary final and lost what many considered an unloseable contest. As I watched from the stands, part of me felt that if I'd been playing we would have won that game. But another part of me was excited, knowing that the boys would be hungry and could go the full hog the following year. I knew from the moment we lost that game that we had a template for success, and a true motivating force – a shocking disappointment to avenge.

I kept having X-rays and MRIs on my foot, and was assured that the crack was closing – I was healing. At the end-of-season footy trip in London I kept training, running in Hyde Park, because I knew that I would need to train constantly to come back from my almost nonexistent game fitness level.

In January 2000, I trained a full session with the boys, and my foot pulled up really well. No problems. Slowing down had been the way to go. Quinny had been right.

In early 2006, Quinny received an email from a London soccer club. One of their players has a stress fracture in his foot, and guess whose names feature after an internet search for gurus on navicular stress fractures? Mine and Quinny's. Quinny is now being contacted by people all round the world about rehabilitation for navicular stress fractures. Recently, he has worked closely with an Australian player in the English Premier League.

In the three years before 2000, I played 22 games out of a possible 69.

In 2004, *The Age* helpfully put together a list of my woes. Under the headline 'James Hird's Major Injuries 1993–2004' it detailed:

- 2004: bleeding in the eye, 2 matches
- 2003: deep vein thrombosis, 5 matches
- 2000: finger, 3 matches
- 1999: foot fracture, 22 matches

- 1997: foot stress fracture, 15 matches
- 1993: hamstring, 4 matches.

The list was by no means comprehensive, but it gave a fair indication.

I think my mother's comment that I have the ability to overcome adversity is true. It's probably fair to say that I've missed the best part of three seasons through injury. In 2004 it was estimated that injuries had cost me around 70 games since 1992. I've had to deal with them mentally as well, because they toy with your emotions. Just when you think you're fine, because the injury has ceased to cause you pain or limit your movement, or when you think you can train and play at full pace without worrying that you will hurt something, or when you think you will have an injury-free season, another one strikes. Essendon club doctor Bruce Reid once said about me: 'He's had all the glory and all the shit.'

There is no doubt that the misfortunes, crisis and injuries in my career – the negatives – have made me a better person and player than success has. They have allowed me to tell better stories, taught me better lessons, and made me work harder and make larger sacrifices than any Grand Final, Brownlow, best and fairest or premiership has. I did more to come back from the last foot injury than I have had to do for anything else in my life.

Muhammad Ali once said, 'Only a man who knows what it is like to be defeated can reach down to the bottom of his soul and come up with the extra ounce of power it takes to win when the match is even.' This could have been the motto of my sporting life: every time trouble has struck I believe I have come back from it a more complete player. It took my facial injury to make me realise I loved this game enough to keep going – and win the last of my four best-and-fairests. It took three possibly careeer-ending foot injuries for me to learn to understand people and lead my team to premiership success.

To me the greatest successes in life are born out of adversity. How much sweeter does something feel when you know you have really earned it? Your first deposit for a house or the promotion you got because you busted you guts and earned it is so much better and more sustainable than fluking a few good sales and getting a promotion but then landing on your backside because you failed to learn how to work hard. There is a picture I have at home of me cuddling Tania and Stephanie straight after the 2000 Grand Final. It shows me crying, in a moment of pure relief. I am relieved not because we won the game, but because at that moment I know that Tania, Stephanie and I jumped every hurdle we had to, both mental and physical, to achieve our moment. This was so much sweeter than the 1993 success, because I had truly earned it.

I hope the injuries I've had don't affect my life too much in later years, but they probably will. My knee already aches all the time. I take four anti-inflammatory tablets a day, which is double the recommended dose, just to play football and be able to train. When I'm not training I don't need them. But if I don't take them, my knee has to be drained – probably twice a year. By taking them, I reduce the need for this procedure. I've had four operations on that knee. The foot injury and the facial injury are what everyone knows about, but the knee is the one that will eventually stop my career. If I do too many weights to strengthen my legs, the knee just blows up. And if I kick on my left foot five or six times in a row, it'll blow up.

Sometimes my knee hurts if I'm lying in bed, sitting in a car for more than an hour or sitting in an aeroplane. There's no doubt I have arthritis in it now.

It's just one of the reminders all over my body of a 16-year football career.

JOHN QUINN ON JAMES

*T*he first player I met when I arrived at Essendon at the end of 1998 was James Hird. It was clear from this very first introduction that James was focused and had high expectations. He was also injured – with a navicular stress fracture.

At this point I had never seen a game of Australian Rules football – I was very much an athletics coach. Navicular injuries are often regarded as an athletics injury; many sprinters are afflicted with a fractured bone in the foot at some stage in their career.

To be honest, I was glad to meet this 'navicular Hird'. It was an injury I knew, and naively, I believed that I could rehabilitate him. I told James this in what was, in hindsight, a fairly nonchalant manner. In short, 'Yes, we can get you right.' From that moment, I worked with James every day, sometimes twice a day, seven days a week for the entire pre-season.

Always the message was the same: 'Work with me, follow the program and you'll be playing AFL by Round 1.'

As any coach will tell you, when you work with an athlete one to one over a period of time, you get to know them well. Very well. And they get to know you well, too!

All through that rehabilitation of 1998–99, we talked about James's return to football. His dreams. My dreams. His *expectations, my goals. His fear of re-injury and my logic as to why this wouldn't happen.*

And then, by March of 1999, the navicular was rehabilitated. He didn't have an injury. Just a good foot and a repaired one. With my promise of his best years in footy ahead of him, James led Essendon onto the MCG for Round 1 against Carlton. Essendon won by 39 points, and James kicked one goal in this game. After a quiet start, he looked more than comfortable by the game's end.

This triumphant return to football was to prove short-lived, though. The following week, again at the MCG, Essendon took on North Melbourne. James didn't make it to half-time, forced from the ground with the all-too-clear pain in the navicular.

He sat next to me on the bench. We barely spoke. We didn't need to. No one that I was aware of had ever overcome three injuries to the navicular. In reality, I knew that this was it for James Hird. His career was over.

At the end of the game, despite a win by 35 points, I was devastated. James left the MCG early, and after the rest of the team had warmed down and packed up, I had to decide what to do. The first thing was to go and see how James was coping. A number of scenarios raced through my mind – all of them not very positive. Maybe he wouldn't even open the front door.

One of the Essendon club doctors, Bruce Reid, and I made our way to James's house. By this stage it was almost midnight. I knocked on the door, feeling a wave of apprehension, guilt and hopelessness. I was sure he would say, 'But you told me . . . you said it would be okay . . . You assured me . . . I thought that you knew what to do . . .' And then the door opened. 'I wondered when you'd come,' he said. 'I've got a good wine out for you.'

So we sat down with a glass of shiraz and James Hird said eight of the most defining words of my coaching career: 'What do you want me to do now?'

There was no blame. No finger pointing. No anger. Just a simple question as to what was the next step – as if this recurrence had been planned all along. 'I've got a few ideas,' I lied. In truth, I didn't really know where the answer was. But it was James's simple question that made the difference. He motivated me to lift the bar.

To me, this is what makes James Hird a champion in one of the world's toughest games. I have worked with a lot of outstanding athletes in my coaching career. But greatness is determined by one very significant distinction. The ability to take responsibility for yourself – regardless of whether what's happening is good or bad. Positive or negative. It's easy to be a champion when you're winning. It's when a person is under pressure, though, that their true mettle, their basic character, is found. On that night, James Hird didn't blame, accuse, imply or suggest. He simply asked a coach the most addictive question in coaching: 'Please help me to achieve.'

I hit every contact known in the world of athletics. Many suggested that James's career was over. One, however, recommended trying a new treatment from the United States. It was called OP1 – osteoprotein 1. The surgeon, Julian Feller, had to get special permission from the government to bring this new treatment into Australia. It's just as well he did.

With the use of OP1, Julian Feller's surgical skills and another 10 months of seven-days-a-week rehabilitation, James Hird would lead Essendon onto the ground for Round 1 of the pre-season cup in 2000. Since that time, he has won a night premiership, a day premiership, participated in two Grand Finals, contested and captained four International Rules series, won a Norm Smith Medal, and been voted 3rd in Essendon's all-time team. The list could go on. And it continues to grow.

As a coach–athlete relationship, ours has had its ups and downs. James is under no illusion, at any time, as to what I might be thinking. We don't always agree, and we are both prone to a streak of stubbornness. We had an almighty blue on a long drive from Barcelona once. We call it 'the Andorra Incident'. To look someone in the eye and tell them how it is is always a risky business. However, the greater the risk, the greater the return.

Coaching sport is about developing better athletes. I believe it is also about developing better people. I have been privileged to work with James for the past eight years. I truly regard him as the best athlete I have ever worked with. And I do not make that claim lightly.

His commitment, drive, dedication and ruthless ambition are second to none. He has an ability to make his goals your goals. He doesn't use you. He journeys with you. I'd have to say that I have loved the journey.

Chapter 7

2000: Triumph and Personal Despair

The decision that nothing would stand in the way of the Essendon Football Club winning the 2000 flag was confirmed and cemented just moments after the siren sounded on preliminary final day 1999. The siren might have ended a game – and our season – but it also started something: a promise among the players to avenge the bitter disappointment we all felt at the MCG that day.

Let me take you back to preliminary final day 1999. It was the day of the Victorian state election, the one Jeff Kennett and his Liberal Party were unbackable favourites to win. There were portents there; we just didn't know it.

Essendon had had a fantastic year, finishing on top of the ladder, and were primed for a Grand Final spot . . . and, we believed, the flag. We thought we had a team good enough to go all the way. And then Carlton got in the way. As you know, I wasn't playing.

I watched the horror unfold from the coaches' box.

In the last quarter we'd made a bit of a comeback. Mark Mercuri had quite a close shot – and missed. That could have won us the game. Dean Wallis tried to get around Fraser Brown and was tackled. If he had succeeded, that could have won us the game. In the last two minutes, everything that might have won us the game didn't work out.

In the coaches' box, Sheeds wasn't critical, and he wasn't swearing; he was calm. 'Well,' he said, looking out at the Carlton supporters going crazy with excitement and the Essendon players trudging shell-shocked off the ground, 'we've got to do it next year.'

And with that he got up and walked out.

There was a terrible feeling around the club in the week after the loss. The burden felt even heavier because we had been such strong favourites to win that game. Most people believed Essendon would beat Carlton, that we were headed for the flag. But expectation is a strange thing. Victorian Premier Jeff Kennett would probably agree with that. On the day we lost, the Victorian electorate very nearly voted Kennett out – in a supposedly 'unloseable' election. A few weeks later, the Independents did the rest. No disrespect to Carlton, but it was said that like Kennett, we had lost the unloseable. It's a ridiculous concept, in politics and football, but it's a phrase that sticks in people's minds.

The next day I rang Sheeds and suggested we make all the guys go to the Grand Final. I said: 'I think it'd be a great way to make it hurt even more.' He agreed.

Our reserves were playing in the reserves Grand Final, so the guys who weren't in the reserves game sat and watched North Melbourne beat Carlton, very aware that we were as good as those two sides. The overwhelming feeling was that that year could have been ours.

My family often used to go to a little restaurant in Wellington Parade, Jolimont, at the top of the MCG carpark, called Gepetto's. It was a homely place which had been there for years, with good pasta and a warm atmosphere. I felt a team dinner there was a good idea. It was: the raw emotions began to flow. I spoke to the boys, and Sheeds spoke. I spoke about how we'd missed out, and how we never wanted to be in that situation again, of having the potential and wasting it. I told the players to use that thought and let it burn in their hearts for the next 12 months. It was an intense night.

A week later we went to London to play Hawthorn in an exhibition game. From there, the whole team went to Barcelona for our end-of-year trip.

It was a true bonding time for us. All through 1999 I had been full of self-doubt because I had played so little footy since I'd won the Brownlow in 1996: I had played just 15 games in three seasons. I was still training really hard, but I kept getting injured – if it wasn't my foot it was a hamstring.

On a beautiful day in Barcelona I was sitting around the hotel pool with Mark Mercuri and Joe Misiti. The three of us had played football together since we were kids. They said, 'Just make sure you're there at the start of the next season. If you're there, we reckon we can win it. If we've got you on the team and we keep our team together, we believe we're a really good chance.'

Those words were a major boost to my confidence. Here were two of my peers, blokes I'd played the most footy with, and they had confidence in me, and would back me. It was really heartening, and it contributed to steeling me for the year ahead. After a year when I'd captained a team I hardly took to the field for, I needed all the support I could get. As much as I'd tried to tell myself that none of the injuries was my fault, and that I'd done everything I could to get myself onto the field, I also sometimes had a nagging feeling that I hadn't contributed, and that if I had been playing on that preliminary final day against Carlton, we may well have won. When you're flirting with self-doubt – which my nature has me do – the mind hunts out the most emotionally destructive material it can find.

So Joey and Mercs's words inspired me. I knew that nothing would stand in my way in 2000.

Almost all of us carry some self-doubt. It can come in many forms: lying in bed at 4 in the morning wondering if you're a good parent or husband, standing in front of 2000 people all waiting for you to deliver a keynote address on leadership at some swanky corporate function, or running on in front of 95,000 people on Grand Final Day at the MCG. Most of it is rubbish drilled into us by teachers, coaches or parents who are in fact passing on their own self-doubt, but some of it is real. The only way to defeat self-doubt is to face it, take it on.

For instance, if your teachers said you were a bad reader, you probably believed it and became one. To remove this doubt, read more. If you challenge yourself to get better, you will – and you'll lose the doubt along the way. The day before a game I always spend 10 minutes throwing the ball against the wall and catching it to remind myself that I have good touch. That way, when the ball comes towards me on the field with an opponent breathing down my neck I know it will land first grab into my hands. Matthew Lloyd, the best set shot for goal in the game, removes his self-doubt by having a precise kicking routine that he follows every time he kicks for goal. Having structure can give you something to hang on to and can keep self-doubt at bay.

My body was right, my foot was fine, and I was set for a great preseason. At a week-long training camp at Essendon Grammar three weeks before the first Ansett Cup match, I got up in front of the boys. I started by talking about where I was coming from and where I wanted to go, spilling my guts about my frustrations over the last three years, that I felt as if I'd been working my arse off but nothing was coming to fruition. 'I really don't want to let you guys down anymore. But you should make sure you don't let yourselves down either.' I finished with a note on attitude. 'If you want to win a premiership you've got to be harder on yourselves. You enjoy beer too much. You enjoy life too much. Let's knuckle down for a year.'

It was nothing revolutionary, but I felt it needed to be said.

The effect of my speech was huge. About 20 of the boys came up afterwards and said, 'Best speech I've heard in ages. That was just great. Thanks for being honest with us.' And from the training camp until the end of that season, a huge wave of momentum carried us through.

On the Wednesday night before our first game for the season, we trained at Windy Hill. Two weeks earlier we'd won the pre-season competition. Things were looking good.

I came off the track after 30 minutes of training – not too long, because I didn't want my foot to get sore. I sat in the lockers and experienced a fantastic feeling. For the first time in three years I was going to go out and play with a body that felt 100 per cent; there was a bit of self-doubt because I hadn't played in a long time, but I would have the chance to test myself at the top AFL level again. It was a great moment.

Everything fell the right way for us in 2000. From the moment pre-season started, I felt enormous resolve among the playing group. There was a sense of inevitability about what we were going to do that year, as if nothing could stop us. I felt it from the most junior to the most senior player. It was the strongest level of commitment I'd experienced in my years at Essendon.

We had the resolve, and I thought we had the players. It was, I thought, the perfect team. Everyone was sacrificing for each other. Everyone was playing their role. We had high-profile stars such as Michael Long and Matthew Lloyd, but everyone in the team knew that success did not revolve around the efforts of a handful. Everyone had a role to play. In 2000 Lloydy kicked 100 goals and Longy was a dynamic rover/forward. But we were all just part of a team.

We had so many guys who had something to prove that year. Dean Wallis was known as a tough man, but he wanted to prove to the footy public that he was a good player too. I was coming back from the foot injury that had kept me out of football for the whole of 1999. Michael Long wanted to show that he wasn't a spent force. We had young guys like Dean 'Solly' Solomon and the two Johnsons – Jason and Mark, not related, but united in their ferocity – absolute brutes when they needed to be. They were aggressive young men who used their strength and force to benefit our side. There was Dustin Fletcher, who won the best and fairest that year, and wanted to make a name for himself. He also wanted to prove something. When you have 25 players who all have something very big to prove, you have a pretty strong force.

My first game in 2000 was the third game into the Ansett Cup. Michael Long and I had always had a lot of respect for each other, and when we were all running around doing a warm-up for the game, he stopped us and spoke up.

'This is Hirdy's first game back in a couple of years,' he said. 'Look, guys, don't expect too much from him. He hasn't played for a long time. It's great to have him here, great to have him back playing with us. Just enjoy it and we'll look after you, we'll give you the ball.'

The first two balls Longy found he kicked to me. I kicked two easy goals. The boys were looking after me. A real camaraderie developed out of that. We went on to win the Ansett Cup Grand Final against the Kangaroos, who'd been our arch rivals.

In the season opener we beat Port Adelaide at Colonial Stadium by 94 points. It was a good omen. Next up was Richmond at the MCG. This time we won by 43 points. At the WACA in Perth we beat Fremantle by 36, then Hawthorn at the MCG by 47, Carlton again at the MCG by 24, and Western Bulldogs at Colonial by 10 goals. We were doing everything right.

In Round 9, Melbourne took it right up to us, and we won by a slender 13 points at the MCG. But then we got back on a roll, beating Adelaide by 48 at Colonial (after being behind at three-quarter-time), then Geelong, St Kilda, the Kangaroos and West Coast, then Port Adelaide again, this time at the dreaded Football Park.

Apart from the Melbourne game, our wins had so far been convincing, but then we started burying teams. We caned Richmond at the MCG by 101 points, thrashed Fremantle at Colonial by 87 and took Hawthorn apart at Colonial to the tune of 83 points. Carlton gave us a run for our money in Round 20, but we were still able to account for them by 26 points.

We felt confident every time we ran out to play. In 90 per cent of the games, the game felt over by quarter-time. It was a great feeling, knowing the game was won so early. Certainly, we had an edge even before each game started, because teams were psychologically scared of us; this also happened with Brisbane in more recent times. We went out to games and obliterated the opposition. Games would be finished by halfway through the second quarter. By about Round 10, you'd run out, you'd look at your opponent, and you'd think, *This bloke knows he's not going to win.* You could feel it.

In the game against West Coast in Round 15, for example, they put everyone on their back half – they didn't even try to score a goal. They had just two people in their forward line. It's rare that a team will flood the forward line like that from the start of the game. It sent a strong message to us. If a team's doing that, you've got them.

That game was the one low moment for me on the field that year: I hurt my hamstring and missed three weeks. But my recovery was good, and it didn't affect my football for the rest of the year.

I found that I was dominating games again. I was playing well and kicking goals, and because the team was so dominant, instead of me getting the key defenders, Mercs was getting tagged, Longy was getting tagged and Lloydy was getting key players. I was running around free, doing what I wanted to do. The abuse I had experienced in other years was eradicated as my teammates – usually Dean Solomon, Jason Johnson, Dean Wallis and Michael Long – protected me.

I formed a bond with Solly one day at a training camp when we were partnered for some basic one-on-one ball skills. In the camp we were doing a lot of really physical one-on-one sessions, and on this day Solly came up and said, 'I'm going to be your partner.' So we went one-on-one for about two hours. Tackle, slam and brand 'em. It was a really fierce contest, but a good one, and I thought, *This kid's going to be a good player*. From then on, whenever I was attacked on the footy field Solly would be there cleaning blokes up for me and keeping them away. And we became really good friends. He is eight years younger than me, but we're terrific mates.

We had some real leaders at the club that year. I was captain, but it was probably the easiest captaincy anyone could experience. Longy was vice-captain, so he and I did a lot of the up-high decision-making stuff. Dean Wallis looked after all the rogues, because he'd been a rogue himself. He badly wanted to achieve something great in his life. He had two young kids and an awesome wife, and had been through some personal difficulties. He made a promise to himself that this would be his year, that he would achieve something. And he did. If anyone got out of line or drank too much, he was straight onto them. He's great with his family, but he's a hard man, no two ways about it. He's seen parts of life that I never want to see, and I'm sure he has a couple of regrets. But he's very strong and has a huge heart.

In Round 21, having dominated the season and with just one more match before the finals, we lost to the Bulldogs. We were hot favourites, but the Bulldogs had opted for the approach West Coast had taken: they flooded our forward line with their players, blocking supply to Lloydy and reducing our firepower. It was a tactic Rodney Eade had developed when he was coach of the Swans, and it often worked. Sometimes it worked so well that commentators would wring their hands and cry that it was the end of football as we know it, and say that flooding should be banned as a blight on the game. It's true that after that game we talked a lot about flooding, trying to analyse what it might mean to the game in future. But as we've seen, flooding alone can't stop good sides. There are ways around every tactic.

We regrouped and prepared ourselves for the finals. The loss might even have had a positive effect, acting as a salutary warning against getting too comfortable, too relaxed, too arrogant. We were extremely aware, all season, that we must not drop our guard. That year, we were the champs and everyone was coming to get us. Guarding against complacency was a critical part of our strategy.

We steamed on, beating the Kangaroos by 125 points in the qualifying final. This meant we were to meet Carlton in the preliminary final – same game, same venue as the year before, but we were planning a different result.

The team was on fire, but September 2000 was about to become the most emotional and difficult time of my life.

'You'd better come and get on the phone.'

It was the Friday afternoon before the preliminary final. It had been a good training session. At 3.30, halfway through our session, our footy manager came over, looking concerned. It was the hospital on the phone, ringing to say that Stephanie, my 18-month-old daughter, had been brought in by Tania after having a lengthy febrile convulsion (she had in fact convulsed on and off for an hour, and it had required a large amount of sedatives to stop it). I was told that Stephanie was still under sedation and probably wouldn't wake up for the next 12 hours. The doctors thought it could be meningococcal disease, which is extremely dangerous, even fatal, for children. They said: 'You'd better come straight away.'

I remember with great clarity the moment I learned the news. All thoughts of football flew out of my head as I made my way towards the car. *Is my sweet little girl all right? What is a febrile convulsion, and how serious is it?* My head was spinning with questions. Stephanie was our first child and I'd had no experience of sick children.

I drove to Epworth Hospital and spent the next two hours there. Then Stephanie was taken by ambulance to the Royal Children's Hospital. It was incredibly emotional for Tania and me. Stephanie needed a lumbar puncture: they take fluid out of the spine with a very large needle. I was asked to try to hold her while the doctor performed the procedure. Little Stephanie, though half under sedation, was screaming. It was a terrible thing to be part of.

'Bend her in half, hold her head between her knees and don't let her move,' the doctor instructed me.

As the huge needle slid into my 18-month-old daughter's back to extract spinal fluid, Tania and I were numbed by fear about what might be discovered. On that cold and dreary Friday night the innocence of a baby and her parents was taken away. Bringing a child into the world was clearly not all teddy bears and hugs: my daughter was screaming and I was crying. This was not how I had envisaged fatherhood. I had always thought I could protect my family, no matter what.

Kevin Sheedy's involvement during that time is one of the reasons I'll back him until the day I die. At 11 o'clock that night, about eight hours after that phone call, Sheeds arrived at Casualty. Stephanie was in the Intensive Care Unit at this point, and Tania and I were waiting in the room outside. Sheeds spent a good three hours at the hospital with me. We weren't really talking; he was just making sure everything was all right. His presence was comforting, and much appreciated. He is a family man, and much more sensitive than some people realise. He understood what I was going through and he was concerned, both for Stephanie and for me and Tania.

We were playing a game the next day at 2 o'clock – a preliminary final. If we won, it meant a place in the Grand Final. The importance of the game didn't need to be spelt out, especially given what had happened in the preliminary final against Carlton exactly 12 months earlier.

'Look,' Sheeds said, 'this game's really important for everyone. I know it's as important to you as any other game is. It's very important to me. But if you don't feel you can play because of what's going on, don't play. I respect that decision – as much as we want you to play. Your kids are more important than any football game.

If we lose a game, we lose a game. Your child's welfare is more important than you playing in or winning or losing a game of footy.'

He finally left the hospital at 2 am.

Sheeds's comments might sound quite normal, like something everybody would say, but I don't think many people in footy, certainly not many coaches, would say that to the captain of the club 24 hours before the second most important game of the year. It gave me a new perspective on Kevin: it proved that he is about more than just footy and that he has perspective in life. To him, people do matter more than football, and family is his number-one priority. I will always be grateful for the compassion he showed. I think it's the mark of the man.

I also left the hospital about 2 am. Tania stayed. At home I grabbed a couple of hours' sleep, had a shower, and then at 7 am went back to the hospital. At noon, the doctors told us that Stephanie did not have meningococcal disease and that she would be taken out of Intensive Care. That news allowed me to make a decision: I would play. I thought, if she was out of Intensive Care, she was going to be all right. I rang Sheeds and said: 'I'll play.'

I arrived at the ground a bit late. Most of my teammates didn't know the seriousness of my daughter's situation. I'd only told them that Stephanie was in hospital for a few tests. The ones who were close to me knew. We won the game, although I didn't play very well. We were through to the Grand Final, the following weekend.

After that preliminary final game I was going to the coach's room for the post-match meeting when Sheeds stopped me.

'What are you doing?' he asked.

'I'm coming to the meeting.'

'Don't. Just go. Go to the hospital.'

So I drove to the hospital to join Tania. Stephanie was slowly recovering, having slept a further 12 hours after a brief moment of consciousness that morning.

At 2 o'clock the next day I was sitting in Stephanie's hospital room with Tania and my mum, Tania's brother, sister, mum and stepfather, and my friend Rod Law. Stephanie had been sleeping now for two days. I was looking at my little girl as she was waking up, recalling how the doctors had told us that she didn't have meningococcal disease – that she was out of danger. The sweetness of that news cannot be described.

The emotions that went through my head then were out of control. There was doubt, because they hadn't yet ruled out epileptic ramifications or the possibility of slight brain damage. And there was sheer exhausted emptiness. I would soon play in the biggest game of the year in the biggest code in the country; normally I'd be pumped, but I felt no excitement at all. I felt powerlessness. In my life I'd always confronted problems and solved them. On this Sunday afternoon I couldn't do that.

Stephanie came out of hospital on Monday night. I didn't do much training that week, even with the upcoming Grand Final, because I was so drained. Two weeks later we got Stephanie's tests back – she was okay, and there was no consequential damage. That report was better than any premiership. The weight totally left my shoulders. *Thank God for that . . .*

But it would still haunt me for weeks to come. A couple of weeks later I was on a plane flying to Ireland to play in the International Rules game. I was sitting next to Steven King, of Geelong, and watching the movie *Gladiator*. At the start of the movie, the Russell Crowe character's wife and child are murdered by his enemies in a very disturbing scene. I was suddenly overwhelmed with emotion. All I could think was, *What am I doing, leaving my family to play footy after we've been through all this pain and heartache?* The film stirred up all the emotion of the previous weeks. I sat there with tears rolling down my face, unable to stop myself, and just hoped no one would notice. I was with 26 footballers I didn't know very well, heading to Ireland to play football, and I was crying during a movie. I covered my face with my arm, then sneaked a look over at Steven King. He was asleep.

Tania and I were extremely shaken by Stephanie's illness. I found it very hard to focus on football, but I was captain of the club and I had to prepare for the Grand Final.

This Grand Final was probably the most important game of my life. After all my injuries and setbacks, this was my big moment, a chance to put all the disappointment behind me. The game could not hold more significance.

We'd beaten Carlton in the preliminary final, and some people in the team might have been tempted to view that victory as revenge for what happened a year earlier. That feeling lasted no more than five minutes after the game. The real focus was on beating Melbourne in the Grand Final, the final hurdle of our season. It was the result that we had felt was our destiny all season.

As usual, that week was full of Grand Final fever and big events, starting with the Brownlow Medal count on the Monday night. We were invited, but it was the last thing I wanted to do with Stephanie just out of hospital. Her health was still up in the air. She'd had tests, and the results wouldn't be confirmed for a couple of weeks, so there was still a lot of uncertainty.

I knew what was facing me that Saturday: the conclusion of my redemption year. I'd had a really good season, but if we lost that Grand Final it would all have been for nothing.

I ran out that day with one purpose – to play as well as I could.

There were two things we had identified about Melbourne: they were quite young and light-bodied, and they were playing on hardened men who'd lost big games and won big games and been through big injuries and had a lot of reasons to win. We also identified the way the Demons moved the ball out of their backline – they handballed it out, almost up to the middle of the ground, using their fastest players to run it out, and then they'd kick. So we focused on countering that tactic. We decided that when they brought the ball out with a handball, we had to stop that handball. We'd chase, chase and chase to break the handball down.

We knew that once we got our hands on the ball we could move it very quickly. We had lots of goal-kickers, too: Lloydy, Longy, Scott Lucas, Darren Bewick (who could sniff out a goal anywhere), Blake Caracella and me. We had six or seven guys who knew how to get a goal when it was in our area. We were confident we'd win the game.

Our other main plan was to play aggressively. It was never said that we should target players, but given that their side was very young, we thought that aggression would break them down a bit. There was an added incentive in that a few of our older players, guys like Dean Wallis, were preparing to hang up their boots at the end of that game.

Michael Long's hit on Melbourne tall man Troy Simmonds in the second quarter didn't look good. Longy hip-and-shouldered Simmonds, who was flattened and apparently knocked unconscious; he was stretchered off the ground. There was some concern that he might be seriously hurt; luckily, he wasn't.

There was some criticism of Longy for that bump. Longy is a tough man, but he's also very gentle. He wouldn't have tried to hurt Simmonds. He went in to bump, and he didn't realise where Simmonds's head was. It was a natural instinct to give a hip and shoulder.

135

I was quite close to it, and it didn't look too serious to me then, but when I saw it on TV afterwards, I thought, *Gee, is that what it was like?* I spoke to Longy about it after the game, and he felt terrible. He said he wished he hadn't hurt Simmonds. Troy's family were critical of him when they spoke to the media, but these things happen with instinctive play. Longy didn't mean to hurt Simmonds. I think you have to assess it in the context of the game.

We were well in front on the scoreboard at the time. The incident didn't change the tone of the game, or alter the momentum. Just before, the ball had been on our forward line a lot. There was a melée after the incident, which we all got fined for, but I didn't mind paying the $2000 – after all, we'd won the Grand Final. We powered on for the rest of the game, playing almost to our potential (we kicked 21 behinds, so we should have won by more than the 10 goals we did). We'd won. Our promises to ourselves had been honoured. All the pain and stress and hard work and passion had paid off. All the crap I'd been through didn't matter anymore.

When the siren sounded I knew where Tania and Stephanie were, so I ran over to them – they were waiting for me just inside the fence. I held them both and burst into tears. I remember feeling overwhelming relief: first, Stephanie was going to be all right, and second, we had won a Grand Final. I'd played a good game, which was icing on the cake. As if my day hadn't been dramatic enough, I won the Norm Smith Medal for the best player in the Grand Final.

Stephanie's illness had put football in perspective. That's probably why I was able to play so well. Footy was still very important, and stressful, but Stephanie's illness the Saturday before had been much worse.

Sickness and misfortune remind you that sport is just sport; real life is different, and is so much more important. Grand Final

A family portrait, 1980. My parents, Allan and Margaret, surrounded by us kids. Amilia and Katherine would later say how much quieter it was at home once I'd moved south to Windy Hill.

Above: Out in the garden at Latham, Canberra, in December 1975.

Right: At home in Latham in 1976, waiting for Dad to come outside and have a kick. There was never any doubt I would support the Bombers: my grandfather, Allan T. Hird, and my dad both wore the red-and-black guernsey of Essendon.

The Ainslie under-11 side, 1983. That's me in the centre, just behind the sign, dreaming of one day becoming the next Terry Daniher or Tim Watson.

Visiting my family in Reid, Canberra, during the 1992 off-season. It was always great to go home. From left to right: Amilia, Dad, Mum, me and Katherine.

'The Baby Bombers', as we were named, early in the 1993 season. At the front of the group on the far right is Ricky Olarenshaw, next to him (holding the ball) is David Calthorpe, then Mark Mercuri; along the back row, dark-haired Steve Alessio is in the centre while Dustin Fletcher stands at far right. Five months later, we'd be part of a premiership-winning team. (THE HERALD & WEEKLY TIMES PHOTOGRAPHIC COLLECTION)

Left: Tania and I at Checkpoint Charlie, Berlin, November 1995. The time away travelling and experiencing other cultures was invaluable to me.

Below: Feeling the harsh cold of the northern European winter, at an Allied war cemetery in Flanders, Belgium. My Great-Uncle Tom was captured by the Germans in 1944, and I've always felt a huge respect for and debt towards the thousands of brave Australians who fought for our country during the two world wars.

Above: Joint winners of the 1996 Brownlow Medal, Michael Voss of the Brisbane Lions and me. I'd always focused on achieving success as a team – the Brownlow win, though a huge honour, was never part of my dream. (NEWSPIX)

Left: Our wedding day, 11 October 1997. This photo was taken as we arrived at the reception, at Ripponlea in Elsternwick. It was a superb day.

(ROBERT D'ARGENT, CENTRAL PARK STUDIOS)

Above: Triumph and relief. No one except Tania and I understood exactly what Essendon's 2000 Grand Final win meant to us after Stephanie had suffered a lengthy febrile convulsion the week before. (GETTY IMAGES)

Left: In the locker room at my beloved MCG, savouring the victory and realising that my childhood dream had come true. Stephanie seems to be developing a taste for success too – namely my Norm Smith Medal! (NEWSPIX)

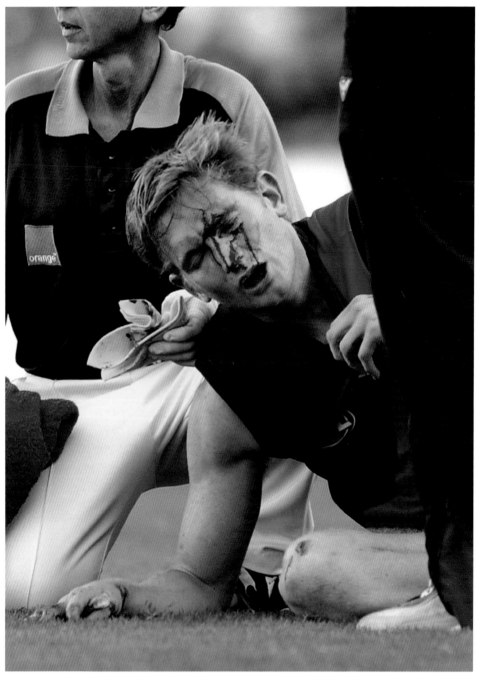

'Plagues and pestilence', Sheeds calls them, and it's fair to say I've had my share. They don't get much worse than my facial injury in Perth, on 4 May 2002. (GETTY IMAGES)

Above: Conferring with coach Kevin Sheedy, early in the 2003 season. I have been very lucky with the role models and mentors I've had at Essendon – people like Sheeds, Tim Watson and Danny Corcoran. (NEWSPIX)

Left: I'll never know whether it was some sort of pressure release or just elation at having kicked the winning goal to snatch victory from West Coast. Me hugging a Bomber supporter, Telstra Dome, 10 April 2004, midway through the umpires saga. (NEWSPIX)

A family affair, outside St Finbar's Church, Brighton, November 2004. My sister Amilia's wedding day saw us all take a role: I gave Amilia away, Tania handled some of the bridesmaid duties, while Stephanie and Tom were flower girl and page, respectively.

My fellow number 5 Thomas and I looking on at Princes Park, Carlton, February 2005.
(NEWSPIX)

25 April 2005, leading the Bombers through the banner for the annual Anzac Day game against Collingwood. Except for the Grand Final, it's the biggest game of the year, and an honour for me to play in. (GETTY IMAGES)

Receiving the Anzac Day Medal – my third – after the 2004 game. (GETTY IMAGES)

Swimming with the kids. Enjoying a break at Coolum in Queensland, January 2005.

With my co-partners at the Red Mullet Fish Caf in Malvern. From left to right, John Stamoulis, Nick Gordon, Helen Stamoulis and I raise a glass. (NEWSPIX)

Tania and I arriving at the Brownlow Medal dinner, September 2005. Once in a while the red-carpet treatment can be fun. (GETTY IMAGES)

I see courage in all walks of life; in the footy world, it's rarely more evident than in the likes of Michael Long and Adam Ramanauskas. This is Michael and me, draped in the Aboriginal flag, at 'the Dreamtime Game' against Richmond in May 2006. (NEWSPIX)

Football has touched our entire family and continues to affect everyone from grandparents to my youngest child. This is my daughter Stephanie's depiction of a game against the Saints.

Above: August 2006, in Fawkner Park, South Yarra – with the kids letting me know who's boss! (NEWSPIX)

Left: Darth and Princess Leia (aka Dad and Mum) help Tom celebrate his fourth birthday, *Star Wars* style.

Thomas, Tania, Stephanie and Alexander help make my August 2006 celebration dinner complete. This is us in our hotel room just before heading down to the Crown Casino's Palladium Room.

day 2000 was a day on which I achieved my football dream. But it came when my focus was not totally on football. This taught me that to perform at your optimum you need to train well and be totally commited to the cause, and to stay in touch with reality. Great skill, hard work and luck count for a lot when a top-level performance is required, but so does a balanced outlook on the place sport holds in your life. It was a lesson I would have to learn again 12 months later.

The win capped off an extraordinary year for the club. We'd made history along the way: we had the most wins in a season (24), we joined Carlton as the team with the most premierships (16), it was the longest winning streak to start a season (20), the highest score in a final (31 goals 12 points against the Kangaroos) and the third-highest percentage for the year (behind Essendon in 1950 and West Coast in 1991).

It was the year I needed to have, after all my injuries. No matter what happened after this, I'd proven to myself that I could play footy.

As Angus Morgan noted in *The Age*:

There is a hint of redemption about James Hird's Grand Final performance. Not that the 2000 Norm Smith medallist is preoccupied with the past; there's too much for him to rejoice about in the present. But those two lost years, when he was sidelined with stress fractures, hobbled with hamstring strains and driven to distraction by the barbs of media hardliners who questioned his value for money, must surely make this among the most romantic of victories.

In the following week there were to be celebrations, media events and club things, including the Essendon best-and-fairest count on the Wednesday night and a tickertape parade on Thursday.

I was very sleep-deprived as a result of Stephanie's illness, and I said to Tania, 'We've got to get out of here.' We jumped on a plane the next day and went to Queensland for four days, just the three of us, to get away. The footy was over; it was only sponsors' functions that weren't done. The club might have missed me, but the three of us needed some time to get over what had happened. To spend time with the two people I loved so much was priceless.

Finally, some peace.

Chapter 8

What Happens Now?

The glow didn't wear off for a while. Winning the 2000 premiership was a special time for all of us at Essendon and a great time in my life. It's impossible to overstate how relieved I felt. My life changed straight away – I had finally accomplished one of the things I had always wanted to achieve. That journey was over. I would start new journeys, with their own pressures, but that one was put away.

A fog lifted off me that day. The fog was the lingering fear that I would never fulfil that dream. When you have a dream for as long as you can remember and things go wrong and people start doubting you and putting negative thoughts in your head, it can be hard to see the way forward. Then you meet people who put positive thoughts back into you and help you rebuild. When we won that game, I realised that the positive thoughts in my head were stronger than the negative ones. I knew that even when things went wrong, if I kept working hard they would probably turn around. Strength would flow from this achievement for the rest of my life.

When Tania, Stephanie and I went to the Gold Coast, my Essendon teammates may have smiled knowingly, but the first thing I did for relaxation was train. So on the Saturday after the Grand Final I started: running on the beach, running along the main street. I needed to relieve the stress of the past few weeks by running. It worked. My break began. I've always been someone who can't not train for more than a week or so. It's a bit of obsessive compulsive behaviour that my doctor and good friend Bruce Reid always has a go at me about. If I'm not training I get . . . not depressed, but a bit quiet. If I don't start the day doing some exercise, I feel flat. It must be some chemical that your brain releases.

A couple of weeks later I joined the boys for a quick footy trip to Ibiza, an island off Spain. We discovered it was a dubious place for a footy trip. It is famous for its drug culture, rave parties and sunburned Poms. I won't mention whose idea it was to go there; that wouldn't be fair.

At 6.30 one morning I went out running, which was unheard of on a footy trip, almost criminal. But we had the International Rules series coming up in Ireland and I really wanted to perform well, for two reasons: I'd been named captain, and I'd never played against Ireland before. As I jogged out the door, three of my teammates – Dean Solomon, Adam Ramanauskas and Mark McVeigh – walked in, returning from a party. Mark McVeigh had his arm in a sling. As captain of the team and a good mate of Mark's, I asked for the story and got my first lesson on foam and water parties.

Mark had broken his collarbone at a foam party. That's where they fill the whole nightclub with foam. He slipped over. It took him 10 weeks to get better, but he didn't miss a game. The foam party wasn't the only treat for tourists. In the same nightclub they also held water parties, where they filled the nightclub with water up to chest height. It sounded dangerous, especially at 4 am when people are inebriated. I was told one of the Essendon boys went under and had to be plucked out before he drowned.

I did think, as I jogged off, that it probably was a bit early to be going for a run – just as my teammates were staggering home from a party. They still, to this day, have a dig at me about it.

Dustin Fletcher and I came back early from Ibiza because I wanted to go to the Olympics with Tania. We had cheap air tickets, and we soon realised why they were so cheap: it took us 48 hours to get back to Melbourne.

When we finally got home, Nike flew me and the other players they sponsored – Matthew Lloyd, Corey McKernan and Stephen Silvagni – and our partners up to Sydney. We were joined by a few rugby guys: Wendell Sailor, Gorden Tallis, Darren Lock-yer and Andrew Johns.

It was a great trip. We were taken by boat all the way to Homebush Bay, where many of the Olympic events were being held. We were able to go through the Athletes' Village, and then we watched Cathy Freeman win her gold medal in the 400 metres.

It was interesting to see the difference between the rugby league blokes and the Australian Rules guys on the boat. They were a lot louder and seemed a lot more confident. They taunted us about our drinking capabilities – as in, we weren't as good, which is not surprising given their size. They were big! There must be such different body requirements and training regimes for them. Lloydy, SOS (Steve Silvagni) and McKernan aren't small guys, but they paled next to Sailor and Tallis. When I was a kid in Canberra you could play any sport – rugby league, union, soccer, Australian Rules. I'm glad I chose Australian Rules, because getting hit by those guys on a regular basis would shorten your life span. That said, they were a lot of fun.

Tania and I spent five days on a luxury ocean liner moored in the harbour as guests of Channel 7. There were lots of celebrities there, including Ian Thorpe and Kylie Minogue. I didn't meet Kylie, although she was sitting only a couple of tables away. I'm pretty hesitant about going up and saying hello to people I don't know just for the sake of meeting them.

We had a ball on the boat. After working so hard up to the Grand Final, it was a great reward for what Tania and I had put in. We'd had a few rough times with my injuries – nothing compared with what other people have been through, but significant for us. We really enjoyed being given the red carpet treatment in a city that was buzzing with the Olympics.

The big event for me to witness was Cathy Freeman's 400 metres final. To this day, Cathy's victory in that race is up there as one of the most amazing things I've ever seen. The race was good, but what I loved was the look on her face when she finished, a look of utter relief. In the 30 seconds to a minute afterwards, it didn't seem that she was ecstatic or happy or that it was the greatest moment of her life, it was, 'Thank God I've won this thing.' You could see the pressure being released from her body.

There were certain parallels with the release of pressure I'd felt just a fortnight ago when we won the Grand Final that we too just had to win. People would say the pressure on her was much bigger, because she's a national and international figure, and it probably was. But still, I knew a little about how Cathy felt. There's definitely exhilaration, excitement and enjoyment, but also you can see the relief rushing out of her when she rips her headpiece off and looks up.

Athletics, to me, encapsulates what the Olympics are. Other people have other favourite sports, but athletics is my love as a spectator. The sense of national pride after Cathy's win was palpable, just as it was when the Socceroos qualified for the World Cup in 2005. I've met Cathy a couple of times. She comes across as a very nice person – a normal person like the rest of us who was given a talent and worked extremely hard and went through a lot of pain to get the most possible out of that talent.

On the night of that race I met Ben Crowe on the boat. Ben was with Nike then. He's now my manager. We only had a three-minute chat that night, but we later developed a strong relationship. It's interesting where life takes you. I wasn't to know what a central role Ben would later have in my professional life, managing me and bringing me in as an equity partner in his business.

Sydney was a great trip. I really like the city. Both my sisters have lived there, and one still does. I think it's probably the most beautiful natural harbour in the world.

It's interesting to imagine what might have happened if I'd gone to Sydney 16 years ago. It would have been so different, living in a non-football city – Michael Voss has talked about being a big name in a non-footy town. I think being away from the football-mad world of Melbourne, Adelaide and Perth probably helped the Lions win those three premierships. One of the reasons it's hard to win back-to-back flags – a small reason, it must be said – is the weight of expectation. After you win a premiership, people get out of control and start saying how good you are; it's very easy to lose perspective. The Lions are an excellent team, and one of the things that might have helped keep them on the edge is that they are probably able to get on with their normal lives. The madness level is rising in Brisbane, but it's nothing like in Melbourne. So the upside of not being in a football culture is that you get some peace, and the downside is that you don't get the support that culture provides. For me, 95 per cent of the time I love being in a football culture, and 5 per cent of the time I wish I could be a little more anonymous.

After the Sydney holiday we joined a three-day training camp at Telstra Dome in preparation for the International Rules competition against Ireland. It was great to meet the Bulldogs players – Brad Johnson and Rohan Smith are terrific guys. The team also included Craig Bradley and Brett Ratten from Carlton – sensational people and great players. Lloydy and Fletcher pulled out, Lloydy because he hurt his ankle, Fletch because after that nightmarish trip to Spain, he decided to stay home with his family. So the Essendon players in the squad were Damien Hardwick, Blake Caracella, Justin Blumfield, Chris Heffernan and me.

On the trip I roomed with Andrew McLeod, who's a good bloke and an athlete with amazing, silky skills. In the Australian side, two guys from other clubs have amazed me – in 2000, McLeod, and in 2004, Nick Riewoldt – mainly because of the speed and the intensity of their training.

Dermott Brereton coached the team that year. He allowed the senior players to have their heads a bit. His philosophy was that if you've been chosen to play for your country, you are obviously a professional athlete at the peak of your career, so he gave us freedom to play as we saw fit. It was a good team.

We beat the Irish in both games. At three-quarter-time in the first game we were a little behind, and looking down the barrel. Dermott put a real challenge to me. During the game, you'd come off for a rest every seven minutes because it was such a hard-running game. He said, 'Can you run the whole last quarter out and win us the game?' Not that I won us the game, but I was able to run it out and I played all right. Blake Caracella kicked all the goals for us to win. It was a good coaching ploy by Dermott.

It was a great feeling to go over to another country with 25 blokes, representing Australia, and captain the team to a win on Croke Park, and then to a second win. We'd beaten the best of Ireland at a game we think is biased towards them (incidentally, they think it is biased towards us).

One of the great days was when Damien Hardwick, Chris Heffernan, Justin Blumfield, Blake Caracella and I went to Trinity College in Dublin to have a look at the Book of Kells, which contains the four gospels, as well as wonderful, elaborate illustrations depicting events in the life of Christ. The Book, whose history stretches back 1500 years, has been at Trinity College since 1661 and is the most important work in the university's library.

Being a group of footballers, our desire for tourist-related activity waned by about lunchtime. Obviously, we couldn't go to Ireland and not experience the Irish pubs, so we found a bar in Trinity College overlooking the cricket ground and surrounded by superb buildings which were probably 500 to 600 years old. We sat there in a dark, loud, atmospheric bar and told stories for hours over a lunch that was fuelled by Irish beer and stretched until 7.30 that night. I can't remember the last time I've done such a marathon lunch. There we were, on the other side of the world, watching Dublin go by, talking to some of the Trinity students about their experiences and talking to each other about how good it was to win a Grand Final and how much we all meant to each other.

It's a day I'll always remember.

We started the 2001 season hot premiership favourites, in as dominant form as we had shown the year before.

We were very aware of the dangers of complacency – we had come too far and played too much good football to let success slip away. The media focused on our dominance. In May, when we were on a roll, *The Australian* published a piece quoting other coaches, or 'victims', as they called them, talk about how to stop us. They quoted Leigh Matthews, coach of the Brisbane Lions:

> I think it is fair to say that they have been the most dominant side of my era in football. I mean, being beaten twice in their last 34 games, there is no other side in my memory in footy that has been quite as dominating as that. They are not robots or super-humans. They have the appearance of being superhumans, I must admit, but they are flesh and blood like everyone else.

Despite all this talk, there were signs that year that weren't good, things we hadn't seen the year before. In hindsight, it's easy enough to see where we lost the 2001 Grand Final. It started in the Round 8 game against Hawthorn. They were unbeaten, and our major rivals, and we were without five of our best 10 players, and had others going down with injuries all over the place. But we still smashed them. Even at less-than-full strength, we were playing imposing football. After that game we thought, *Here we go, we're on our way again*. Maybe we were being too optimistic.

The next week we were to play Brisbane. In the build-up to the game, Leigh Matthews returned to his 'flesh and blood' and 'superhero' theme when he told a press conference, 'If it bleeds, you can kill it', a line delivered by Arnold Schwarzenegger in the 1987 film *Predator*.

It must have given them a lot of confidence, because they belted us around the park. We had a young side and were missing Dean Wallis and Michael Long, who weren't playing the best football of their careers, but they were our enforcers. It's odd, I suppose, to describe Longy as an enforcer, because he's only 80 kilos dripping wet, but he had the ability to hit someone at the right time with a hip and shoulder. Wally, on the other hand, was a fierce competitor, an aggressive bloke people were scared of.

The Lions had been thrashed by Carlton a couple of weeks before, but after they caned us they got on a roll. That victory was a turning point for them. We'd been the benchmark, the ones to beat. We'd lost two games of footy in 40. From that game on, the Lions didn't lose a game for the rest of the year. We knew they were good, but we didn't realise how much better they were becoming.

Some football writers said that that Round 8 game was the one in which the Lions replaced us as the competition's predator. They were probably right.

The loss wasn't the beginning of the end for us, but the injuries were mounting. In patches we played very good football, but it wasn't like 2000 by any stretch of the imagination. We lost a few games, and had a few more injuries. The players weren't as fit as they should have been, and I don't think we had the absolute killer instinct we had in 2000 – though it's hard to have that when you don't have the quality players available. We didn't feel shaky, but we certainly didn't have the iron-clad confidence we'd had the year before. Leigh Matthews's pilfer from *Predator* was clever, graphic, and probably spot on.

But there were still days of power. In Round 15 I played in one of the most incredible games I've been a part of, against the Kangaroos. We were 10 goals down in the first quarter, playing like absolute dogs. I was on Glen Archer. The ball came to us three times, and Archer beat me point blank three times. Every Essendon player was getting beaten. Shannon Grant and the midfield were unstoppable. They had kicked 12 goals straight in a scoring blitz, made even more remarkable by the fact that they were without three key players – Wayne Carey, Anthony Stevens and Mick Martyn. It was a game the Kangaroos looked to have well in their keeping by quarter-time. Early in the second quarter they led by 69 points.

But we came back, kicking nine goals in the second quarter without reply from the Kangaroos – Lloydy kicked five of his nine goals in that quarter. By the end of the third quarter we were down by only seven points, and from there we held on to win.

To come back from nearly 12 goals behind – and against such high odds – made us feel we were still on our roll. We felt we still had the measure of our old rivals. But a great side should never allow itself to get 69 points down, even if it does come back and win. It was not a good sign.

We were to play Carlton three weeks before the finals. We had a lot of history with the Blues. They'd been our arch rivals for a long time, but things had intensified after we lost by a point in the preliminary final in 1999 – yes, the 'unloseable' preliminary final. In 2000 we had some great contests with them. They had a really good side, I believe the second-best side, in 2000.

As it turned out, we lost to Carlton, then to Port Adelaide a few weeks after that. We were losing to sides that were about even with us. We were lucky that we played Richmond and Hawthorn in the finals, because while they were good sides, they weren't, to my mind, as dangerous as Carlton, Port Adelaide or Brisbane.

When we first played them in 2001, in Round 3, we got to the ground and Robert Shaw, our assistant coach, said: 'Bradley's out, Ratten's out, Kouta's out.' Their best three players. We thought we had their measure anyway, but hearing this news we were rapt. We'd beaten them the year before, by around 20 points each time, with their great players playing.

I played on Simon Beaumont. I'd played on him in the preliminary final the year before, and he'd beaten me a couple of times. So I badly wanted to beat him. We all had personal battles we wanted to win. It came as a nasty surprise when Carlton beat us in that third round.

Winning the August return match against them became a mission for us. As they say in football, we 'set ourselves' for it. I again had a personal mission to beat Simon Beaumont.

The game felt good. I was getting some fitness back, and my body was responding well after a calf injury which had interrupted my pre-season and a groin injury mid-year which had forced me out for a couple of weeks. For three-quarters of the game I felt I was back. And I was getting on top of Beaumont.

Then just on three-quarter-time I went for a mark in the wet and landed awkwardly coming out of the contest. I'd rolled my ankle. My initial fear was that I'd broken it. Tests showed no break, but I'd torn the ligament badly, which meant a recovery on crutches.

So while it was satisfying to beat Simon Beaumont – which I think I did – it was frustrating to be injured.

When I was on the ground we were two goals up, but we finished up losing the game by 15 points. That could have cost us a top two spot. Luckily, it didn't.

But for me the damage was done. The injury meant that coming into the finals, I couldn't do the work I needed to do to get fit. I think that's why I hurt my groin again in the finals: I just wasn't match-fit.

In the last match of the season, against Richmond, we all played like dogs and lost.

We were struggling. Come finals time we were missing two or three of our best 10, including Wallis, Long and me. Justin Blumfield was struggling with injury, as was Chris Heffernan. Every team has injuries, but this was a crucial time of the year, and we had injuries to the players we needed out on the park.

We just beat Sydney – Steve Alessio kicked a goal after the siren – and then we beat West Coast (in Perth) and Collingwood. We ended up on top of the ladder, even though we were not playing great football. There weren't 22 players out there playing well; there were four or five – and a different four or five each week – carrying us over the line.

On 11 September 2001 I woke at 7 o'clock and turned on the TV to check the news. I saw what was happening in New York. I stayed in bed until about 9.30, not moving. I drove to training, where it was of course the big topic of discussion. It struck us all how incredible it was that we were still taking our footy so seriously even during such overwhelming world events.

As tragic as the news from the United States was, our lives had to go on.

For us, this meant trying to stay focused on the job at hand: beating Richmond in a return match a week after they'd beaten us. This time we won easily. The victory meant we had a week off before the preliminary final, which was handy for me. I might now have time to get my ankle right.

The next Friday night at Windy Hill we did a drill called match simulation, a hard training session with a lot of running. With about 10 minutes of the session left, I was coming through the middle of the ground when I turned and felt a pop in my groin. I'd strained it.

We were to play Hawthorn in the preliminary final, and I needed to play. The problem was that Lloydy had been rubbed out on a charge of head-butting, and Longy and Dean Wallis were also out. There were too many senior guys sidelined. I knew I had to play, no matter what my groin was like. I figured I'd be beneficial even as a presence on the field, even just standing there and taking a few marks, plus giving guidance and occupying a key defender.

Hawthorn's centre-half-back, Jonathan Hay, picked me up. At that stage, Hay was one of the quickest players in the competition.

I would lead out for the ball, running at three-quarter pace, and he would spoil everything away. I didn't have the confidence to really motor towards the contest. I could feel the groin, but it wasn't totally inhibiting me.

In the second quarter I went for a mark, the ball hit the ground, I turned, and felt as though a really sharp knife had been plunged into my groin. I knew I was in trouble.

I went off the ground and my suspicions were confirmed: a strained groin. There was nothing the physios could do to fix it. It just needed time to heal. We were three or four goals up at that stage, so we were confident of getting through to the Grand Final and I was optimistic that something could be done to fix me up in time for it.

Then Hawthorn started to come back. Things were looking ominous. Sheeds said, 'Get out on the ground. I don't care how you are, just get out there for the last quarter and see if you can do something.'

I didn't touch the ball, but I made a couple of good tackles. We won the game and I was rapt, but I'd torn my groin and I knew I had only six days to get up for a big Grand Final.

I spent all week down at the beach walking in the water and receiving treatment (twice a day). It didn't do much good. The newspapers reported me in deep discussion with club doctor Bruce Reid. If the Lions could lip-read, they would have been confident that I was going into the Grand Final injured and worried.

The big day. The Grand Final. As usual, Melbourne stopped for the day. Red and black balloons had been tied to trees and lamp-posts in Essendon. It seemed to be all anyone talked about. Even people who are not heavily into football schedule their day around the game at 2.30 pm at the MCG. There's a fantastic spirit in the air, the same spirit I remember on Grand Final mornings when I was a kid.

But I wasn't enjoying it. I knew – as did Bruce Reid – that I was vulnerable going into the game. It was a roll of the dice. And I've never been much of a gambler.

As the morning wore on, I continued to feel tentative because of the groin. I wasn't confident it would stand up to the pace and intensity of a Grand Final. In the warm-up before the match it didn't feel good, but I had no choice: I had to hope like hell it would hold together for three hours.

Brad Scott, Brisbane's feisty stopper, picked me up. The first ball I went for resulted in a bang – and a knife-like pain in the groin. I played on, but I was running around on half a leg, and Scott capitalised on it. He made me look absolutely stupid, running me up and down the ground. He did a good job on me.

It wasn't the only good job he did on me. Twenty minutes into the second quarter, I was down getting the ball when his knee went into the back of my head.

I went into the rooms at half-time feeling crook after the knock to the head, and not able to calm down. I was really hot and flustered and I couldn't relax. At half-time, being able to relax is important. Whether your team is winning or losing, you have to relax. You've probably got about five minutes when there's no one talking to you, and there's no cool-down and no warm-up, where you can just sit and compose yourself. I couldn't do it. I was edgy, and my head felt like a pressure cooker.

We were in front, but in the third quarter the game started slipping away.

And then it was all over. We'd lost. All the work in 2001, for what? For me it was worse than just losing a match. I felt useless because I couldn't do anything. I couldn't make my body run. Every time I tried to change direction, I'd feel my groin again. It's not like a pain you can carry; you have no power in your legs because you can't move properly.

Courtesy of Brad Scott's knee, I have no memory of the actual play in the second half of the game, which in some ways is a blessed relief. It's not something I would want to remember. I do remember the siren sounding and walking off the ground feeling hugely embarrassed. I was as embarrassed as I'd ever been on a football ground. It took me a long time to get over that, because I'd always prided myself on giving 100 per cent. Even if you played badly, you put your body on the line. I tried 100 per cent, but there were things I just couldn't do.

Losing that game was the most disappointing moment I've ever had in footy. There are photos of me on the ground afterwards, barefoot, disconsolate, in stark contrast to the over-whelming high of the year before. I've never seen a sorrier sight. I felt I hadn't worked hard – I couldn't run, couldn't do a number of things. I came away with just 10 possessions, and I'd had limited influence on the game. I remember standing on the ground thinking, *It doesn't get much worse than this in footy.*

After the game I didn't talk about the injury. People asked me if I'd been injured and I said no, I was fine. There was press speculation that I'd been injured, but I chose not to confirm it.

In the *Herald Sun* the following Monday, former Melbourne captain Garry Lyon wrote:

> Modesty will no doubt forbid either player [Mark Mercuri and me] from blaming their quiet games on injury, but I've seen enough of both almost to guarantee they were not close to their physical peak. If I was Kevin Sheedy, I would have played them, such is their quality and importance as on-field leaders. But it was always going to be a risk, and their returns of 10 possessions each would suggest that the risk backfired.

Afterwards Tania wanted to know why I said I'd been okay. 'Why would you say you were fine?'

'There's nothing to be gained from saying you're injured. It's just a cop-out. We lost, I played badly, we'll get over it.' She disagreed.

I was slammed in the newspapers. Every article seemed to be not about the fact that we'd lost, but how poorly I'd performed, that it was basically my fault. I have never blamed anything or anyone other than myself for anything bad in my life. I believe that if you take the easy option – such as saying you were injured – once, it becomes easier to make excuses next time. I have always believed that if I choose to play with injury I cannot then use it as an excuse. If I don't believe I can play with it, I shouldn't play.

Losing the 2001 Grand Final was my fault. Not entirely, but enough to mean it is a sore point that time has slowly healed. But it is also a day I learned from. If 2000 taught me not to lose perspective on things, 2001 taught me the same lesson, just in a different way. This may sound strange, but I took 2001 too seriously, and let football control me rather than the other way round. I worried about protecting my and the team's reputation instead of aiming to build a better one. Sometimes, no matter how important and enticing an activity is, you need to step back from it and look at it from a different angle, otherwise you won't see the full picture.

Hindsight has helped me analyse my mistakes and the club's, but it has also given me a sense of pride: I have never shirked my responsibility about that day. This is a common theme in my life. I believe that at all times we need to take responsibility for our actions. If we don't do this, we can never truly grow and improve as people. I will never get another chance to play in a Grand Final, but taking responsibility for the 2001 loss means that no other high-profile challenges in my life will ever control me; they will find a place in my life, but they will never come before my family and the moral fabric that defines who I am.

As I said, there was some savage press coverage, about both the team's performance and my own. Some mentioned the obvious contrast between my emotional embrace of Tania and Stephanie after the 2000 Grand Final, the huge joy, relief and sense of destiny of that game, and me exactly a year later, trudging along bootless, dejected, white-hot with anger and frustration. One report even brought out the old 'roosters and feather dusters' line.

The next day all the players went to Windy Hill to meet the Bomber fans. After a win, this is a great day. Having lost, it was difficult, but the fans deserved to see and hear us. It was about sharing the pain, I suppose.

From the stage I told our supporters: 'It's very disappointing. I was embarrassed with the way I played. You lead a team and you expect to do better than that. They're a terrific group of players. We'll be here having another crack next year.'

There was some blood-letting after that game. It was suggested in the media and around town that despite three years of finishing on top of the ladder and being the dominant side (by winning 63 of the last 73 games), Essendon had underachieved. I was stunned when I read that. Was it underachievement, or were we beaten by a better side? Certainly, we didn't play well on the day, but I didn't feel that any of us underachieved.

In 2003 I delivered the keynote address at the launch of the Essendon–LaTrobe University management seminar and spoke about what I believe was a contributing factor to our loss in the 2001 Grand Final:

People with level heads make excellent leaders. In hindsight it was something we lost sight of in 2001 when we lost the premiership to Brisbane. We went into that final series farewelling Michael Long, Dean Wallis and John Barnes, and I think we got too emotional. From a leadership point of view,

155

I think it took our focus away. Personally, I got very emotional about saying goodbye to two very good friends and blokes I'd played a lot of football with. We took our eye off the ball and paid the penalty.

On the Monday night before the Grand Final, Dean Wallis told us he wasn't going to even try to play, that he was finished. That was emotional enough. A guy I absolutely loved because of his passion wasn't going to play in the big game. People might see it as melodramatic, but there was a bond in that team: we'd done so much together, and one of our key members was saying his body wouldn't allow him to play.

Then, on the Wednesday night, Longy did his hamstring at training, so he too was going to miss the Grand Final. I thought, *I've got a sore groin, but at least I'll get to run out there and we might win it. This bloke has torn his hamstring; he can't even walk.* I spent an hour and a half looking for him. I couldn't reach him on his phone, I drove to his house but he wasn't there, I drove to somewhere I thought he'd be, but I didn't get hold of him.

The departure of Longy, Wally and Barnesy built up around the club and everyone became quite emotional. I think now that it would have been better to try to put all that aside for three days, to try to leave the emotion until after the game.

Michael Voss, the premiership captain, and I had spent a week in 1996 living in each other's pockets after we'd shared the Brownlow Medal. I got to know him reasonably well and have subsequently admired him from afar as a player. The one thing he has over me is the 2001 Grand Final. I've never liked someone having one up on me. On the day I didn't feel glad at all that it was him; I was upset that it was anyone. But if someone is going to be in that position – someone who's not attached to the Essendon Football Club – I guess I'm glad it's him.

Losing the 2001 Grand Final was hard to live with. But when you lose a Grand Final, you also appreciate how hard it is to win one. The disappointment turns into motivation in a pretty big way.

And that's what we all took away from 2001: a hunger to atone.

Chapter 9

The Plumber from Prahran

He's the self-described plumber from Prahran, I'm the middle-class boy from Canberra. He was the dour back-pocket player in Richmond's powerhouse teams of the 1960s, I'm the on-baller/forward who kicks goals. He's the coaching genius, eccentric and brave, willing to try anything once; I'm the cautious, sometimes-too-seriously-minded perfectionist. We are both headstrong, strong-willed and determined, and in our own ways, we have both spent our football careers as leaders, but we have vastly different styles.

My friend (and Essendon' former football manager) Danny Corcoran once said of Kevin Sheedy and me, 'They're very different people. They look through the same window and see a very different picture.' But Kevin himself commented, 'We are not as different as he thinks we are.' And Tim Watson once wrote in *The Age*, 'They probably won't ever be mates, but both have an admiration for the other. That's healthy in its own way.'

There have been many attempts to describe our relationship, but 'the odd couple' is probably the best. Not that either of us is odd, though we probably both have our moments. Kevin Sheedy is the man who has been my sole coach as an AFL player, a man whose addresses I've heard hundreds of times, a man given at times to eccentricity and provocativeness (especially when dealing with the media), a man who is the second-longest-serving senior coach in the history of the game after Collingwood's Jock McHale, a man towards whom I will always feel a deep gratitude and loyalty.

At 17 years old, just drafted, I walked into the dressing rooms at Essendon, very emotional about starting on my life's dream journey, my parents in the car outside. There I was, among players I had watched and admired, and who would now be my teammates (if I made the seniors, that is). I'd been shown my locker, given my jumper and socks, and had said hello cautiously to these big, professional footballers. All I needed to do next was meet the coach.

When I did I was scared of him. Here was the man who had led the club that I had loved ever since I could remember, a man who had been coaching Essendon's premiership-winning teams when I was still in primary school. I had a huge amount of respect for Sheeds – so much that I had to dig deep to find the courage to talk to him.

After shaking my hand he asked me which player I most resembled. I couldn't think of one. At that very moment, Mark Thompson walked past. 'I'd say it's Bomber Thompson,' I replied.

And with that our two-decade-long close relationship began.

We've had our disagreements, but mostly it's been a good relationship, especially considering how many times I've heard his addresses, and heard him outline a game plan.

He has often taken me aside and said that he realised that I'd already heard what he was going to say, but it needed to be said to the team as a whole.

Kevin is aware that there can be an issue with over-familiarity and players becoming stale. Late in 2005 he told me that he didn't want me to come to the club and train until January. He felt that I would benefit from a longer break. I think this shows what a wise coach he is: he recognised a potential problem and had enough confidence in me and in his judgment to let me loose for a while.

Sixteen years of listening to the same coach every day could get boring, but I still respect his message. Sheeds doesn't believe in having too many rules or giving too many precise instructions. Instead, he provides a loose framework. As long as you stay within that framework he's happy for you to show your style and do it your way. A lot of other coaches couldn't cope with that.

I've been very lucky to have had Sheeds as my coach, because I don't respond well to being constrained and dominated. I tend to rebel a bit when people tell me exactly what I have to do. I respect rules and I understand that you need to do things a certain way, but I don't like being told what to do in minute detail. I work best when I'm given the basic principles. Sheeds sets the environment, the timing and the philosophy, and senior players take what they need and want from that. Of course, this freedom means that players must then take responsibility for their mistakes as well as their moments of glory.

Many teams have very strict game plans. At times we have been criticised for our lack of one. But I think it can be seen as a positive. I would find it very hard to play in such a rigid structure. Sometimes, if you over-intellectualise things, you take all the creativity out of a player. This is not a good thing to do to an individual or a team.

In 2003, Kevin wrote in *The Australian*:

Hird, like any champion, is a fascinating player to coach. You don't tell him how to play, except in terms of talking about the way he and the team should play. The same would have been the case when Tom Hafey was coach of Geelong. He would never have tried to tell Gary Ablett what to do. James knows how to play this game; how to read it and on days like last Friday against Collingwood how to control it, to turn it into his personal domain.

Sheeds has always had very good people around him. David Wheadon, for instance, was an inspiration as an assistant coach during my early years at Essendon. He was a fantastic intellectual coach and probably one of the main reasons we won the Grand Final in 1993. His ability to analyse the opposition and give us insights and on-field strategies to use was invaluable.

Sometimes David would turn his insights on us. One day he called Mark Mercuri and me into his office. He started by telling us that we were playing some good footy. Then he proceeded to explain that there was one difference between the words 'flair' and 'lair' and that was the letter 'f'. He crossed the 'f' off 'flair', looked at us both and said, 'You guys have taken the "f" away and become *lairs*.' It was a big lesson for me. Mercs and I thought we were playing well, but we had become a bit cocky.

Sheeds would use David to deliver those sorts of messages. It had the desired impact. It's a highly effective strategy. Sheeds will set the broad framework, but he'll use his assistant coaches to work with individual players on specific issues.

Sheeds is the most positive person I've ever met. Even if we lose by 20 goals, he will find a positive in it. He'll come in and say, 'It was a bad loss and you guys could do better, but if we do this, then we'll win the next game.' Meanwhile, I'm sitting there thinking that it doesn't matter what we do, because the basic problem is that some players are just not trying hard enough. When I've later voiced the opinion that he's being too easy on some of the guys, he'll point out that totally crushing and humiliating them will not help them perform better. His way is to address the issue with the individual players who aren't giving 100 per cent.

In hindsight I can see that that is the way to do it: you don't embarrass the whole group if it's not the whole group's problem. You find the individual and you speak to him.

Sheeds has savaged some players, though. In the early 1990s we were playing a practice match in Hobart and Sean Denham, a rover/forward, had just come over from Geelong. We were playing pretty badly and Sean was looking at the ground while the coach was talking. Sheeds ripped into him and ordered him back to the dugout. Sean then had to walk the whole 100 metres from the huddle in the middle of Hobart Oval to the dugout while the whole crowd was going mad. Sheeds had embarrassed him in front of the spectators and all his teammates.

Sean Denham went on to become a very successful player for us, winning a best and fairest and playing in a premiership team. I suspect now that Sheeds knew Sean was the sort of guy who could cop it, and gave it to him as a way of telling the rest of the group that they weren't performing. Sometimes he would single out one player for a spray, knowing that the rest of the team would get the message.

One day I copped the full Sheedy onslaught. There was certainly nothing subtle about the way he delivered his message that day. We had been playing Geelong, and I was playing at half-back. Sheeds sent a message out that he wanted me to play at half-forward. I knew he wanted me to go there, but the ball was still in my area so I didn't run back straight away. We lost the game by 10 goals. I didn't think my action or inaction was the reason we lost the game, but later, in front of the group, he came up to within a couple of centimetres of me and abused me mercilessly. There was spit coming out of his mouth and it was hitting me on the face.

Tania and I were going to her mum's house for dinner that night. When I got home I was in a very angry mood. Tania asked me what was wrong and I told her that I had been abused by Sheeds. We went upstairs to talk about it. Tania listened and supported me, as footballers' wives and partners do so well. I was angry, and had a few upset days.

On the Monday, at training, Sheeds pulled me aside and asked me if I understood why he had acted the way he had. No, I said, I didn't. He told me that I'd done the wrong thing by not following his instruction immediately. He had carpeted me so that the other players would realise that they could not do the same thing and get away with it. We were playing badly and it was important that they were all aware of it. He needed to send a message to every player in the team, but there were players who lacked self-confidence, and if he'd had a go at them directly, they would be unlikely to bounce back. Kevin had been using me to get at the group. Once I understood what he'd been trying to achieve, I handled it better.

Sheeds has mellowed a little over the years, but not much. As he's matured I think he's got the mix right. But he can definitely still abuse some of the players. Players from the early 1980s tell stories about how he would savage blokes, and they say that he was the hardest task-master you could imagine. You probably can't do that for 25 years. If you did, you'd end up killing yourself and your players.

There has always been a volcano within Kevin Sheedy, and you never quite know if it will erupt. He has the ability to keep a lid on things, and to mask his feelings with a calm exterior. But every now and then he'll show the world a side to him he'd rather he hadn't.

The incident involving Mitchell White, a West Coast Eagle at the time, is one of those. We were playing the Eagles in 2000. I was on the bench. One of our players went down, and Bruce Reid told us all that Mitchell White had just come up and whacked our guy, behind play. Sheeds took the club doctor's word for it. Unfortunately, Reidy was wrong. I think White had knocked the player down, but it wasn't a deliberate and vicious act.

As Sheeds walked across the ground to the huddle, he looked angrily over in Mitchell's direction and dragged his finger across his throat. The incident was picked up by the TV cameras and broadcast widely. Sheeds was cited and had to front the tribunal, where he was fined $7500.

There was some sparring between the two clubs in the ensuing weeks, but it eventually faded.

I believe that Kevin genuinely cares about his players, even if he doesn't always show it. He has talked to me about his concern for his guys and the difficulty that it can cause. It is his job to bring out the best in each player and to develop the whole team, and that often involves telling footballers things they don't want to hear. Some players can't handle it. Some get angry with him. This must be hard when he believes that he's acting in their best interests.

I think he also gets great satisfaction from taking young men with undeveloped ability and turning them into great footballers. There are a lot of blokes out there who have a lot to thank Kevin Sheedy for.

Nothing gives Sheeds more satisfaction than giving players from other clubs a second chance if he believes they still have some good football left in them and that he can reignite their passion. For any number of reasons, some players leave their clubs; they then have a point to prove, which can be a very powerful motivator for them.

Sean Denham, for instance, from Geelong, turned into an excellent small running player. And Sean Wellman came over from

Adelaide as a trade for Paul Salmon. I'm sure everyone thought he was going to be a good player, but I don't think Adelaide realised how good he would turn out to be. John Barnes, a ruckman who started at Essendon, went to Geelong, came back to Essendon and played in our 2000 premiership side. I hope that expunged the memory of the four Grand Final losses he'd endured. At the Grand Final dinner in 2001, after we'd lost to the Lions, I said to him: 'Barnesy, I don't know how you've done this four times. This is one of the worst feelings in my life.' He said, 'At least I've won one.'

Sheeds has a sharp eye for finding players in unlikely places. He will also take a punt on a player whose reputation off the field is not too good. Martin Pike, the wild boy who went to the Brisbane Lions via Fitzroy, Melbourne and the Kangaroos, is one example.

When Pike left Melbourne in 1993, Sheeds was very keen for him to come to Essendon, but the board at the time were not. I think they had some concerns about his off-field antics. Unfortunately for us, he went to the Kangaroos and then Brisbane. He won one premiership with the Kangaroos and three with the Lions. A good result for him. Needless to say, the off-field stuff doesn't seem to have been an issue at Brisbane. Sheeds is always throwing up the Martin Pike story and saying that we should have got him.

Players he has managed to get include Scott Camporeale, who came across from Carlton at the end of 2005. I still find it hard to believe we were able to get someone of his calibre from Carlton. It would be like Scotty Lucas, Matthew Lloyd or myself walking out of Essendon. Justin Murphy and Matt Allan also came from the Blues in 2005, and Ty Zantuck from Richmond.

Sheeds also takes players in the draft on their second time around. He recycled Paul Salmon back in 2002, which was a success. Camporeale, Murphy and Allan were seen as under-performing at their clubs, but they all had footy left in them when they came to us.

Sheeds shows enormous loyalty to and faith in his players. We saw that famously with Kevin Walsh in the 1980s. Kevin was an unfashionable defender who many believe had his career prolonged because of Sheeds's belief in him. Some spoke of it as favouritism. That may be true. But to Walsh's credit, he worked very hard and repaid Sheeds with some good football.

It's harder now to pick up the players you want, because of the draft system. Not so many players slip through the net these days. You have to do more trades and cross-trades than Sheeds ever used to do. Ever the non-conformist, he doesn't always go for the obvious pick. Luckily, he has a great eye for spotting a promising player. I was picked at number 79 in the 1990 draft; Matthew Lloyd was swapped for Dale Kickett, Todd Ridley and Tony Delaney, who would have been lucky to have played 50 games between them. Sheeds secured Adam McPhee of Fremantle for a draft pick, and Adam won a best and fairest two years later. He grabbed Damien Hardwick from the under-19s at North Melbourne, and Damien became a hard and skilful player for us. I'd be interested to look at the draft statistics to see which clubs have drafted the best players. We would certainly be well represented.

Things haven't always gone our way, though. Essendon has been forced to lose players we didn't want to lose, most notably star defender Gavin Wanganeen. Gavin wanted to go home to Adelaide and was offered a huge amount to do so. Paul Salmon leaving us for Hawthorn was another blow. It was also a blow to me personally, because he is a good friend and confidant. I didn't understand why he was leaving until he explained. As Fish tells it, Essendon were playing at Waverley in 1995, in the second semi-final against West Coast, and he was struggling with a groin injury. He told me that Sheeds said he had to play. Fish didn't want to, because he knew he couldn't run. When he came off the ground in the third quarter he was greeted by Bronx jeers from the Essendon supporters.

Fish felt passionately about Essendon. He had played a lot of games with the club and even when he was injured he had still performed well. He was tired of that type of treatment and I guess the Bronx jeers were the final straw. Paul Salmon received criticism he didn't deserve.

I was very happy when he decided to come back to the Bombers in 2002 for his final year of football. We made the finals and Fish had a pretty good year. I think that having a successful return cleansed his soul. He made his peace with the Essendon people, which I'm very happy about.

I have been very lucky with the role models and mentors I've had at Essendon. The first major figure at the club for me, apart from Sheeds, was Danny Corcoran. Danny started out as Essendon's footy manager and fitness trainer; when footy became more specialised, he gave up the fitness trainer role. For some reason he took a very special interest in me and spent a lot of time training me and getting me fit from a physical point of view.

Danny encouraged me to take it on myself to get super fit, because he understood that the fitter you were, the easier football became. It was invaluable guidance. It meant I didn't have to worry about getting to the contest: with my increased endurance and aerobic capacity, I just got there. I'd always known how to win the ball, and I knew that I put my body on the line, but I had to build my fitness to get to more contests. I credit Danny with putting a bit more steel and endurance in my game.

He used to tell great stories, too. When he trained me, I'd be running, absolutely exhausted, with my tongue hanging out and my muscles hurting, and he'd start telling a story, just to get my mind off training. He knows when someone's hurting, and he knows how to continue to motivate them.

Danny also made sure I was okay away from the club. He acted as an adviser, watching over me. He knew my family was miles away in Canberra. If I was at training a bit early, he'd want to know why I wasn't at uni, and I would have to admit that I'd missed my lecture; he would point out that if I missed too many, I wouldn't get through. Danny wasn't as strict as a dad, but he definitely looked after me. I could ask him questions. I'd go and sit in his office and have a chat, or go over and talk to him at his house. I got to know his wife Maxine and their kids really well. Brigid, their daughter, was the flower girl at our wedding. It's a longstanding friendship.

Danny's time at Essendon ended sadly. An investigation in 1999 by the AFL into salary-cap breaches by Essendon resulted in Danny being reprimanded for having a minor role in the breach. It was reported that then league boss Wayne Jackson proposed to Danny that he accept a $10,000 fine for an infringement involving Mark Thompson in 1996. The irregularity involving Bomber had something to do with part of his contract being paid after he retired and joined the Essendon coaching staff. Danny refused Jackson's terms. Wayne Jackson wouldn't confirm that the offer had been made, telling *The Age*: 'We just don't broker deals, whatever that is supposed to mean . . . we don't work that way. There is rumour and speculation flying everywhere, but we've settled the matter with Danny Corcoran and said all we're going to say.'

The AFL Commission's statement acknowledged that Essendon did not exceed the salary cap during the period in which Danny held responsibility for contract negotiations and, according to *The Age*, 'registered the fact that he [Danny] attempted to clean up the club's books'.

On 19 April 1999 – by which time Danny had left Essendon and joined the Melbourne Football Club – the league announced its decision to reprimand him and, as *The Age* again reported, to 'hang over Melbourne, or any other club he should work for, a minimum penalty of the loss of a third-round draft pick for any subsequent infringement'.

When Danny left I was disappointed, from a personal point of view, because I knew that the club would never really be the same without him. He was my confidant, and such a good bloke to have around. I could always talk to him about things, no matter how bad they were.

I think he left partly because he had had enough of the environment, and partly because he needed a change. I respect that. All professionals need opportunities to grow and develop, and Melbourne had offered him new challenges and a greater role. I understand why he left, but I still miss him.

He was very hurt by a lot of what happened around the salary-cap investigations and by the accusations that were made. I felt he was made the scapegoat for it because he had just left the club. Danny's not bitter, but it took a while for him to renew some of his friendships at Essendon.

I went around to his house just after the issue blew up. Essendon had placed an injunction on him, which meant he couldn't work for Melbourne for six months. He was shattered by that. He felt betrayed. I loved Essendon, but I certainly saw his side of the story.

It was the first time I'd felt in conflict with the club. I didn't say anything, but I wrestled with the issue. Danny Corcoran was a mate and had done so much for me, and I felt really badly for him. And I was disappointed with the club.

* * *

John Quinn is another person who has had a big influence on my career and been a great help to me. In late 1998, Quinny joined us as fitness coach, and since then we have become great friends. John is a control freak, but so are most good coaches. He's passionate about what he does. If something is not done the way he wants it done, he becomes quite upset. When I had my injuries in 1999, 2000 and 2001, Quinny worked with me day in and day out. His commitment went beyond what was required. He helped me to a point where I was back playing footy and confident in my own body. It's unlikely that I would be where I am without him, and there are not many people I can say that about – my mother and father, Tania, Sheeds, Danny Corcoran and Quinny.

I've had disagreements with him. We've had some arguments around training and other issues at the club, but nothing that has affected our friendship. The one big disagreement that I can remember was when we were in Sydney in mid 2002, five weeks after my facial injury. I wasn't playing, but I had a bit of adrenaline running through me, and wanted to train at Telstra Stadium with the team, so I did.

Quinny let me have it. 'What do you think you're doing?' he yelled. 'If the ball hits you in the head, your face will crack! You're not only hurting yourself, you're hurting your teammates.'

I hadn't thought of that. I was focused on what I wanted to do, not on any possible consequences. He pointed out that I was the captain of the team, and if I wasn't playing, the whole team was affected.

However, disputes between John and myself are rare and we respect each other enough to speak our minds.

I've always found that the best trainers, fitness guys or coaches are the ones who physically train me and also get into my head. Quinny trains me physically and mentally. He doesn't tell me how to do everything; he helps me make my own decisions. He inspires and leads me in a powerful way.

Mark 'Chocko' Williams, now Port Adelaide's coach, was our assistant coach at Essendon for two years, 1995 and 1996. He was terrific. He'd take me out and kick me the footy and just chat. Once he told me about the goal-kicking contests he used to have at Collingwood with Peter Daicos, the legendary 'Macedonian Marvel'. Daicos could kick a dribble goal from any angle – seamlessly and effortlessly. Chocko told me he always used to beat Daics, and that it was him who taught Peter how to kick those freakish goals.

It was an outlandish claim, so one day I asked Daics about it. He laughed and said, 'Well, that's Chocko for you.' He added: 'He didn't even beat me once.' Who are we to believe?

I still speak to Chocko now and then. He's a very funny man, but he's intense when you're training and he demands that you train hard. At one period, I'd been doing extra daily individual skill sessions with him – hours and hours – but I was developing a hot spot in my shin, which is sometimes the symptom you get before a stress fracture. The doctor said he wanted me to stop the extra skills sessions for two weeks, which I did. At the next training session, Chocko got up in front of all the players and told them they were not training hard enough and then had a go at me for giving up my extra sessions. I was embarrassed and angry, but I let him know that I was under the doctor's orders to stop. He is just that sort of coach. He demands excellence. That's his strength.

The factor uniting all this coaching talent is, of course, Kevin Sheedy. It's his vision. Everyone has their job, and Sheeds pulls the show together. Sometimes he does it in an eccentric way. He doesn't mind that description – I think he quite enjoys it. There's nothing colourless about Sheeds. In 1993, for example, after we'd beaten West Coast, Sheeds took off his jacket and waved it around in a manic fashion. After that, every time we played West Coast and lost, their supporters would madly wave their jackets around. It went on for five or six years. It was a pretty awesome sight from the field.

I suspect that Sheeds loves his image as a nutty professor, and even tries to enhance it. The way Sheeds played his footy was as a dour, ruthless professional, but underneath that there's a lot of flair. For instance, he loves dancing. Whenever he and his wife Geraldine are at a club function they're twisting and turning on the dance floor. At Adam Ramanauskas's wedding, Sheeds had just had a hip operation. We called on him to show us his moves, knowing full well that he wouldn't be able to dance. He laughed, and within a matter of weeks he was up on the dance floor spinning Geraldine around again.

The attempt in 1998 to remove Kevin Sheedy as coach was the most difficult and sensitive period in my 16-year involvement with him.

There had been some rumblings among players that it was time for Sheeds to go. There were players who were disenchanted with him, and a couple who were agitating against him. There were a lot of behind-the-scenes meetings. A faction on the Essendon board tried to unseat him.

The talk was that Sheeds wasn't turning up for meetings, or he was always late; he was running his own show. It was the same type of talk that gets bandied around about him every now and then. Kevin definitely has interests outside the footy club, but perhaps that's why he has been able to stay in the game for so long. These are things he enjoys, things that motivate him – they enrich and broaden him.

It was a tough time for the club and for me. I'd been captain for a mere six weeks, yet many of the issues were being passed through me. I was getting calls from board members, from players, from people around the club, all asking what I thought of Sheeds. I had a meeting with Graeme McMahon, our new chairman, and he asked me what I thought. The chief executive officer, Peter Jackson, also came down to the gym and grabbed Gary O'Donnell and me and asked us what we thought.

It was all pretty difficult. I knew that whatever I said could be misconstrued or taken out of context, so I tried to be very careful. I probably wasn't well established enough in my leadership to say, 'Boys, cut it out.' I didn't want to be part of a putsch that got rid of the coach – I didn't want that legacy as part of my career. In the end I simply said that, in my view, Kevin Sheedy had coached the Essendon footy club well for a long time and I didn't want to hear any more about it.

Eventually, we all went to a meeting with Graeme McMahon, and Graeme told us: 'Sheeds is the coach, and you blokes pull your heads in.' I think that was the right thing for him to say.

In *The Age*, Stephen Rielly and Rohan Connolly reported:

> The long reign of Essendon coach Kevin Sheedy will continue for at least one more season. The widely anticipated attempt by a faction of the 13-member Essendon board to unseat Sheedy last night did not materialise . . . According to (chairman) Graeme McMahon, a motion to terminate Sheedy's tenure was not put at the meeting . . . and therefore the matter was not even put to a vote.

We played the preliminary final the next year, 1999, and then two Grand Finals in a row. We've missed the finals only twice since 1998, in 2005 and 2006. I'd say keeping Sheeds was the right decision.

There was a fallout: Mark Thompson, the assistant coach, and Loris Bertolacci, the strength and conditioning coach, both left.

Bomber went to North Melbourne and Loris to Geelong. That was hard for everyone, because they had been Essendon stalwarts.

Two years earlier, Danny Corcoran, David Wheadon and long-serving recruitment manager Noel Judkins had left, and then Mark Williams had departed. They were all good people who had contributed much to the club.

I guess that is one of the marks of a healthy club: people join, bring new ideas, develop those ideas and themselves, then move on, and they are replaced by others who do the same. If you want a good, progressive football club you have to keep moving people through: you find other good people and the culture grows. Essendon has usually had Essendon people in coaching roles, but I've always felt it was useful to get perspectives from outside.

Former Hawthorn champion defender Gary Ayres joined Essendon at the beginning of the 2006 season. When it was mooted in the newspapers that Gary and Sheeds might work together, there were questions about how well the two men and their egos would gel. After only a few weeks there were indications that it was one of Sheed's more inspired moves. That Gary is new to the Essendon culture is one of the things we need.

When Mark Harvey left for Fremantle everyone was disappointed. Harves was very popular among the playing group because he cares for the players . . . in his own gruff way. Harves would never tell anyone he loved them. He wouldn't even tell you he liked you. But we knew he had a genuine affection for each of us. To take the next step in his career, he had to leave. Let's hope he doesn't coach too well against us.

Being captain under Kevin Sheedy has been a great experience. I have been allowed to develop my own style, my own way of showing leadership. Sheeds has left me alone to do this. I believe that as a leader of the club I have two duties on the field: one, to get the ball myself and play my best game; and two, to make sure the people around me are playing a better game because I'm there.

I don't like to see players fooling around on the ground, nor do I like to see their teammates berating them for it. Yes, you get frustrated, and yes, sometimes players do the wrong thing. But there are ways to address all that, and verbal criticism on the field is not the way. You need to show respect for your teammates on the ground, no matter what; you shouldn't demean a teammate in front of everyone. It gives too much comfort to the opposition. The change room, behind closed doors, is the place to let someone know you're not happy.

Mind you, it does happen. We all get frustrated now and then when a player makes a mistake or doesn't kick you the ball when he should have. Even if all you do is spread your arms wide, it says to everyone: 'Come on, mate! Kick me the bloody ball!' When you watch it back on TV, you can see it doesn't look good. And when a side's doing that a lot, it means they're not as close as they should be.

There was one moment when my body language wasn't what it should have been. It was in 2005, when we were playing Geelong, in my second game back from injury. I'd played the first half, and I'd played only all right. In the third quarter Sheeds told me to play at half-back, so I went there. Five minutes later he sent out the runner to tell me to go to half-forward. So I did. Then he told me to come off. Fair enough – coming off for a rest, I could deal with that. Three minutes later he said, 'Go back on.' So I went back on. Five minutes after that, it was 'Come off.' I was starting to get a bit agitated. I know this kind of rotation happens all the time, but at that point I felt that it shouldn't be happening to me. The only time I'd ever been taken off before this was if I was playing badly or if Sheeds wanted to give me a rest. This didn't feel like a rest. I couldn't get any rhythm. I was pretty annoyed by this time. We were walking out on the ground to the three-quarter-time huddle when Sheeds came up to me.

'Come on, we need a bit more from you,' he said.

'Well, I can't give you anything if I'm sitting on the bench.'

I wouldn't advise any player to talk back to their coach like that. I felt that, being 32 and pretty experienced, Sheeds and I could have a rational discussion about it, but in the heat of the game you probably can't. Even if you are 32 and you've played footy for 15 years with someone, he's still the boss. You just have to take it and get on with it.

The last quarter started, with me back on the ground again, and the ball came down and I kicked a goal. I remembered how Darren Bewick had responded after Sheeds had put him through the same on-again/off-again treatment a few times. 'Boris' kicked a goal and gave Sheeds the finger, then kicked another one and held up two fingers; then another one, and held up three. I think he kicked four or five that day, and held up his hand. Now I knew how Boris had felt. So I gave Sheeds the same message that Darren had given him – only with dark looks and mumbled curses instead. In hindsight, I shouldn't have.

Tim Watson wrote in *The Age* that 'you didn't need to be a lip-reader to understand his phrasing, or have a degree in orienteering to know where it was directed'. Tim reassured me in the article, though:

> It's not the first time he [Sheedy] has been on the receiving end of a verbal discharge by one of his captains. The very laid-back and mild-mannered Terry Daniher gave him an almighty gobful down at Kardinia Park one day at three quarter time . . . To Sheeds's and Terry's credit, it was forgotten after the game and to my knowledge has never affected their relationship, both

agreeing it was said in the heat of the moment, when emotions are raw. It had an effect on the rest of us, though – a tighter, more attuned bunch of blokes never stood to attention to hear a coach's address.

As a past Bomber champion himself, Tim understood what was going on:

> For Hirdy, sitting on the bench was a new experience and one he obviously didn't enjoy. Sheeds would not have been wanting to humiliate him, but even after nearly a quarter of a century, he is the boss. What would have pleased him was the response, excusing the expletives. Hird came back on, played angry and kicked two match-winning goals. The old coach would have retired . . . a very happy man.

The best thing about Sheeds is that he lets this stuff pass quickly. We had a club auction the next night and the two of us sat down and had a few red wines. We had a bit of a laugh and it was all forgotten. He moves on well. I'm probably the same. Give me 24 hours, and I'm normally pretty right.

Sheeds has been a major figure in my life, and there would be a lot of players who'd say the same thing. Much is made of the differences between us, but we respect and admire each other, and we have shared many of life's highs and lows. Kevin has always been there for me during my own and my children's crises and we are both passionate about our great club, Essendon.

I've no doubt that Kevin Sheedy will outlast me. He has coached Essendon for over 25 years. In 2005 he celebrated his 500th game as coach, and he seems set to continue for quite a few years.

It has indeed been a remarkable career.

KEVIN SHEEDY ON JAMES

James Hird is the best player I have coached in 25 years. I rate him very closely with Wayne Carey, Gary Ablett, Michael Voss, Leigh Matthews and Kevin Bartlett as the handful of greatest players I've seen play. Jim's had a remarkable career, one that he should be very proud of. He's a player with huge natural talent and the desire and capacity to exploit it with hard work.

But I didn't see his talent straight away. When James arrived at Essendon in 1991, he looked knobby-kneed, skinny and slightly anaemic. I wasn't surprised that he was from Canberra – there's no beach or surf or sun there. When I first saw him play I saw he could read the play well, but I didn't see the player that James Hird would become. I thought he could be a very good player, but in that first year you couldn't see that he would end up being named in the top three players of the Essendon Football Club.

What I did see straight off was his courage. From the start he was always good at hard balls, which is unusual for young players. He always had ferocity for the ball. It helps if your great players have it, because you can use them as an example to others – I could point to Hird and say, 'That's the sort of player you want to be.'

There came a time when James just coached himself. A lot of the great players of the day don't get coached much. In my own playing career at Richmond it would have been very hard for Tom Hafey to tell Royce Hart how to be a great centre-half-forward or Kevin Bartlett how to have pace and read the play. You can instruct them on technique, but great players have that thing where they know they can go over the head of the coach. Not all players are the same. Some, like James, have special talents which need to be nurtured and allowed expression. The charismatic brilliance of a sportsperson really shouldn't be taken off them.

James has had a shocking run with injuries and has shown enormous character in dealing with them. Injury has robbed him of probably two-and-a-half to three years. When James had his bad foot injury in 1999 it was always a concern that he wouldn't come back. His future was even more doubtful after that grotesque injury in Perth in 2002. A lot of players wouldn't have come back from that. In the end, he always gets his act together. He can look back and be very proud of what he's been able to achieve in overcoming these obstacles.

He's shown courage beyond the call of a footballer. The stamp of his character stood out in his first match back after that fractured skull. There was no way known that this major operation on his skull was ever going to deter him. He went for a super hard ball – straight at it as if it were his first game. We all cringed in the box. They're the sort of qualities you admire. I never considered telling him to take care. You'd be knocking your head against a brick wall talking to him like that. He'd look at you and say, 'Forget about it, coach.' Jim gives you these looks down the barrel of his eyes. And I sometimes say, 'It was only a piece of advice I was trying to give you.'

In the end it doesn't matter how many games he's lost through injury. Anyone would love to have had James Hird's career anytime.

When Jim and Tania's little girl Stephanie fell ill in 2000 it was of course a deeply traumatic time for the family. I was concerned about how Jim was coping, and that's why I went to the hospital to see whether there was anything I could do, and to see whether Jim was all right. There are times coaches should be there and times they shouldn't. I've been to hospital with my kids. I would be there for any of my players if their child was struggling in hospital. As a coach, you want to make sure the player is coping with all of these stresses that families can go through.

I would have understood if he'd pulled out of the preliminary final against Carlton during that time. A coach has to put up with lots of abnormalities, barriers and confrontations along the way. You have to try to handle those situations and show the player that you care for him and feel for him, his family and his extended family, because you never know what's going to happen in this game. It's not just about Friday night and Saturday and Sunday afternoons; it's the whole task of building a club. And James Hird has been a part of building Essendon from a great club in the VFL to a great club in a national competition.

By 2000, Jim had been through a lot – both on and off the field – and his desire to captain the side to a premiership that year was fierce. It was a powerful feeling. That year I saw a very determined man get what he wanted. I saw the killer instinct in him, and not many see that in James Hird. I've said before that he looks like a male model but hits like a killer. And in 2000, after the disappointment of injury in 1999 and watching his side lose a preliminary final, I saw that determination and killer instinct a lot of people forget he has.

Football can be all-consuming, and it's important that Jim gets away. That's why I wanted him to stay away from the club for a few weeks over the 2005–06 summer. We needed to keep him fresh. I'm sure he was revitalised after spending the summer with his family. Nobody enjoys time with their kids as much as Jim does. I remember Dustin Fletcher and Jobe Watson arriving at Essendon – both sons of famous former Essendon players, including one, Tim Watson, I had coached for many years. And Jim's son Tom is often around the club. I have a great photo in my little book at home of Tom and James. When the players get tested after a game for their fluid intake, four-year-old Tom lines up with the whole team to be tested too.

I fell off the couch when I heard Jim say what he said about the umpire in 2004. That's probably how I injured my hip (which required an operation) – I blame Hird for that. It was a tough time for him; it's always hard when you say what you feel and the whole world jumps on you. That's a lot of pressure. There was a lot of pressure on the umpire, too, there's no doubt about that. Sometimes in this game you're not allowed to say what you feel. Hird responded pretty well. In the Eagles game in the middle of that frenzy he said, 'It's not fazing me. I'm going to go out and play the game I need to play.' That's championship material.

It's not always easy being Jim Hird. The hardest thing has been that he is shy and private. You can't give every one of your thousands of fans every minute they want. In Melbourne the game's practically a religion, so when you become iconic as he is it's a time-bomb. It can be a burden. If I see a number of fans here over the holidays I make sure that everybody – Jim and Matthew Lloyd included – give them 10 minutes of autograph signing, and then we get on with business.

Jim was appointed captain of the club in 1998. He was an obvious choice. When you appoint a captain you say to yourself, 'I hope this bloke's got it all together.' He was captain for eight years. That's a hell of a long time never to do much wrong. Jim's the longest-serving captain in my time as coach. As a captain he has done everything he could and shown great leadership. But he's still an individual. He's never liked analysing the stat sheet after the game. Most brilliant players don't. I don't think many of the great players I coached took to analysing the game. Most great players don't quite know why they play so well. He's got sharp hands, an ability to read the play, and instinct. You can develop instinct along the way, but you have to know when to use it, the right moment. Some players have instinct but look back at a game and say, 'I could have done that.' But the game's gone, the moment's missed. Champions don't miss the moment.

The right question to ask Jim in 2005 was: 'When do you want Lloyd to have an opportunity to be captain?' If Hird had gone on, Lloyd wouldn't have ended up captain until he was 30, and I don't think that would have been fair on Lloyd. I said, 'Consider it.' I think that's what good leadership is: knowing when to release a little bit of the pressure and instead focus on enjoying an opportunity to get another premiership. He doesn't play any differently after relinquishing the captaincy. To me, 'captain' is just a title. Leadership is the way you live and act. You'll never see James Hird not lead. I don't think he wants to coach, even though he would be a very good one. He's a bloke who wouldn't put up with some of the stuff coaches put up with.

James has been a great role model at Essendon. The younger players know James is very dedicated about how he trains; he wants to be top class at everything he does. He commands attention on a ground and around a footy club. I've got young players who want to be in the same side as James Hird while he's still playing.

It's been a fascinating relationship between us over the years. I don't live in Jim's back pocket and he doesn't live in mine. We don't share the great fun times that some people do. But it's often difficult for coaches and superstars to be best mates. I think we'll be the best of friends later on; you can't be best friends as coach and player.

I don't accept that 2006 is his last year. It's all about whether Jim wants to go on with it and what kind of a player he would be. As you're coming down from the mountaintop it's always going to be awkward; it's hard not to expect yourself to be the player you were at 26, in full flight. It's about the standards you set yourself. Are you prepared to play at a different level or play a different type of role from the one you once had?

Having said that, though, I think we push retirement onto people too early these days. I played with a bloke called Kevin Bartlett who at 31 years of age was asked, 'Is this your last year?' He went for five more. He was over 30 when he kicked more than 80 goals from a half-forward flank. Champions are very hard to understand, and you never know what their capacities are.

James Hird has been a loyal and outstanding Essendon person. He has given so much to the club. It's been a pleasure to have coached and watched him over 16 years. I would love to have played with him. I wish James and his family every happiness for the future, at the club and beyond.

Chapter 10

Courage

As a professional footballer, I've seen a lot of examples of courage over the course of my career. The physical nature of the game demands it, and the external pressures of media and public expectation often require substantial reserves of inner courage. The ability to stand up for yourself, to do what you think is right, to overcome the fear of what others might do to you, are vital attributes whether you're a footballer or a parent, a plumber or a prime minister. But there are a couple of examples that I've witnessed in my years at Essendon that go way beyond the norm, and seem to me to define something about courage, something that we should all aspire to.

In 2003, our teammate Adam Ramanauskas was diagnosed with a malignant tumour in his neck and shoulder region. The first we knew of it was when Rama told us he had a lump on his neck and he was going to see a doctor. The doctors didn't think it was serious, initially: it was just a lump, it would go away, they said. Then he saw a surgeon who told him it could be serious. He had a biopsy and was told it had to be taken out, but it was growing around a lot of nerves in his neck, all entangled, so it couldn't just be cut out – there was a risk of damaging the nerves. He was in a dilemma.

It was a pretty rough time for everyone involved. Rama had two operations. In the first, the most serious one, midway through the 2003 season, they cut most of it out. The surgery caused nerve damage and a second operation was required.

Rama underwent that first operation on the same night our third child, Alexander, was born. Given that Rama was in the Royal Melbourne Hospital and Tania and Alex were next door in Francis Perry, I went to visit him that night to see how he was. I wasn't allowed into his room because he'd just had the operation, but I was told by the nurses that the surgery had gone well. I went back to be with Tania and our newborn. Unbelievably, by 8 o'clock the next morning, we received flowers from Rama and Belinda, his fiancée, congratulating us on Alex's birth. I was amazed, and hugely moved, that the two of them, just after Rama had had such major surgery, could even think of me and my family, let alone send us flowers.

That Sunday we were going to play the Bulldogs. About 10 of the boys, all of Rama's really good mates, came over to my place on the Thursday, and they were really struggling with the blow that Rama had been dealt. We decided to have a few beers, which we would not normally do on a Thursday with a Sunday game coming up. We needed a release, and we needed to talk.

We were there until 3 in the morning – about five hours. It was good for us to just talk about Rama, about his future and about how we could help and support him and Belinda. And not just for six months or so: until he was absolutely clear and his life was back to normal. This intense feeling that we have for Rama is partly due to the person Rama is, but also because of the camaraderie of a football club. It's like a brotherhood, which is one of its truly special attributes. We are very close, and what happened to Rama just brings us even closer.

We absolutely smashed the Bulldogs that Sunday. Dean Solomon, who is one of Rama's best mates (and was later in his wedding party), has been to a few radiation treatments with Rama and has seen a little of what he went through. Solly carries a footy card of Rama around with him. He put it in his sock during the game, but it fell out. One of the runners picked it up and said: 'I think you lost this, mate.' I thought that was a pretty special moment.

Belinda and Rama got married in January 2006. It was probably one of the best weddings I've been to – an enormous amount of love, a great party, and a lot of fun. His family and Belinda's family are terrific people, and they just wanted to embrace everyone in their world.

We believed Rama was going well, that his cancer was in remission. After his wedding he was back at training. His body was great and he was keen to get into the action. His future was looking good.

I wrote the above words on 8 February 2006. In a horrible coincidence, the next day I learned that Rama's cancer had returned.

There was a message on my mobile from Dean Solomon, to ring him as soon as possible. I was in a meeting and couldn't, but Solly then sent me a text message repeating his request. Solly's not normally as insistent as that, and at first I thought there must be something wrong with him. When I called him he told me Rama's cancer had come back. I couldn't believe it, but my immediate thought was that like last time, he would soldier through and the doctors would make it better. That was until I found out that it's not something he's going to get over in a hurry.

Solly told me Rama wanted about eight of us to go over to his house that night for a drink so he could talk to us himself. (There's a group of eight or nine guys who are very close, and Rama's at the centre of that.) Solly explained that Rama would probably have his collarbone broken to get to this very rare tumour. The cancer is contained within the tumour, but it grows extremely aggressively. The problem with Rama's tumour is that it's under his collarbone and wrapped around his carotid artery, so it can't just be cut out. If it was in his leg it could be cut out, or his leg amputated, and it would never bother him again. But the carotid artery is too important to risk cutting near.

I immediately rang Reidy, our doctor, who confirmed the seriousness of Rama's cancer. He talked me through the issues. Rama had told Solly, and Solly needed to tell someone. I was glad he turned to me.

We went to Rama's house with a couple of bottles of red wine. We walked in the front door and there's Rama with a big handshake and a big smile. 'How you goin', boys? Good to see you.' It was hard to know how to behave. After a few seconds of awkward silence, some social sense kicked in. I smiled back and attempted normality, but it was hard. My gut was raw inside.

In the room were Lloydy, Damien Peverill, Mark Johnson, Mark McVeigh, Andrew Welsh, Paul Barnard, Joe Misiti, Sean Wellman and Scotty Lucas. I took the wine and put it in the kitchen for whoever wanted a glass, and found Belinda. I had seen her three-and-a-half weeks before at their wedding, which had been magnificent. She hadn't had a worry in the world. They went on their honeymoon, had a terrific time and their future looked bright. Why had these superb young people been dealt this hand?

Rama stood up and talked us through the past few days. He had had a routine scan, not expecting anything abnormal, but the results showed that his tumour had doubled in size. He had known this was a possibility (the doctors had warned about the possibility of this sort of development in, say, five years). The suggested mode of attack was to break his collarbone, get in there and try to cut most of it out. This would be followed by an intense program of chemotherapy. 'There's a 99 per cent chance I'll never play footy again,' he said, 'but it's more serious than that – it's about my life. I've got to get rid of it, no matter what it costs me.'

The 11 of us sat there stunned and didn't speak.

'Come on, boys, you've got to cheer me up,' Rama said. 'I've been through this before. I'm strong, I'm ready to go, let's have a good time.'

So we started telling footy-trip stories and Rama stories. It was like one of those clichéd movie moments where someone announces they're ill and everyone acts happy and talks and laughs because they don't quite know how else to act. Then you walk out the door, reality hits, and you turn to water.

There was a definite weirdness about that night. We weren't footballers then. For so much of our lives we're together as footballers, self-absorbed (and team-absorbed), thinking about the next day, the next training session, the next game. But that night we were together just as mates, trying to deal with an extraordinarily frightening situation.

The next morning at the club, Gary Ayres was named as our new assistant coach. He was bubbly and excited, of course; not 30 seconds later, CEO Peter Jackson told the team that Rama's cancer had returned and his career was probably over. Rama then said a few words to the boys. There were a few wet eyes. To have one of our own fighting for his life is pretty hard to take. What a day of contrasts.

Adam Ramanauskas is an incredible person, one whom everyone loves, but it wasn't always the case. When he first came to the club, in 1999 as an 18-year-old, he was a real smartarse, probably the biggest smartarse we've ever had. I remember, for example, Rama as a rookie with three months' experience telling Matthew Lloyd that he would never kick 100 goals until he wasn't scared of Micky Martin, the Kangaroos' ferocious full-back.

In 1999, when we were weights partners, he kept criticising my technique. Okay, my technique probably *was* wrong, but you don't expect a teenager to criticise the club captain like that. And when he was asked by Sheeds whose position he was going to take, he said, 'I'll take Michael Long's spot.' This was when Longy was on fire. It's no wonder Adam got himself knocked around a bit by the other players, in an effort to help him pull his head in (footy clubs are good at that). Barry Young whacked him one in a practice game, Damien Hardwick hit him in another, and Gary Morecroft in another. Looking back, he wasn't trying to be a smartarse; he just said what he thought.

Among the players, our awareness of what cancer sufferers go through has increased ten-fold because of Rama's plight. As has our respect for him as a person. His strength and positiveness are an inspiration. Aaron Henneman, who also plays for Essendon (and who is Belinda's cousin), has been incredible as well: his girl-friend, Jo, contracted leukaemia about six months after Rama was diagnosed, so they have had to cope with similar issues.

There is so much we'll miss about having Rama on the team, both as a player and as a personality. It won't be the same for me: at every meeting we had at the club, Solly, Rama and I would sit up the back taking the mickey out of the coaches. He can't be replaced, but I know I'll carry the lessons of his courage and the way he's dealt with his illness with me for the rest of my life.

Rama has a terrific family and great friends at the footy club, and whatever happens, there are 10 of us there who will look after him and his family forever.

If Rama to me personifies courage on a private level, Michael Long shows just what it takes to stand up for your beliefs in public.

On Anzac Day 1995, Essendon played Collingwood in what was to become an annual event. There was a sell-out crowd of 94,825 people packed into the MCG – those numbers are equalled only at the last game of the year, the Grand Final. But this game always has a special feeling because of the importance of Anzac Day to all Australians, and because of the fierce, long-held rivalry between these two old footy clubs.

Just before the final siren, Collingwood ruckman Damien Monkhorst was over the ball on the wing when he was tackled by Michael Long and another indigenous footballer, Che Cockatoo-Collins. As Monkhorst got up, he allegedly turned to Longy and said, 'Get off me, you little black c—.' Michael and Che appealed to the umpire, but the ball was bounced and the game went on. It ended in a draw.

In the rooms afterwards, Longy told football manager Danny Corcoran what had happened. He was angry, sick of the abuse handed out regularly to Aboriginal players. And Monkhorst had not even been reported for misconduct. Longy was adamant that this treatment of indigenous players had to end, and he wanted to make an official complaint.

Longy felt deeply about racial abuse. His mother and father were part of the Stolen Generation: they had been taken away from their parents and placed in a Catholic mission on the Tiwi Islands; Michael's father had been born in Central Australia. 'Racism denies people the fundamental human right to be judged by their character, by what is inside,' Longy said later. 'This is why it's not easy to experience a lifetime of racial abuse, to be constantly reminded of it and yet be expected to simply ignore it.'

The AFL's response was ham-fisted. After negotiations, the AFL reported that the two clubs had reached an agreement, and a press conference was held to show that everything was fine. But it was a farce. Longy said later that Monkhorst had not apologised.

The racial vilification rules that were brought in as a result of the pressure Longy brought to bear are one of the greatest changes to the game in my time as a player. Longy lit the fuse that day, and football is better as a result. Until then, the problem had been ignored by both the AFL and the majority of players, who felt that what happened on the field should stay on the field. Some, such as former Collingwood captain Tony Shaw, in what became an infamous comment, felt that any tactic that upset your opponent was valid. Racial abuse was just another tactic.

It was an emotional time at Essendon. We knew what a sincere and genuine person Michael Long was, and we heard what was being said to him on the field. Other people could not understand why he was hitting players, and why he was so often being suspended by the tribunal. But his teammates knew! What we heard on the field, directed at Michael, was completely unacceptable. It was abusive and dehumanising. One club was particularly shocking: 'Your mother's this, she's that, go back to your home, you f— black' was the gist of it. The thing that amazed me about the players who were saying these things was that they had Aboriginal teammates at the other end of the ground. How could this team work if some of its players harboured racist thoughts? It struck me as totally wrong that someone would consider it okay to say such things to any fellow human being, but especially strange that the people saying them had Aboriginal teammates.

Longy was regularly reported for aggressive behaviour in the games when he was racially abused, and he was criticised fiercely in the papers. Even Sheeds had a go at him. One day I heard the coach tell Longy that he was letting the whole team down by being so aggressive. I was only in my second year of footy, but I went to Sheeds and told him what was happening on the field. Sheeds nodded. The rest was between them.

In 1993 Longy won the Norm Smith Medal as best player on the ground for his superb performance in the Grand Final victory over Carlton. To add to the significance of that acknowledgment, he was presented with the medal by his childhood hero, former Richmond star and fellow Tiwi Islander Maurice Rioli. Everyone agreed that Longy had had a great year, even though he'd missed eight games through suspension. He had already started to take a stand – and paid a price for it.

I was 20 years old in 1993. It was the year when another indigenous footballer, Nicky Winmar, famously held his jumper up to the Collingwood supporters who were abusing him to show he was a proud Aboriginal. It was immortalised in a photograph, taken by *The Sunday Age*'s Wayne Ludbey, that has become an iconic image in Australian football. It's extraordinary to see the effect that photograph had; there was a great deal of courage involved in taking that stand at that time. It was a brave gesture by a young footballer.

A decade earlier, the North Melbourne player Jimmy Krakouer had endured similar abuse and taunts. He had retaliated, naturally, as Michael did, and Krakouer too had been given suspensions. It was only much later that the football community started to understand.

Nicky Winmar's action in 1993 and Longy's two years later started the movement for change. The AFL was under pressure to act. At the end of 1995, they introduced Australian sport's first racial vilification rule, with severe penalties for anyone who breached the rule.

What Michael Long and other Aboriginal players endured on the football field had been a stain on our game, a silent evil. Before Longy and Nicky took their stand, there was a sense of inequality on the football field. Sport can be seen as a microcosm of society, so we shouldn't tolerate things in sport that we won't tolerate in society. Michael Long and Nicky Winmar were telling us what the rest of the community also believes: racial vilification is *not* okay.

At the primary school I went to in Canberra there were lots of kids from different ethnic backgrounds. Some went to the Introductory English Unit at the school when they first came to Canberra, to learn English. After a few months they'd leave my school and go to their neighbourhood school. They were in a separate classroom, but at lunchtime we'd all play together. There were kids from Asia, Africa, Eastern Europe and South America.

I developed a close friendship with a couple of Croatian kids. That's one of the reasons I played soccer so often, and developed such a love for it. (Actually, I don't think I had much choice – they were much bigger and stronger than I was! They also insisted that I barrack for Melbourne-Croatia. Who was I to refuse?)

Not far from our house was a big block of government flats where people of many different nationalities lived together. It seemed natural to have such a diverse group of people around me. My sister's best friend's dad came from Malaysia. Amilia would often have dinner at Indi's house, as she loved the food they ate, and Indi would join us for roast lamb and baked potatoes. We had a real appreciation of the richness difference brings.

I suppose that's why, when all the comments were being directed at Longy, my first reaction wasn't to feel sorry for him; it was indignation. No one should ever treat another person like that. I didn't even think about how Longy was feeling. I just knew that you didn't say that sort of thing. It wasn't right.

When I was a bit older, I sat down with Michael over a few drinks and had a talk about racism and football. It was only then that I got some real understanding of the impact it had had on him and his family. He gave me a much better insight into what it meant to belong to his culture, and into the things that had happened to his immediate family.

In 1994, I went to Darwin with a teammate, Michael Symons, to play a match against the Aboriginal All Stars, a Northern Territory side. Symons and I went up a week early and spent a couple of days in the Tiwi Islands with Michael Long's father. We did a bit of fishing and a few footy clinics and I was able to spend some time in Aboriginal communities in Katherine and the Tiwis. It was one of the great experiences of my life, and I'll always be grateful for the time Michael's family spent with me, sharing their stories and showing me a very different part of Australia.

Longy has a heart the size of a football and the build of a greyhound. He's used both to great effect, unafraid to stand tall on the field and act as a protector of his teammates. But he is also blessed with dash and guile, and these have made him a remarkable footballer.

He is also possessed of a self-deprecating, mischievous sense of humour. You never know when Michael Long is serious. He'll sometimes look serious and sound serious, while having the biggest joke of all time with you.

Longy once invited Mark Harvey and a couple of Harves's mates for a shooting trip on a property up in Darwin that Longy's family owns. Longy told Harves that before he and his mates could come onto the land, which was sacred land, they would have to do a special Aboriginal dance. Harves was onto him. He knew this wasn't the case, and that Longy was having him on. So Mark protested that he'd already done the dance – the time before.

Longy shrugged. 'Yeah, no worries.' He then turned his attention to Harves's unsuspecting mates.

Michael carefully showed them what they had to do. I think he even painted their faces. And the dance began. It was full of the most exaggerated and weird moves Longy could think of, arms and legs going all over the place. All of which was captured on video. Nice one.

Early in my career Longy came to me and in a very convincing way told me that he was desperate. He needed someone to help him out by going to a function at the Essendon Town Hall early one Sunday morning. I was a raw 18-year-old, eager to help out, so I offered to go. Down I went to the Town Hall at 8 o'clock that morning. No one was there. I waited an hour or so, and still no one turned up. At training on the Monday he quietly asked me how the function was. My reply was certainly not suitable for printing.

Michael was picked up by Essendon in the 1988 draft. There's a story that Essendon recruiter Noel Judkins, having heard about this fabulously talented speedster, told Kevin Sheedy he might have found the Pelé of Australian football. After the 1993 Grand Final win, Patrick Smithers from *The Age* wrote:

Essendon's hijacking of the 1993 premiership stands as an indelible testimony to a series of bold initiatives at Windy Hill. None was bolder than the signing in 1988 of an Aboriginal teenager from Darwin who was little more than knees, elbows and an over-sized heart. Every recruiting officer in the country watched

Michael Long dance and baulk his way through the Bicentennial Carnival in Adelaide in that year, a performance that earned him All-Australian selection – but amazingly, only one club pursued him.

Longy was vice-captain for three years of my captaincy, and was a natural leader on and off the field, always guiding the younger players and supporting the older ones, including me. In 1999, when I was struggling with my foot injury, Longy was appointed co-captain with me. It was an obvious choice.

He genuinely cares for everybody. Perhaps because both his parents were part of the Stolen Generation, Michael will immediately gravitate towards anyone who has had a wrong done to them. He wants to support them and help them work it out. We are so lucky to have people like Longy around the club. He's the sort of player who is a leader not just at a footy club, but in the community, and not just in the Aboriginal community. He is a leader for all Australians. I believe his walk to Canberra to talk to John Howard was one of the most courageous things anyone has done in a long time. He just left his uncle's house one night and said: 'I'm going to see him – bugger it. He won't talk to anyone else, so I'll go and see him.' He then proceeded to walk from Melbourne to Canberra to talk to the prime minister.

Michael Long has had an important and lasting influence on the whole football club. There are certain people you meet along your journey in football who cause you to examine your own belief and values. Longy is one of those people. I have a better understanding of other people because of him. Football clubs are lucky when they have people like Michael Long around. I will always admire him as a player and a man. I loved watching him play. I enjoyed his wry and occasionally out-there sense of humour, and I can even tolerate his guitar playing.

It was a pleasure and privilege to know Essendon's number 13 and to play alongside him for 10 years. I know that his courage in standing up against abuse and intolerance, whatever the personal cost, will act as an inspiration to me forever. Our club – and football as a whole – is better for it.

Chapter 11

The Umpires Saga

I had no plan in my head; it was going to be just another night on *The Footy Show* (except it was a Wednesday, not the usual Thursday). I'd go in and sit on the panel with Eddie McGuire, Sam Newman, Trevor Marmalade and the team. But a couple of things I said that night unleashed a firestorm unlike anything I've experienced in my career. It totally dominated at least my next two weeks, if not more. It caused me sleeplessness and anxiety. As captain of the team, I felt the full weight of responsibility for the team's performance that week.

Let's go back to the fateful evening on 7 April 2004.

We'd won the first two Wizard Cup games before being knocked out by St Kilda. We'd lost our first two games of the proper season and were to play West Coast in Round 3 at the weekend. We were under a fair bit of pressure: losing the first three games of the year hadn't happened to Essendon for a while.

I was sitting on the panel when Sam asked me about the umpires. Now, I know that players have to be careful when talking about umpires, because there are rules, but I felt we'd been getting a really rough deal. We had been to the umpires a couple of times and they'd explained why they'd made certain decisions. We had also talked to the AFL about umpiring standards. The umpires' interpretation and our interpretation seemed to be different too often, and we felt we weren't getting a fair hearing. In a split second – that's how quickly your fate can be sealed – I decided to say what I felt. So I did. I said that Scott McLaren 'hasn't been our favourite umpire . . . That's something that the club and he have to come to terms with, because at the moment there's a feeling at Essendon that he's not doing the right thing by us . . . hopefully the club and he can come to some arrangement where the umpiring is a bit better.' I went on: 'I thought the umpiring was actually quite disgraceful on Saturday night . . . I just didn't think the free kicks that were there were paid, and some of them that were paid weren't right, I suppose . . . I'm not alleging incompetence. We all have bad days; he had a bad day.'

Eddie McGuire's jaw swung open. I'm sure the jaws of many of the show's 650,000 viewers did too. Kevin Sheedy, watching at home, later said he nearly fell off his couch. Sports reporters across the city reached for their pens and tape recorders. James Hird, known to be a man of moderation and caution, had given them their back-page lead, soon to move to the front page.

Adelaide veteran Nigel Smart was a fellow panellist that night. He was obviously taken aback by what I'd said. 'James, I think you're totally wrong by hanging your dirty laundry out on national TV about the umpires,' he spoke up. 'If you're saying he's had one bad game and you're taking the mickey out of him here . . .'

I replied: 'I'm not taking the mickey out of him, Nigel. I feel very strongly about the way he umpires. This is maybe one way of bringing it to a head.'

Nigel responded with a certain amount of understatement: 'Well, I think it will.'

What was I saying and why did I say it? I wasn't challenging Scott's fairness. It was just that I thought a few of his decisions had been going against us and I didn't like it. From my words, some people in the media thought I was doubting Scott's integrity. I definitely wasn't. It was simply that I didn't feel we were getting the run of decisions going our way. I went home after the show, and around 11.30 I started to get text messages from my mates. 'What have you said? What have you done?' A good friend of mine, Rod Law, was working at sports radio station SEN, which had just been launched. He rang and asked whether I'd appear on their morning show. 'Sure,' I said. I went to bed. The next morning the show's hosts, Garry Lyon and Tim Watson, asked me questions about what I'd said, and I began to get the feeling that this might become big. I picked up the *Herald Sun* and was rapt to find that there was nothing about it on the back page or the front page. But then I picked up *The Age*, and there it was. It just grew and grew from there.

At half-time in the Channel 9 broadcast of that Thursday night game, Eddie McGuire and his co-commentators pumped it up, adding their thoughts and opinions. They really went to town on it, replaying a clip of what I'd said. That only made things worse.

Matthew Lloyd had been reported the week before for head-butting and I was a character witness for him at the Thursday tribunal. The cameras were waiting for me. I was photographed and filmed all over the place and my car was followed by a number of journalists. A journalist and a photographer followed me for a whole week – I don't know why. It was ridiculous.

That same Thursday I went into Essendon chief executive Peter Jackson's office after training. He was talking to someone at the AFL on speaker phone. Jacko had rung to see what was going on, and the AFL guy said, 'What's your captain done? What's his story? Why's he going off at the umpires? This is a major issue!' That was probably the moment I realised it could all be fairly serious. It was also the moment I realised I might get nailed for it.

In the newspapers the following day I got hammered. Patrick Smith of *The Australian*, Caroline Wilson of *The Age* and Mike Sheahan of the *Herald Sun* – the big names in the football media – all had a crack.

Wilson wrote:

> McLaren will face sledging from crowds at every game at which he officiates, thanks to Hird. The AFL rightly fears that young children around the country – and *The Footy Show* averaged 500,000 viewers on Wednesday night – will be further turned off umpiring as a result of Hird's bleating.

It was the first time anyone had ever really attacked me, and I found it hard to deal with. I got really defensive about it, in fact. I thought, *This is just ridiculous. I had a strong view, voiced it, and yes, it was about Scott's umpiring, but I haven't attacked his character. I just said that I didn't think he was doing a good job, that he had a bad day. In any other profession, individuals can be criticised about their performance.*

I knew by now that I was likely to get into a little trouble. I expected to receive a call from Andy Demetriou saying, 'You know that's unacceptable. We're going to fine you a few thousand dollars.' But I never thought it would blow out to the extent it did.

I was told that the backlash was greater because of my high standing in the game. I'd always been fairly measured and reserved in my comments, and because of this and my public profile, my comments would damage umpiring forever. Mike Sheahan wrote in the *Herald Sun* that Michael Voss, Nathan Buckley and I had been the game's unofficial ambassadors, so 'Coming from such an exalted figure, it was the worst possible publicity for umpiring . . .'

I don't think there was much perspective in the coverage. It was just: 'Umpiring must be protected. What was he thinking?' I hoped that even if the powers that be disagreed with my opinion they would have a look at why I'd said what I did – was the standard of umpiring what it should have been? Particularly, as Sheahan had said, because I had been playing footy for 15 years and was not known for coming out with outlandish statements. It's not as if it came from nowhere either: I have been to the umpiring department and the AFL a number of times representing the club in talks about umpiring standards. It wasn't the first time I had brought up the subject; I'd just never gone public about it before. And I have to say that when we'd talked about it privately, nothing had been done. It seemed nothing would ever change.

Scott McLaren's response was: 'I was surprised and disappointed by the comments he made. This has deeply affected my family and friends . . . but I have every confidence in the AFL rules and regulations and that they will deal with the situation appropriately.'

There was talk of deregistering me for four weeks for bringing the game into disrepute. Interesting, really, given the rather high number of footballer scandals over the years, many of which I would have thought would bring the game into more disrepute than saying an umpire had had a bad day. I would have been the first player in 20 years to suffer that fate – Hawthorn's Leigh Matthews was deregistered in 1985 after an off-the-ball hit on Geelong's Neville Bruns.

My teammates took the level-headed, measured approach, and just laughed at it all. They supported me and backed me up – but they also laughed.

That same day, which was Good Friday, a good mate of mine told me that he'd heard that AFL chief Andrew Demetriou was filthy. He advised me to phone Andrew – not get down on my knees and beg, just give him the reasons why I'd said what I said. I followed that advice and rang Andrew. He took my call, which was a good start. I apologised for what I'd said, and acknowledged that I'd made a mistake. I told him the umpiring standard was still not what I wanted it to be, but that I realised that *The Footy Show* wasn't the right place to say that. He was quite chilly on the phone, but he was probably on holidays, spending Easter with his family, and the last thing he wanted to do was speak to me. He was okay about it, but he certainly didn't tell me that everything would be all right.

A few players had spoken out in the newspaper and said the slamming I was getting was ridiculous, but I was disappointed in the Players' Association response. I don't think I was given enough support from them. I hadn't hurt anyone or been found taking something I shouldn't take, but I felt as if I was in the middle of a police investigation.

We called a press conference in a function room at a city hotel, and I read out a statement:

My comments were a spur of the moment thing, not premeditated, and do not reflect the attitudes of the Essendon Football Club. In voicing my opinions, I had no comprehension of the potential impact my comments could have on either Scott or the umpiring community, and if it has caused him or his family any grief, I am truly sorry. I have been involved in AFL football for 15 years and I now realise I do not fully appreciate our game from an umpire's perspective. This is one of the bigger lessons I have learned from all this.

When I was asked a quesition about the harm I might have inflicted on myself, I responded: 'My kids still love me, my wife still loves me, and I still believe I'm a good person. So other people can decide whether they like me less or more. I can't decide that for them.'

Everyone had a view about it, an angle on it. Umpires were the topic of the month. Brisbane coach Leigh Matthews sprang to the umpires' defence: 'If you don't have umpires you don't have games,' he told *The Australian*. 'I am incredibly disappointed when I go to a game of footy and if they introduce the umpires, everyone boos. Even before the game starts, they boo.'

There were many meetings between me and my management group and my management group and the AFL, and there was advice coming in from the AFL and Channel 9's lawyers, Corrs Chambers Westgarth. We decided, after legal advice, that I should appear on *The Footy Show* the next week and read a prepared statement.

There was, of course, a huge build-up to the game against West Coast at Telstra Dome three days after the storm began. From that Wednesday through to the Saturday I was upset and exhausted. It was all I could think about. But I knew I had to captain Essendon in the game, and I knew we needed the win. My focus had to be on that.

I'd played some really good footy during the first two rounds of the season, and I was really keen to make sure I didn't let the events of the past few days interfere with the way I performed or the way the team performed. If I played poorly, I would be criti- cised for letting myself and the team down. I felt that if I played well, I would insulate myself a little from the criticism. I felt a huge weight of responsibility. If I went out and had a shocker, and we lost – meaning we'd lost three in a row – I knew the blame would be squarely laid on me. And probably fair enough, too, because I'd taken the team's eye and my eye off the ball.

So I was determined to play well and I was determined we wouldn't lose.

We started sensationally, kicking the first six goals. They kicked the next six goals. At half-time, the score was level; then in the third quarter they got in front. At three-quarter-time we were one point up.

I was having an all-right game, but not a great one. In the last quarter I wanted to go all out and play my best footy. Until then I'd been tagged by Andrew Embley, and he'd kept me pretty quiet for three quarters. For some reason they dropped the tag off me at three-quarter-time, so I started to get the ball at stoppages, and I was able to run and play with more freedom.

With a minute to go we were six points down. It was make or break – we had to get it out of the middle. I said to David Hille, the ruckman: 'Push the ball to this spot, I'm going to be there.' Hilley got the ball down to me, I kicked it forward and kept running.

There was a stoppage, a ruck contest, and the ball travelled to our right forward pocket. That was lucky, because I had practised incessantly from the right forward pocket at Windy Hill. Every time I walked off the Windy Hill ground on the way in from training, I would kick 20 balls from each pocket with Colin Hooper, an assistant. He'd roll them along the ground to me, and I'd pick them up and snap them through. On a good night, I might kick 18 out of 20, and on a bad night, 15 out of 20. It's a kick I'd been practising for the last 15 years, over and over again.

There was a ball-up. I could see it was coming out to the pocket, so I ran around the pack. Mark Bullen got it, and I called his name. When I got it from him, I was in the exact same spot that I've kicked the ball from hundreds and hundreds of times. I had the feeling that this kick was mine.

Normally I dribble it along the ground, but there was someone in the goal square, so I had to loop it. I knew the type of kick needed. If you kick it so it spins away from the goals, making sure it fades at the last minute, it will go through. To get it to fade, you lean forward a bit. It sounds technical, but it works. I kicked it. It spun, then started to fade . . . straight through the goals.

I instantly thought, *We've won the game!* I was running towards the boundary, and was so excited that when I saw this bloke on the edge of the crowd, I just hugged him.

God knows why I hugged him. I suppose it was like a pressure valve being released – out poured the emotion. After the stress of the week and the build-up to this game, the win was something positive to hold on to. I knew the week ahead was going to be a shocker. I knew I was going to get canned again. I'd been charged with 'conduct unbecoming to the game' and was probably facing a three- or four-match suspension (that's what I'd been told). So there was no holding back, I gave it my all.

I remember when Essendon beat Hawthorn in the 1984 Grand Final and I was at the game with my dad and my uncle. Leon Baker kicked a goal which put us in front, and Dad turned around to the bloke behind us, who he didn't know, and hugged him. That's how I felt when I kicked that goal – pure relief. It was totally instinctive. I'm not usually a huge celebrator of goals, but relief is a funny thing.

But then, of course, we realised that the game wasn't over. We were six points up, but there was another centre bounce, and who knew how much time was left? The ball was bounced, and was kicked towards the Eagles' forward line, but Rama spoiled it. That spoil was as good as my shot for goal, because if it hadn't been successful, the Eagles would have marked and had a shot. Fortunately, the siren then sounded; we had indeed won.

It was a dramatic, emotional way to end an extraordinary week.

That night I got a call from Garry Lyon asking whether I'd come on *The Sunday Footy Show* the next day. I thought it was a good opportunity for some positive press, so I went. They'd also organised for the guy I'd hugged to come into the studio. I felt a little embarrassed, because hugging a bloke is not really in my personality, but he was a nice guy and it brought a moment of fun and levity into a pretty heavy saga.

On the following Monday, the newspapers who'd canned me the week before couldn't resist the agony and ecstasy angle. Here's Patrick Smith in *The Australian*:

> James Hird was breathtaking on Saturday night. In the real sense that he took your breath away. You gasped as he resisted West Coast in defence, gained possession at stop plays and won the match with a goal in the last minute . . . He was breathtaking in the sense that he winded the Eagles every time they huffed and puffed in the final quarter. The Eagles would be set to win the match only for Hird to wrench it back off them . . . Commentators, almost to a man and woman, said they had not seen a player perform better in 30 minutes of football. He is one of the greatest footballers we have seen.

And Mike Sheahan in the *Herald Sun*:

> You just had to warm to James Hird on Saturday night. It simply was the perfect package: bravery, persistence, brilliance, emotion, humility and contrition. Hirdy made a mistake last Wednesday night, a blunder, yet responded three days later with a performance that reminded all of us he is both a great of the

game, and for the game. He was superb from the moment he exuded such warmth to field umpire Darren Goldspink at the toss of the coin. Then he worked like a navvy until the most stunning individual quarter in a long time.

Sheahan even complimented me for embracing the Bomber supporter and then meeting with him on *The Sunday Footy Show*: 'It was Jimmy Hird as we rarely see him. To hell with the measured responses we usually get from him on telly; let's have more of the bloke that everyone at Essendon knows and likes so much.'

I received no Brownlow votes that day, which a lot of people argued was ridiculous; it was contentious at the least. I suppose it serves me right. You can't criticise the group of people deciding on the votes and then expect to get votes. The umpires acted naturally. If someone had a go at me, I probably wouldn't look at them the same way either.

There was competition for the votes, too. They went to Lloydy, who kicked eight goals, Ben Cousins, who had 30 disposals and kicked three goals, and Chris Judd, who'd had 23 disposals. Chris went on to win the Brownlow that year.

I had that night to relax. I'd bought myself a little time, time to get myself back together and regain confidence. There was a bit of positive publicity in the paper, but then the onslaught started again.

The umpires saga was still being given heavy coverage in the newspapers. In *The Australian*, Patrick Smith was scathing about what I'd said and suggested ways in which my comments could do harm:

A perfect example of the harm Hird's comments can do to the integrity of football was evident yesterday. AFL football operations manager, Adrian Anderson, was forced to step in and appoint McLaren to tomorrow night's Essendon–Carlton game. Previously, the umpiring department had removed him from that game, presumably concerned about the pressure McLaren would be under. Had that been allowed to happen, then a player would have been able to dictate which umpires officiated at his games. That would make the system so compromised as to be unworkable. Each week a coach or player would name and criticise an umpire they didn't particularly like. That is why the penalty for Hird must remain fearsome despite his apology.

Smith called on the AFL Commission to suspend me. The judge-and-jury tone of Smith's column prompted a letter to the newspaper from my father. I had no knowledge of the letter, but I greatly appreciated his support. He wrote:

I am James Hird's father and I would like to comment on Patrick Smith's article . . . I need to say at the outset that Jim has no knowledge of this letter. In fact, he and I are estranged. The last time I saw him was when I flew to Perth after his injury against the Dockers in 2002. Mr Smith says the AFL Commission should consider a four-match suspension for Jim for two reasons. First, Mr Smith claims that in Jim Hird's 'considered opinion' McLaren umpires Essendon with prejudice. And second, because Hird 'is so talented, so respected, has such a high profile, and is capable of captivating all of us'. Leaving aside the false claim that it is Jim's considered opinion that the umpire is prejudiced against Essendon, let us examine the crime Smith considers deserves a four-match suspension. Jim holds a considered opinion and his ability at playing football is widely recognized and acknowledged. Well, we can only be grateful that Smith writes for *The Australian* and isn't employed in the judicial system. Imagine if he was a

judge and he determined his sentences based on a person's considered opinions and their fame.

It was a surreal experience, picking up the newspaper and reading
Dad's letter. It made me quite proud. Any other time I would have
been annoyed with him for doing it, but I was copping such a
hiding that I appreciated the support. I hadn't spoken to him for
about two years when that letter appeared. I didn't like the word
'estranged' – I thought that was too strong. But Dad's always been
about the most honest and forthright person you'd ever meet. He
tells it like it is.

I met up with Scott McLaren on the Tuesday after the West Coast
game. He was visibly upset. We had a very frank discussion and he
explained to me how what I'd said had hurt him and his family.
He said it might cause bad feelings towards his kids – that was, of
course, the last thing I wanted to do.

We received notice that Scott was going to take legal action if
we didn't apologise on *The Footy Show*. I was happy to apologise
for hurting his family, if that's what I had done, but I didn't want
to apologise for having a point of view. I had to eat my pride,
though. I felt I was being gagged and I didn't like that.

On *The Footy Show* Sam and Eddie wanted to make a big
deal of it. I asked them not to. Channel 9's legal people said,
'Guys, you can't say anything. There's a chance you're going to get
sued here.' Wording was worked out, mainly by Scott's people,
but also after some negotiation with me, Ben Crowe and Channel
9's lawyer, Jeff Browne, and I delivered it:

I accept that my remarks have unjustifiably questioned Scott's
integrity as an umpire. I have had the opportunity to reflect on

what I have said and I wish to withdraw my remarks without
any reservation. I sincerely apologise to Scott. I've taken steps to
understand where Scott is coming from and I've reviewed a video
of the game with Scott. I now agree that Scott's umpiring was of
a more than acceptable standard.

On the Thursday morning the case was heard at the AFL Commission. They decided against suspension. I was advised that offering
a 'donation' would reduce the possibility of being deregistered
for four weeks. A figure of $10,000 was mentioned, but about
10 minutes before the hearing, we were told that $20,000 was the
amount. The Essendon Football Club was fined $5000 under
the AFL rule that allows the club of an offending player or official
to be penalised. I would also commit to three years as an umpires'
ambassador. I had no problem taking on the ambassadorial role.
I've always had a lot of respect for the umpires.

Our next game was against Carlton at the MCG. There was
another huge build-up, because Scott was scheduled to umpire the
game.

I wrote on the Essendon website that I would be bitterly
disappointed if Essendon supporters gave Scott a hard time:

> I know he will do his job as an umpire as professionally as I will
> as a footballer. I certainly hope our fans will do the same, as well.
> I would be bitterly disappointed if Essendon supporters treated
> Scott any differently this Friday night. Let him do his job. It will
> achieve nothing if Essendon supporters do anything other than
> support us as they always do. It would make things awkward for
> Scott and it would embarrass me.

As it turned out, they didn't boo him. But there were some other
reactions, a few of them funny. At the MCG you walk down the

race and there's a cage above you; this time a Carlton supporter was holding a $50 note down through the cage. 'Come on, Hirdy,' he said. 'This might help!' And I thought, *Bugger this bloke, I'll try to grab it*, but as I did he pulled it away.

Even today, I hear comments from the crowd: 'That was $20,000 well spent, Hirdy. You got a lot of free kicks today.'

After our win over Carlton, in which I didn't get a kick until the seventh minute of the second quarter but ended up with nine kicks, six handballs and two goals, Sheeds conceded to reporters that the pressure of the umpires saga had affected me, and then spoke of the talk we'd had during the week:

> It is not all about how fit you are; it's energy burnt up, it is energy and time. Probably didn't help him on Thursday night after *The Footy Show* when I was at his home having a nice red with him. Sometimes the best thing to do is put your captain to sleep, have a nice bottle of red and say, 'Forget about it, pal.' It was his red, which is probably more important. Just the one. Sometimes you need to sit down and have a talk to your captain and say, 'Look, move on and enjoy life. You haven't gone and blown up or robbed a bank. You have just made an error. I've done it about 10 or 12 times. Just keep going along with your career and enjoying your life, and the same goes for all parties concerned.'

I can understand why there are restrictions on players commenting on umpires. For a start, you want to keep junior umpires in the game. If only there was a way for an umpire's performance to be . . . not criticised, but *discussed*. If there was, I don't think you'd have outbursts from players and coaches.

I've subsequently done a lot of work with the umpires. I think there should be open discussion, and the umpires I've spoken to are responsive to that. It's about respect: you don't get respect when people are untouchable, protected. You get it when you're in this thing together.

I have a lot of respect for the umpires who umpire our games. The ones I have the most respect for are the ones who I can talk to, during a game or after a game or even in the heat of battle, and who talk back to me as a person, rather than ignore me. I've been playing footy a long time and they've been umpiring a long time. I'm not going to abuse them, but I will ask the question if I don't think it's right. I know they're not going to change their decisions, but at least they know what I think – and then you get on with it. Ninety per cent of the time I get an excellent response.

The ones who frustrate me are the ones who just look at me blankly or ignore me, and obviously don't want to develop any rapport with me. Some don't want to be challenged. Maybe they don't feel comfortable with that. But we all make mistakes, and part of life is accepting what others say, or at least listening to them, about those mistakes. I think part of umpiring should include having a relationship with the players.

Being an umpire's ambassador has been all right. I didn't want to deal with current umpires because I'm not going to be telling them how to umpire a game. But I like dealing with young umpires. I ring them sometimes and am involved with their camps, because I believe I have something to offer. My message to young umpires is, you're going to make mistakes and you're going to get criticised by supporters, but the way to be the best umpire you can be is to build rapport with the players. It's simple, really: it's much harder to abuse someone you have a rapport with or like. If someone behaves like a robot, you can say whatever you like to them, vent your frustration – you forget that they feel.

The reaction on the street after the umpires saga was interesting. My profile rose enormously. And to this day, because of it, people recognise me more. Supporters from other teams feel that they know me a lot better, are more accepting of me and seem to feel warmer towards me. I think it's because they have frustrations with umpiring too. Also, I suspect I seem more approachable as a result. To go from being a player who has been pretty aloof, pretty cut and dried and measured, to one who shows his emotions, makes me more of a normal person in their eyes, someone they can relate to.

Before the game against Carlton, I'd said:

I will not answer any further questions about my remarks or the incident, but I can say Scott McLaren will be umpiring the Essendon versus Carlton game and I personally wish him well for the game, and I'm confident he will umpire fairly and profession-ally, as he always has . . . The AFL's judgment I think was pretty fair and reasonable and I'm quite happy to accept that and get on with life.

And that's what I did.

ROD LAW ON JAMES

*J*im and I have little in common, and I have no idea how we
became friends. I first met James Albert Hird (I've always
wanted to say that) back in the summer of 1995, on my first day
of work experience at radio station 3AW. I was making coffees
and Jim was about to do the first of what would become a regular
segment with Garry Lyon. He was already the golden boy of the
AFL, a year away from his Brownlow, but with a Premiership
Medal in the bank. There was no way this boy from the west was
going to like him. We were, and still are, very different.

He has the perfect family. I'm still single. He lives in
Melbourne's most required suburb. I live out west. He collects
expensive wine. I buy beer to drink, now. I'm seen as loud and
brash. He is thoughtful and measured – except for that one
occasion relating to an umpire, but I can probably take some
responsibility for that, which I will explain later.

To meet us in our environment can be confusing. If you dropped in on one of our chats, you could be excused for thinking we
were not friends at all. We argue and challenge each other on everything: politics, current affairs, our lifestyles, fashion choices, haircuts
and occasionally – but usually for the benefit of whoever is
listening – sport.

215

I barrack for the Western Bulldogs, and Jim obviously grew up barracking for the Bombers. More often than not the debate is about E.J. Whitten v Dick Reynolds or Tim Watson v Doug Hawkins. He has a challenging tendency in arguments – he makes up 'facts' along the way. It's his form of bluff. But when I'm getting beaten and I really want to stick the knife in and get nasty, I turn into the mug supporter in the front bar of the pub and start bagging the current Essendon team, including him . . . especially when he goes to half-back, the retirement village. It works every time. Privately, I've always said (but never to him) that he is the only player I have seen who looks as though he could play in a dinner suit, but it is his commitment to his family and close friends that I truly marvel at.

Jimmy is the most loyal and protective person I have ever met. I have no doubt Jim is happiest when he is around his kids. His first child, Stephanie, was born in 1999, the year we both joined Channel 7. When Stephanie was tiny, you would often see Jim struggling up and down the stairs on his crutches, with his foot in plaster, holding his newborn. As well as Stephanie, Jimmy came armed with bottles and nappies, and the entire sports department had to be quiet so she could sleep under his desk.

That year was a personal highlight for him, with the birth of Stephanie, but it was also the toughest year of Jim's career. At times he thought he would never play again. It was during 1999 that we started spending a lot of time together. He couldn't train and was very frustrated. Much of our time was spent goofing off go-karting (I would always win), renting a table tennis table (he would narrowly win), or spending time together up late, drinking beer and watching English Premier League soccer, while debating the problems of the world. We still do this: sometimes I get a call after a night match, because he struggles to get to sleep until the early hours of the next morning.

The competitive streak we share, along with our general desire to want to know more than each other on some of the most bizarre topics, has led to us being nothing other than brutally honest with one other; but when it matters, we are incredibly protective of each other.

Aside from what goes on between him and Tania, I don't reckon there is too much we don't know about each other. We lead very different lives, and I know at times he worries about some of the choices I've made – a career choice, or what I'm doing, or not doing, with my money, or that I have broken up with a particular girlfriend again. Whatever it is, he has a great sense of when things aren't going too well for me. Unlike me, he doesn't preach; he just has this way of making a phone call at the right time and asking me about what's going and then suggesting how things might be done better . . . Sometimes I might not realise what he had said until a week later! I take more of the sledgehammer approach when he has issues, but more often than not he looks to me for perspective – which I'm never afraid to offer. I constantly remind him that whether it be his footy or his work in the media, he hasn't been asked to come up with a cure for cancer.

Jim and I were stockbrokers together for a while, and our old boss, David Evans, said to me during the Scott McLaren incident that I was partly responsible for it. He said Jim and I spent so much time together that we had begun to adopt a similar, and at times lazy, use of the language. He reckons we went through a stage of describing anything we weren't happy about as 'disgraceful'. Describing the sandwich you ate at lunchtime and weren't happy with as 'disgraceful' is over the top, but in that situation, harmless. The same can't be said for when you are describing the umpiring on the weekend and you are on national television. As Jim found out.

He shouldn't have said it. It was, as David said, lazy and thoughtless, but I don't think his comments deserved the reaction they received. Having worked in the media for many years, and being so close to Jim, it was a real eye-opener for me to see how it unfolded, particularly the long list of ridiculous suggestions that flowed from the media, and on the radio waves: he was put up to it by his coach . . . his comments were premeditated . . . Knowing the truth of it all made these reactions laughable. I know Jim would never have meant the harm it caused to McLaren; he is too considerate of the feelings of others to have done that. The irony was that he, James Hird, was very much affected – it was his integrity that was now being questioned. It knocked him around a lot.

The following Saturday night he played the game against West Coast at Telstra Dome. I was in the roof of a mate's place helping him rewire his house to get the power on. All of a sudden my phone started going nuts. It was downstairs and out of reach, but it rang so often I thought my house must be burning down – so I thought I'd better get down the ladder and answer it. The first call I answered was from Garry Lyon, who asked me if I was watching the game. I said no and asked him why: my immediate concern was that Jim must have injured himself again. Garry told me that he thought he may have just seen the greatest individual performance by any player in a game of footy. The game was on delay, so I thought I should rush home to see if I could catch the last 15 minutes or so, where I was told he had kicked a miraculous match-winning goal.

By the time we packed up and got home we had missed it, but my phone was still running hot. So many calls were like Garry's. One person also told me Jim had hugged a supporter (disgraceful!); and my friend Nick, who is in TV production, said that he himself had run into an umpire on the way out of the ground, and

Nick was sure, based on the conversation, that Jimmy would have got maximum Brownlow votes.

The phone rings again and it's Jim, on his way home: 'Did you see it?'

'No,' I said, 'I missed it. I was helping rewire a house . . . I heard you had a cracking game.'

Jim: 'No, did you see me carry on like an idiot and hug a supporter? It's the second stupid thing I've done this week!!'

I must admit now that it was silly of me to think he would call to ask about his performance. He has never done that before, but he must have been feeling so battered from the week's events that he was worried about how this perfectly understandable, but unlikely, reaction would be scrutinised.

I headed over to his place and we assumed our positions, one on each couch with a beer in hand, watching the English Premier League. We talked for a long time about what had happened during the week and I tried to tell him that he should be enjoying the moment, including hugging the supporter. I also tried to make him feel better by telling him my mate Nick had spoken to an umpire and reckoned he got the three votes. Given what had happened with the umpires all week, that didn't seem to be any sort of consolation. I think, at that time, he thought this controversy was never going to pass.

After a few weeks it did die down, but it got rehashed at the end of the year during season highlights programs such as the Brownlow Medal night. I was watching the Brownlow with Nick at a pub I had never been to before. There was hardly anybody in the pub and it ended up being me, Nick, the barman and the chef sitting at the bar, watching the count on a little telly in the top corner of the bar.

They got to Round 3, and the votes were: C. Judd (West Coast) 1, B. Cousins (West Coast) 2, M. Lloyd (Essendon) 3. The chef and the barman were outraged, not knowing that I knew Jimmy. One said: 'This is bloody disgraceful. Did you blokes see that match? Hirdy should have gotten three.' My phone rang. The barman saw the name flash up and looked amazed. I looked at the TV screen as I answered it and saw a shot of the Essendon table with Jim with his head down. I said, 'Hello.'

Jim said, 'I thought your stupid f—n' mate Nick said that I got the three votes!'

Chapter 12

Leadership

At the start of the 1998 season, at the age of 25, and seven years after arriving at Essendon as a shy kid from Canberra, I was appointed captain. It wasn't a big news story the way these things are today. Now, it's a press conference. I was told by either Sheeds or Gary O'Donnell, who was giving up the captaincy. It was pretty low-key. Not many people knew until the season was almost under way that I was going to be captain.

It was what I had always wanted.

Now I was the one the young kids looked to for guidance and support; and I was, in my turn, the cause of some mumbles and stumbles from the rookies. That's the way it works.

I was excited by the opportunity, and it felt right. For me, it was a major step on the road to achieving my dream: captaining Essendon to a premiership.

The first year as captain wasn't easy. My official duties began with a week-long pre-season camp at Mt Kosciuszko and Canberra. I found it difficult to relate to the players as captain, and they found it hard to relate to me. I had to get up and talk in front of them, tell them what the schedule was, invite them to meet for a couple of beers that night, but make sure they knew the curfew. It wasn't as easy as it sounds.

I grew into the role. Being captain helped me and inspired me to play better footy. As captain I was even more passionate about the club I had loved since childhood. In a new role, there's always the feeling that you need to do that bit extra, but I never felt that was a burden. There was a trick to it, though.

I was usually able to compartmentalise my roles on the field and off. But to do it I had to build some invisible protective layers to ensure that my administration duties didn't kill my football. Sometimes I'd frustrate our footy manager, Dominic Cato, when I wouldn't return his calls. If I felt I needed to concentrate on my game and he rang me about administration matters – say, about a guy who hadn't turned up to a session or some other mis-demeanour – I'd say, 'Nup, enough. I've got to worry about getting a kick as well.' If a captain doesn't have the capacity to compart-mentalise, he would always be saying, 'I'm worried about this . . . I'm worried about that . . .' and he wouldn't protect his own game.

I loved the simple rewards of being captain: putting on the jumper, running out first, leading the team, doing inspirational things, running the show on the ground – who wouldn't love that? I didn't like it as much when it came to attending all the sponsors' functions, however, or disciplining players who'd been out till 5 in the morning. That stuff wears you down, especially when you take the captaincy role seriously. I'm quite a serious person in some ways, and the captaincy did nothing to change that. A captain needs to be serious, I believe, but as I have got older I've learned to relax a little more.

Some people at the club would say I struggled to deal with off-field matters in the first few years. On-field, I think I always had a sense of leadership in the way I played and the way I directed people, but away from the footy ground, leading and telling guys who were 30 and 31 what to do, particularly when you really respect them, could be a bit tricky. I was a much better captain when I got a little bit older.

There is no rule book for how to be captain. As well as borrowing from all the qualities Gary O'Donnell had brought to the job before me, and Bomber Thompson and Tim Watson before him, I had to sit down and decide on what would be the best way for me to deal with the players, many of whom were older than me. In 1998, when I'd been captain for only a few weeks, I went to Sydney to have lunch with Mark Taylor, who was then Australia's Test cricket captain. I remember watching Mark when I was a young kid. I had always held him in very high regard as a captain. He seemed always to be on the players' side and to operate in an unselfish way.

I asked Mark how he had the confidence to do it.

'Well, basically you've just got to say what you believe and not worry too much if they don't agree with you,' he replied. 'If you say things for the right reason, most people will follow you; and for those that don't, you have to work out why they're not following you, and if it's a legitimate reason, try to resolve it. If it's not, well, it's their problem.'

I got a lot out of that meeting. Mark had come into the Australian Test side when there were a lot of more experienced players around him, including Steve Waugh, so he had faced the same challenges that I was now facing. I thought his advice was pretty good.

It was tough at times being captain of your mates. Especially when your mate's not getting a game and you're on the selection panel and have to tell him he's been dropped from the side. Or when he's taken off the ground, and he asks why Sheeds took him off – when you say, 'Well, I probably agree with the coach', he'll get the shits with you, guaranteed. It's tough, but it's all part of being captain.

Taking on the captaincy role made me think a lot about styles of leadership. You can only be yourself, and use the methods you think work best to inspire those around you, and, where necessary, to set parameters for behaviour and methods of preparation, especially for the younger players. It is a delicate balancing act between being an authoritarian and one of the boys. It's about managing the rowdier ones, and enlisting the support of your senior group.

Some guys you pull in time after time and they just keep doing the wrong thing, whether it's staying out too late or drinking too much or just not showing the required discipline. There's a point where you have to be brutally honest with someone and say, 'If you do that, you're not only hurting us as a team, but your career will go down the tube.' In my time in footy there have probably been five or six blokes who have, shall we say, enjoyed life too much. They've gone from being okay players (there were a couple who were really good) to nowhere because they didn't have the commitment they needed. Their careers just went off track. As captain you feel a bit of responsibility for that, for not tapping into their heads properly. But I also think that professional footballers need to be self-motivated to be successful on a long-term basis. They should not need to be motivated by the coach or always prompted into action by the captain.

And sometimes, towards the end of my time as captain, I didn't feel we were getting enough leadership from enough people: players were not stepping up and assuming that role. Maybe they had become used to me dominating, and just stopped trying to improve. There were certainly some frustrations involved in being captain.

Also, leadership can be an elusive quality. Some people clearly have it, while with others it might not be obvious at first. Dean Wallis, for example, was a huge support to me as captain, and showed remarkable leadership throughout 2000, proving to me that the best leaders are not necessarily the best players. On the face of it, Wally was a most unusual leader. I told a management seminar about Wally's contribution:

> I played a lot of my career with a bloke by the name of Dean Wallis. Wally would be the first to admit that he wasn't the most talented player ever to run onto the MCG. He was also anything but a leader when he first arrived at Windy Hill. 'A ratbag' is probably the best way of describing him. He got himself into a lot of trouble. But if someone was to ask me who the most important player was in 2000, I would say Dean Wallis. He was a sensational leader that season. On the field he created an environment where opposition players felt uncomfortable because of his physical presence. Consequently, his teammates stood taller, played more confidently, took calculated risks, took on challenges, helped each other out and persevered. Off the field, the thing I admired most about Wally was his honesty. He would tell me how it was; he wouldn't pull any punches with someone who was going to be told something they weren't going to like.

Being captain of Essendon was a multifaceted, hard-to-define role. It meant showing an example, of course, advising, encouraging and sometimes rebuking – all done in the appropriate context. You have to treat everyone differently, because there isn't one method that works for everyone but you need to get the best out of everyone.

On the field there are judgment calls to be made, usually quickly. There is a lot a captain can do at the coalface. Very often, a captain's call can be expedited immediately, without waiting for a runner's instruction. In *The Age*, Greg Baum wrote about examples of my captaincy role during the elimination final of 2003 when we played Fremantle in Perth:

> First, he took Damien Cupido aside, after the young Bomber had given away a foolish 50-metre penalty and goal, to warn him to keep his mouth shut and his mind on the bigger prize. Coach Kevin Sheedy was about to drag Cupido, but saw this and put the phone down. Hird was, at least then, captain-coach. Second, at the end of the game Hird used national television to say to dropped teammate Mark Mercuri that he would be back with them this week. Finely argued, it was a pledge that he alone was not entitled to make, but most took it not as a pre-emption of the selectors but as an affirmation of togetherness.

Cupido, incidentally, went on to kick two goals in that game and played a solid second half.

One of the challenges for a captain is to understand the balance of the team, to make sure it doesn't rely too heavily on key players. In football you rely 100 per cent on your teammates; great sides consist of a group of really good players who look after each other and share the play. You don't really want one bloke kicking 140 goals. You want someone kicking 80, someone kicking 60 and a couple kicking 30 – I guarantee you'll win more games that way. The same principle applies with on-ballers.

David Wheadon, one of our assistants in 1993, revolutionised the way we played footy, by simplifying it. His adage was that your strength can be your Achilles heel. If you're too strong in one area and not others, a side can attack that strength and work out a way to hinder it – then you're gone. You need to be better than average all round, he said; and you don't want to have all your eggs in one basket.

It's about the team. Hawthorn in the 1980s is a great example of a club that boasted huge stars, but its success was based on being a powerhouse team. They had champions such as Leigh Matthews, Dermott Brereton, Chris Langford, John Platten and Jason Dunstall. And these stars brought other players into the game. They were great footballers, but they excelled as part of a team structure. Hawks coach Allan Jeans knew it was important that everyone had a role.

No team should ever be too reliant on one player when there are 18 players on the ground. Phil Jackson, the former coach of the Chicago Bulls, has written about his time there coaching the great Michael Jordan. He said that when he got to Chicago the team was too Jordan-conscious – all the team cared about was how many points their superstar player scored. If Jordan scored 40 or 50 points, the team were happy, even when they'd lost. Jackson had to turn that mindset around. Instead of Jordan scoring 45–50 points, other players on the team needed to score 20–30 points and win titles. It took Jackson a long time to convince Michael Jordan himself of that, but once he had, the Bulls went on to win four championships and become arguably the best team ever.

One of the skills of leadership is delegation, which Kevin Sheedy has always acknowledged. He makes the final call on most issues, but many decisions are made along the way by a team of highly efficient assistant coaches. We're lucky at Essendon to have some highly motivated assistants in former champions Gary O'Donnell, Gary Ayres and Dean Wallis, all of whom work closely with the players. Sheeds has a lot of promotional and other duties away from the club, so assistants are imperative.

To be a good captain you also need to be a good listener – I think listening is probably the most important skill in communication. You can't communicate until you've learned, and often the only way to do that is by listening. In some ways, listening is my greatest skill, and I try to use it not only in football, but in business and with my kids. With children you have to listen to what they're saying and watch their actions if you want to understand what they mean, because often they can't express themselves as well as they want to. In business, too, you can sit in a meeting and listen to what someone's saying, but if you're not perceptive in reading their body language you might miss half of what they're trying to communicate.

These skills are probably more important than ever today, with the rise of political correctness in football. I think it has gone a little too far. We don't want to hurt anyone's feelings now. We all have to be equals, we all have to be nice and considerate to everyone. But in footy you have to make quick decisions. Sometimes on the field you don't have time to be nice. People get offended when they're being shouted at, but in my opinion, if you don't want to get shouted at, don't come and play footy. Stress is high and things have to be done in a matter of seconds. You can't put your arm around everyone, speak considerately, wait half an hour, go and have a coffee . . . the game would be long over.

Sheeds's balance is very good – he knows when to bucket blokes and get into them, but he's also very positive, and can actually be quite sensitive. My style is to say, 'Let's get on with it, let's do it, let's make a decision straight away.' I don't think you need 85 meetings to make one decision, which is what is starting to happen.

Back in the early 1990s it was more brutal. Especially in 1992, when we reserves were coached by Denis Pagan. He was the most brutal bloke in the world. You knew exactly where you stood with him. He was tough and honest. I like that: tell me where I stand.

By August of 2005, with my five-year contract coming to an end, I had to start thinking about the captaincy. I wasn't sure whether I wanted to relinquish it or not. I had been captain for eight years and I loved doing it. I felt I still had a lot to offer the group, including the new guys coming into the squad, such as Kepler Bradley, Jason Laycock and Andrew Lovett, who starred in the Anzac Day game against Collingwood that year and won the Anzac Day Medal. I was excited by the potential of these new kids coming through, but I needed to look at everything in context.

I would be signing a one-year contract and would almost certainly play for only one more season. Was it the responsible thing to give up the captain's spot and be out on the field and around the club for that final season, helping my successor, Matthew Lloyd, settle into the job? Would I find it difficult to play not as captain and under Lloydy? I had to think hard about these questions.

Matthew Lloyd had been vice-captain for five seasons. He was ready, willing and able, liked and respected by the players, a genuine superstar of the game and one of the most dedicated professionals I've ever met. Succession wasn't a problem, as Sheeds had often noted.

I first spoke to Lloydy in 2003 about handing over the captaincy while I was still playing. At first he was taken aback at the thought that he could captain while I was still around. Midway through the 2005 season I invited Matthew and his wife around for dinner; I suppose that was the night I unofficially handed over the reins to him. There are plenty of precedents for this. Terry Daniher passed it to Tim Watson and kept playing;

when Mark Thompson took over, Tim was still playing; and when Gary O'Donnell took over, Mark was still playing. It's been a successful tradition at Essendon, and I was sure it would work for Lloydy and me.

Lloydy, 27 years old and with 209 games behind him, 'a local kid from Avondale Heights', as Kevin Sheedy called him, was officially appointed captain on 27 September 2005. He was the first 'local' captain since Bomber Thompson. He became the ninth skipper in Sheeds's 26 years with the club, following Simon Madden (1981), Neale Daniher (replaced because of injury in 1982 by Ron Andrews), Terry Daniher (1983–88), Tim Watson (1989–91), Mark Thompson (1992–95), Gary O'Donnell (1996–97) and me.

Lloydy told a press conference: 'I feel the time is perfect. I wasn't ready 12 months ago . . . [the prospect] probably overawed me.'

We had a pretty frank discussion just before pre-season started. I rang him and said there would be times when he and I were not sure who was in what role, so we should talk it out before it got messy. We both decided we'd just try to trust our instincts. If I felt like saying something, I'd just say it, and if he thought I'd stepped over the mark well, we could talk about it later. We wanted to present a united front.

And I did step over the mark, unfortunately. In early 2006 I found myself saying things like, 'Guys, I really want you to follow what I'm doing here.' I should not have been saying that. I caught myself, but (obviously!) too late.

I had to take a step back and let him lead in his own way – and he went really well even in his first few weeks as captain. He brought a different style to the job. I captain the way I play: with feel rather than structure. I'm very disciplined in some areas, but in some ways I like to let it flow, and leave things to players' individuality and intuition. I didn't want the captaincy to be too structured, because it would then be a burden to me. Lloydy structures it a lot more, which is the way he plays. He's brought a lot more discipline into the place, which I think is exactly what we needed with our young group. The captaincy has also brought Lloydy out of his shell, which is good.

I think Matthew and I have a very good relationship. It is honest. There are times when it has been slightly tested, but not over anything serious. And I think that's good for a relationship – disagreements and differences of opinions – because he's not me and I'm not him. I'm probably a much more easygoing person in some respects but much more particular in others.

Training attire is one area where the two of us have different approaches. I couldn't care less if some of the squad train in blue singlets, some in green and one in pink. To me it's unimportant. But Lloydy's more fastidious – he wants everyone wearing the same uniform.

Another slight variance in style is the point at which I go full-bore into training. I need to have a certain fitness level first; if I'm not at that level I don't want to play in practice games. Lloydy will say: 'Well, we're here to play footy. I don't care where I am fitness-wise, just let me play footy.' It might be a full-forward trait; it might also be a personality thing.

It's been said that it's difficult to captain effectively as a full-forward, because you're usually too far away from the heat of the action to be able to give direction. One of our former assistant coaches, Robert Shaw, used to say that to be captain, Lloydy needed to play at centre-half-forward.

I don't think that's a problem. The reality is that when you're out there on the ground as captain, you're not telling everyone what to do. There are leaders all over the place. I had strong back-up when I was captain – from Dean Wallis, Sean Wellman, Lloydy, Scotty Lucas and Darren Bewick.

A few final thoughts on leadership. A leader of any group needs to create an environment that encourages every individual in the team to best achieve the common goal. That final goal needs to be the same for everyone. In football it is winning a premiership; in business, it's usually profitability. The difficult part comes with the realisation that every person has a different reason for wanting to achieve that goal – and different experiences to draw from to help them go about it. For me, the passion was to achieve a childhood ambition. For some it's about fame and the recognition that comes with being part of a successful team; for others it's a way to change their life and make it better for them and their family; and to a few it's simply about making money. Whatever the reason, a leader who does not understand each individual's motivation to achieve the common goal will find it very hard to inspire and truly lead their team.

By listening to a wide range of people at Essendon and in business, I have discovered that certain traits are essential to good leadership. In short, a good leader needs to:

- have passion for the cause;
- be approachable and good at listening to what their people are really saying;
- follow through on promises;
- set a framework that people can adhere to and get strength from when times are tough;
- show loyalty to the people in the team;
- follow their instincts to some extent and not second-guess themselves too much;
- settle for being respected rather than liked; and
- get to know people on a personal level.

Chapter 13

The Footy Show

'Welcome to *The Footy Show*! And what a big week it has been in football!'

That was the cry from Eddie McGuire that until recently would ring out every Thursday evening during the football season. And the thing about living in Melbourne is that it is *always* a big week in football. Soon afterwards, the consummate host would introduce 'the 300-game champion from the Geelong Football Club and all-round nice-guy, John "Sammy" Newman' (cue James Bond music). Then he'd welcome Trevor Marmalade 'over at the bar'. It was a Melbourne ritual, and still is, in its new format, one that I've been very happy to be a part of for about half of its 14 years.

In 1995 I signed a contract with Channel 9 to appear on the show once a month. For someone who was a shy kid, walking onto a set in a television studio wasn't the easiest thing to do, but I was okay if I could just be myself. During my time with Channel 7 (in 1998–2000) I appeared on their ill-fated football variety program *Live and Kicking*, which they had conceived to try to grab back some of the hundreds and thousands of viewers who had fallen for *The Footy Show*'s mix of footy pie-night humour and vaudeville. That experience taught me a valuable lesson: always be yourself. Wearing women's clothes and singing on television is a long way outside my comfort zone.

Which is why I've enjoyed *The Footy Show*. I play the straight man, I suppose. I get called 'Gentleman Jim', and that's all right. I don't get too involved in the shenanigans; I say what I think, play a straight bat and let the people who are comfortable clowning around make the jokes – Dougy Hawkins in the early years of the show, and Glen Manton and Billy Brownless later on. I just play it down the middle. There's no point pretending to be what you're not.

Eddie was the ringmaster of all this for 13 years, until he took on the job as chief executive of the Nine Network in February 2006. Eddie is an extraordinary presence on TV. He's a natural – quick on his feet, able to pour oil on troubled waters (and *The Footy Show* has certainly needed that at times), and blessed with a steel-trap mind that he can pluck information out of at will. He comes under a lot of criticism for being 'Eddie Everywhere', but he's been our biggest star on TV for the past 10 years, certainly in Melbourne. He's a driven man, the most driven individual I've ever seen, and I think that spills over to the way he handles his production people at times – he has been known to yell a bit and carry on, but that's because he's passionate and because he works hard. I think most people understand that.

The general public sometimes get the wrong idea about Eddie McGuire. They think he's trying to manipulate things, and maybe sometimes for Collingwood he is, but in general I think he's pretty even-handed for a media figure who is the president of a footy club. He certainly made Collingwood a cut above the rest in terms of their financial viability. As one commentator has said, before Eddie they were going 100 miles an hour in the wrong direction; they'd always had a supporter base, but they weren't capitalising on it commercially. He's done a great job with the Magpies.

Eddie was very good at giving me hints and a leg up: he'd go through my tape of the show and tell me how to present and which camera to look at. He gave me the confidence to jump in with a comment whenever I wanted to. He'd say, 'Even if I'm talking, if you want to say something, just jump in and say it.' There's no way I would ever have done that unless he'd given me his okay.

He did blow his stack a few times, and that was interesting to watch. If the three panellists weren't giving him what he wanted, or he didn't think we were into it enough, he would come over during the ad break and say, 'Come on boys, pull your heads out and have a crack. You're letting us down.' I received a couple of substantial serves from him. I was taken aback at the time, but now I view it as a good learning experience. Perhaps I was looking bored. The show is filmed at 9.30 at night and always after a hard training session, so sometimes by 10.30 I'd be pretty knackered. You wake up pretty quickly when Eddie gives you a spray.

I think he's been good for football, and he's definitely been a positive influence on me. Everywhere I go, people ask what Eddie is really like. And I can tell that some of them expect to hear something negative. He's not everyone's cup of tea. But I think a lot of the animosity comes out of other's jealousy. I've seen him around his wife and children and he is very loving.

Sam Newman can be an odd one. I like him and I enjoy spending time with him. He has got a lot of interesting things to say about footy. He's very smart with his ruck comments and he understands the game very well. Given that he's been doing the same thing around footy for probably 25 years, I believe his outbursts stem from boredom and frustration. If he sees a great game or a great player, he gets excited, but if he sees an average game or an average player he switches off.

Sam is pretty savage on Geelong at times. I think that's because he is so passionate about the Cats succeeding. He has a lot to do with the club, but on *The Footy Show* he's never afraid to say precisely what he thinks about them – and woe betide them if they've had a bad game. I have a lot of respect for the Geelong coach, Bomber Thompson, who was one of the great leaders at Essendon when he was there, so I don't like it when Sam gets stuck into him. It might be funny when it's not someone you know, but with Bomber I just become defensive. Sam is a very cynical man. He'll say anything. He doesn't tolerate fools. If things aren't done really well, he can be brutal.

Working on the show has been good for me: the people involved have always understood that my football career comes first, and they don't ever impinge on that. I know some clubs have had issues with their players appearing on the show. Hawthorn have – and Jeff Kennett particularly. When Jeff nominated for the Hawthorn presidency, he made it clear that he had problems with what he saw as Eddie's conflict of interest, being the Collingwood president. For that reason, Jeff said he wouldn't go on the show. He also remarked that the Hawthorn board might consider banning the club's players from appearing on it. Shane Crawford is the one who would be most affected. Not only is he a Hawthorn champion, but he's also one of the show's favourite panellists. He had a starring role in 'The House of Bulger', the show within a show – he played 'good guy' Hank Bulger opposite the 'evil' Garry Lyon.

Al Pacino and Dame Judi Dench can rest easy: it wasn't the acting that gave 'The House of Bulger' its cult status – it was watching footballers *try* to act. It was a lot of fun, and I don't think the segment hurt anyone's football career. Crawf is the sort of guy who needs to do that sort of thing to play footy. He loves it, he's passionate about it. He was a much happier person doing 'The House of Bulger'. I did a walk-on in the show, which was a bit of a laugh, and I actually enjoyed doing it. It was a five-second piece every three weeks, where each time I'd get whacked by a door (a take on my propensity to get injured). Crawf hounded me to have a go at it. I have a lot of time for Shane, he's a good guy.

Although current *Footy Show* co-hosts Garry Lyon and James Brayshaw are doing a terrific job as his replacements, it's a different show from when Eddie did it. Still, I'm sure that from his new home in Sydney he'll be keeping a close eye on his baby. And on panellists not putting in.

Chapter 14

Anzac Day

I'm standing in a line of Essendon players, facing a line of Collingwood players. The Last Post is playing. I'm thinking about the people who died in war, fighting for Australia. There's a massive silence in the MCG, a silence with a great power, more power than the roar of the crowd. I'm standing next to Kevin Sheedy, looking over at the Collingwood footy team in their black and white and looking at the red and black of my teammates, and the crowd is a sea of red and black and white. There's nowhere else in the world I'd rather be. It's an awesome experience, genuinely moving, almost spiritual in the weight of its sadness and the respect you feel for those who didn't return from war, and the families they left behind.

The ball is bounced, the game's away. The crowd's noise and energy fill up the MCG. You hear the roar in waves, ebbing and flowing with the pace of the game.

It's Anzac Day, for me the greatest day to play football apart from the last one in September.

April 25 means a lot to me on several levels. It's a chance to reflect on what it must have meant to be 18 or 19 years old and going off to a foreign land and the terror of war, and to honour those men and women who didn't return.

As a football player the day is special because we've played Collingwood that day every year since 1995, in front of about 90,000 people. It's a day game, which I enjoy, and it's at the MCG, a place I love playing at. It has never mattered where Essendon and Collingwood were on the ladder; it is always a tough, bruising game that both sides are desperate to win. Playing on 25 April, there is a huge sense of occasion. The Grand Final aside, it's the loudest game you'll play in for the year.

And Anzac Day is Stephanie's birthday.

Our family has a strong link with the two world wars, which adds poignancy to the day for me. My grandfather on my mum's side, Jack Lawson, was a brigadier in the army in New Guinea during World War II. My mum was part of an army family. My grandparents, Myrtle and Jack, were Brisbane people. They moved down to the barracks in Melbourne and Mum lived there almost until she moved to Canberra with Dad.

My grandfather died quite early in my life, when I was seven. My grandmother doesn't talk about the war very much, but she gave me and my cousin Jack's brigadier's cap.

On Dad's side of the family, my grandmother's brother Tom was a bomber pilot in the RAAF. He was shot down over France and was hidden by the French Resistance for three or four weeks, but was finally caught by the Germans and sent to Buchenwald, a Nazi concentration camp. He spent a year there. Because he was captured without his uniform on they decided he was a spy, which is why they sent him there at first, rather than to a POW camp.

Interestingly, Tom lived in Moonee Ponds, 500 metres from Windy Hill, and was Essendon's weatherman for years. He was in charge of making sure the coach knew about all weather conditions.

When I was boarding in Melbourne I realised I was living close to my great-uncle, so I spent a bit of time with him. He was big, a gruff man, but always good fun. He wouldn't talk to me about his time in the services, though. He had a fascinating story, but the details had to remain sketchy. Like so many men who'd been to war, he was reticent about it.

Anzac Day is a day for heroes. Tom's story of heroism and survival is one I would like to share.

Warrant Officer Tom Malcom from Hawthorn, Victoria, was the bomb aimer on Lancaster LM571. On 24 June 1944, 112 aircraft attacked the Proville Road junction in the Pas-de-Calais area of northern France. Immediately after dropping the bombs on the target area, Tom's plane was attacked by a swarm of fighters and burst into flames. Tom was blown clear of the aircraft; the rest of the crew were killed instantly. He pulled the ripcord of his parachute and landed safely on French soil. He then set off, hoping to meet some friendly French people who could put him in touch with local members of the Resistance.

Tom's route towards the Resistance took him through Flanders (I would later visit there with Tania) and on to Beauvais, 60 kilometres north-west of Paris. Here he drifted into an ancient cathedral, where he asked a woman sitting on a pew for help. She was startled and uneasy, but she did go for help. She returned with a man who identified himself as the captain of the local Maquis (Resistance). He took Tom to his house, and then organised Tom's path to freedom. The captain arranged transport to Paris in a local furniture van, in which he travelled concealed under boxes as the Germans were checking for identification papers outside the capital. Once in Paris the man assigned to look after Tom, and who turned out to be the chief of the Paris Gaol, gave Tom accommodation within the gaol for Tom's first night. After a stroll around the city the next morning, Tom was transferred, under the nose of the Germans, to numerous safe houses by the local Resistance group, which was called the Pericles.

On 19 July 1944, Tom was transferred once again and introduced to a young man called Captain Jacques, who said he was with the British Secret Service. Jacques told Tom to follow him along the banks of the River Seine to a truck that would take them to the south of France and freedom. Tom jumped into the back of the truck with another 17 Allied airmen, all eager to drive to safety. However, 10 minutes into their journey the truck stopped. The doors were thrown open to reveal a brace of Germans armed with machine-guns. As Tom told it (in Colin Burgess's *Destination Buchenwald*):

> Our truck was in an enclosed courtyard, strangely called the court of sausages, and most of the available artillery was trained on us. Our friend captain Jacques had cleverly passed us on to the Germans. Thus ended my chance of escape at the time, and the joys of life under the Nazi heel were to be mine for a few months.

Tom was transferred to Buchenwald, where he spent most of the time in a state of delirium due to high fever, pneumonia and other sicknesses. He was later transferred to a POW camp and finally liberated at the end of World War II.

Tom's memories of Buchenwald are limited, but the following provides an insight into the terror he lived through:

To this day I have no memory of what happened to me during the time I was seriously ill in hospital, nor of my move across to the air force camp to join the others. What I do remember, quite vividly, is being cocooned for what seemed an eternity in sopping wet blankets.

Another of the airmen talked of an early morning ritual whereby Russian prisoners would enter the hut and haul out those who had died during the night, sometimes as many as three dozen at a time.

After Tom's liberation he walked back to the French coast before catching a transport back to England. Some six months later he returned to his home in Hawthorn – a different man, and much more of a hero than any footballers we loosely use that term for today.

A national day is important, and in our country, Australia Day doesn't quite do it. I think Anzac Day is the one where we get a little bit patriotic. To me, Anzac Day feels like our national day because it is so infused with meaning and genuine emotion for so many people.

On Anzac Day 1999, one of the great moments of my life happened: our first child, Stephanie, was born. There weren't many highlights that year for me professionally, but I did experience the joy and wonder of seeing my first child come into the world.

Unfortunately, I wasn't in tip-top shape. I was on crutches, because the operation on my foot had only happened three weeks before. The night she was born was a Saturday, and we had some friends over for dinner. The baby wasn't due for three weeks.

At 11 o'clock we were lying in bed and Tania said she was feeling a few contractions. We rang the hospital. 'No, it can't be coming yet. Don't worry about it – go back to sleep.' Tania woke me up at 1 o'clock. 'I think we're on here,' she said.

I had borrowed a friend's car – an automatic – to make it easier for me to drive with the plaster on my leg. So there I was, driving to the hospital using my left foot on the accelerator and the brake. Luckily, the hospital wasn't very far from our place.

We got out and Tania had to carry her own bags because I was hobbling along on crutches. It was 2 am, and outside the hospital there were a group of women smoking, as always. We walked past them, with Tania carrying her bags, and they all looked at me in disgust. Every so often Tania would stop, having another contraction. If you're a man, there's a certain helplessness at the time your partner is giving birth; my crutches and foot in plaster did nothing to alleviate it.

Tania had not had time for painkillers. I've been through some pain in my football career, but having a baby without pain relief would have to be as bad it gets. It puts my pain into perspective. Tania showed huge courage that night. I felt overwhelmed and helpless: watching her go through so much pain was challenging. Tania's not a complainer, even though she had agony written all over her face.

At about 11.30 the next morning I thought I'd better go to the game the boys were playing at the MCG. Tania was fine with Stephanie, and her family were there. I'd organised for Barry Young, a teammate, to pick me up. When he arrived, I was sitting on our front step. I must have looked pale and tired.

'What's wrong? Are you all right?'

'Yeah, fine,' I said. 'I've just had my first child, Stephanie.'

It was a great thing to be able to say.

I sat in the coaches' box watching the game, but to this day I can't remember a thing about it. I kept running through different stages of the night in my head. It was a very powerful experience, and I wanted to savour every moment.

One year later, on Anzac Day 2000, Tania organised a big party for Stephanie's first birthday, after the game. I knew I had to play well, because if we lost and I didn't get a kick, I would not be in a good frame of mind at my daughter's party. I did play well, and I won my first Anzac Medal. Stephanie wore it to bed. When I won my third one, in 2004, it was even better, because she was five, Tommy was three and Alex was one, so they each had a medal. They walked around the house with them, proud as punch. I thought that was fantastic.

Needless to say, Anzac Day morning is always a special time at our place. The Anzac Day when Stephanie turned three was one I'll always remember. We'd bought her a trampoline, and it was my job to assemble it. Before I left for the game at the MCG.

Now, anyone who has ever assembled a household item or toy from those stores where you buy it in pieces will know that putting something together, straight out of the cardboard box, against a deadline, can be a challenge. I thought I was going okay, but when it got to 11 o'clock I realised I'd either have to turn into one of the guys from *Backyard Blitz*, or finish the project later, thereby running the risk of disappointing my little three-year-old. Not an option. I ploughed on, pretty anxious, and managed to get it done with just enough time to get shifters and allen keys out of my head and concentrate on our game plan. A little too close for comfort!

Another reason that I look forward to Anzac Day so much is because the MCG is easily my favourite ground. The first game I saw there was the 1982 Grand Final between Carlton and Richmond (which Carlton won by four goals). I feel very close to it, and not just as a footballer and a fan. I lived in Berry Street, East Melbourne, just off Wellington Parade, until late 2005. For three years Tommy and I used to go down and kick the footy in the shadows of the MCG. That's a long, strong connection to the ground – I hope I see many more Grand Finals there.

Perhaps it's because I enjoy playing on Anzac Day so much that I've usually played pretty well. But not every Anzac Day has gone Essendon's way. In 2002, for instance, we kicked only four goals, and for the first time in three or four years we were beaten by a side we didn't think was as good as us.

The next year, 2003, was much better. I won the Anzac Medal. Two years later, in the pre-Anzac Day media session, Collingwood coach Mick Malthouse would be saying: 'The James Hird Medal? It may as well be.' He added:

> I just wish he would grow older quicker. You never doubt champions. We have tagged him, we have sat off him. We have had double tags on him. We have tried to move him to full-forward, we have tried to move him to full-back, we have tried to manipulate it, but he ends up winning the James Hird Medal. Another year, another game. He is a year older and hopefully we are a bit wiser for it.

I was flattered to hear an opposition coach talk about me that way. Kevin Sheedy spoke about why I tend to play well on that day: 'He probably just lifts for certain reasons in his life that only he will know. When you get to the big games you just shouldn't ever fail. Maybe Hird had got a bit of that in him, because that is what champions have.'

On Anzac Day 2004, after I'd won my third Anzac Day Medal, Sheeds, speaking to reporters, invoked the Anzac spirit:

The young kid who lived across from the War Memorial [in Canberra] has collected three medals. It's a fairytale story. He's a very strong-willed person. He's got a bit of soul in him, too. There's a fair bit of soul in the way he wanted to play for Essendon. He hasn't let the club down since he's been there. He's come through some fairly treacherous injuries that would probably have dispirited a lot of people. I annoy him. I keep saying, 'You've only got a year [left]', and he keeps shoving it right through my brain. His willpower, I think, is one of his greatest strengths.

I was proud to have won those three medals, especially because I knew exactly where they were going.

Chapter 15

In the Zone

Some days, everything goes to plan. One of those days was against Collingwood on Anzac Day in 2003. It was the last quarter and the scores were about level. There was a crowd of around 80,000. There was a fantastic atmosphere and I felt great. I felt I could find the ball, so I went up to Joey Misiti.

'You go to the middle and I'll go half-forward,' I told him. 'I believe I can get a couple of goals.'

They say that on a clear day you can see forever. On that day I could see the ball coming down towards me as though it was destined to land in my arms. I was on James Clement – he and I had had some very good contests, and the year before he'd given me a bit of a shake-up. But on that Anzac Day, I knew I was going to get the ball. I knew before I got the ball what I was going to do with it. I would tell the story my way. I kicked three goals in 10 minutes and the game was all over. It was incredible.

That feeling of control occurred more often in the 1996 season, when I won the Brownlow, than in any other year. If you experienced that feeling 20 times in your career you'd be rapt. It's happened to me probably 10 times; it's as if you can almost see the future. You know where the ball's going, you know that if you get the ball you're going to kick a goal . . . and you know that if you could access that feeling at will you would be a champion player every week. But sport is about variables, which is why it's so dramatic. You're kidding yourself if you think you're going to play 22 games at 100 per cent.

Playing football is about recognising the moments, and adjusting your thinking accordingly. But sometimes it seems that an inner force is doing the thinking for you, even the playing. Whether it's an automatic pilot born of long experience, or you're being channelled by the footy gods, I cannot say.

Whatever it is, it's come to be called 'being in the zone'.

You often hear people talking about players being in the zone. Tennis champion Billie Jean King was quoted in *The Age* as saying:

> It usually happens on one of those days when everything is right, when the crowd is large and enthusiastic and my concentration is so perfect it almost seems as though I'm able to transport myself beyond the turmoil of the court to some place of total peace and calm. I know where the ball is on every shot, and it always looks as big and well-defined as a basketball.

In his book *My Life and the Beautiful Game*, the great Brazilian soccer player Pelé wrote that one day he had felt 'a strange calmness' he hadn't experienced before:

> It was a type of euphoria; I felt I could run all day without tiring, that I could dribble through any of their team or all of them, that

248

I could almost pass through them physically. I felt I could not be hurt. It was a very strange feeling and one I had not felt before. Perhaps it was merely confidence, but I have felt confident many times without that strange feeling of invincibility.

The *New York Times* noted the comments of the former quarter-back of the San Francisco '49ers, who told Michael Murphy, the author of *The Psychic Side of Sports*, that there were moments in every game when 'time seems to slow way down, in an uncanny way, as if everyone were moving in slow motion. It seems as if I have all the time in the world to watch the receivers run their patterns, and yet I know the defensive line is coming at me just as fast as ever.'

For me, in a football context, you will only get to be 'in the zone' when you are physically and mentally prepared and ready to fire. You have to be well rested and excited and motivated. That sounds very obvious, but it's all about atmosphere and feel. When you run out onto a ground, it can just *feel* right. Even when another player runs into you and hits you, the way you bounce off them can be just right – you land on your feet with perfect balance and run off. Or you're running hard and you know you're exhausted but it doesn't feel as hard as other days.

There's a flipside to those days when everything goes your way, of course. They are the days when you can't get there no matter how hard you try, the days when you know you're not going to kick the goal – and you don't.

One part of the solution is to think positively. There are plenty of days when you feel terrible running out onto the ground, but 90 per cent of the time you still play all right, because you push yourself through it. The other 10 per cent of the time you're in damage control: *How do I not play as badly as I might today?*

You have to learn how to push yourself through the bad days

if you aim to be a consistently good performer. The champions who play well week in, week out, or the people in the office who always give quality work, are the people who have figured out how to push through the bad days, how to make good days happen instead of just waiting for them to happen.

Recognising the signs of being below par is the first step. Combatting them is the second. When I am playing well I can run all day and get to as many contests as I want to; on the bad days I feel as if all the oxygen has been drained out of me and just walking onto the ground makes me lose my breath. When I realise this is happening, I force myself to run, and I actually count the number of contests I am getting to.

It's hard to pre-empt those off days. Before every game you do exactly the same training, have exactly the same lead-up and eat exactly the same food. One weekend you run out and you feel powerful and mentally alert; the next you run out and your legs are like jelly, you've got nothing in them and you're flat and uninterested. That's life for us humans.

One bad performance is disappointing, two is frustrating, but in my book, three means there is something wrong. Three in a row means it's time to delve deeper. Talent cannot be lost overnight, so it has to be something else. perhaps there's something wrong with your training or your diet.

Why do people in sport – and at work – put in a series of bad performances? In football there are two main categories of reason. First, internal factors: perhaps there's something wrong with your training or your diet, or the way you're preparing. Are you working hard enough on the track? Have you studied the opposition closely enough? Or have you trained too hard, and so lost your spark and need a rest? Second, external factors: perhaps the coaches or your teammates are taking your confidence away by criticising you too much, or the other teams have put strategies in place that are negating your play. It is important to work out what is inhibiting your performance, quickly.

I have a checklist that is a major weapon in my fight against performance slumps. I know what I should weigh in the morning and at night; I know what my optimal body-fat percentage should be; I know how fast I can run 30 metres and how far I can run in 12 minutes; and I know how strong I need to be to be at my optimum level. Testing these things regularly and making sure I am within 5 per cent of my baseline figures gives me something to fall back on. It helps give me the self-confidence I need to get out of a slump. For me, having a set of standards that I need to maintain prevents lengthy form slumps.

Preparation for a game is a balancing act. You need a certain amount of nervous energy, but too much can send you over the top. There are many books written about performance and nervous energy and how much you need. And for everyone it's different.

It's telling to look back at how football teams warmed up in the 1970s and '80s: they all ranted and raved, even the blokes who didn't want to. Back then it was expected, and people were almost made to do it. Nowadays, it is understood that each player has his own method of mental preparation, and that is accommodated and encouraged. If you want to rant and rave, there's a corner where you can do it, and if you want to sit quietly, there's another corner for you. Mark Harvey, for instance, would never join the warm-up. He just sat in the doctor's room. Joey Misiti jokes and mucks around. An outsider would look at him doing that and think, *There's no way he'll play well today*, but he'll come out and have a blinder. Mark Johnson needs to box for half an hour before he goes out to play. Personally, I couldn't think of anything worse – it would be using up my energy.

As I have said, everyone's preparation is different. I like to have a swim three hours before a game to loosen my body up. I don't really like to talk to anyone except the guys at the footy club. If Mum rings me two hours before a game, I'm really short with her, almost rude. With Tania and the kids it's different because they're around all the time, but they know to pretty much leave me alone. As soon as I get in the rooms, I'll have a joke and a muck around with the guys who are going to be playing; they're on the same level. Strangely, I can't do it with the guys who aren't playing that day.

I try not to have a joke around blokes I know might be put off by that. If I'm going to have a muck around with Joe Misiti, we'll go somewhere else, rather than do it where, say, Lloydy is preparing. Lloydy is very tense in his preparation – he needs to be very focused. Three or four of the Essendon guys prepare by spending time with Alan Dunn, the club chaplain. They will quietly go off and pray.

It's about getting into a frame of mind. But the timing has to be right. I don't like getting into my required frame of mind too early. If I'm mentally preparing at 10 in the morning for a game that starts at 7.30 at night, by 7.30 I'm exhausted. The later I get into it the better, but it's hard to delay it, because it's a natural progression. I try to stay fairly relaxed until we run out, and I try not to think about what I'm going to do out on the ground until five minutes before then. The adrenaline's running, I'm talking to my teammates, the coach is talking to me – my intense thinking happens just moments before I start playing.

The different preparation routines you see around you reinforce the fact that not everyone's the same sort of player. And there is room for different types of players. When I started, if you didn't use your fists or bleed during the warm-up, you weren't ready to play footy. That's definitely changed.

Tania and I lived in East Melbourne for six years, and every time we played at the MCG I would walk to the ground – just as I'd done that first time back in 1993, before a game against Fitzroy.

For me, it's all part of getting into the zone. These days, I still walk to the ground from the car park, down the tree-lined paths, past the doughnut sellers and the boys selling *The Footy Record* and the crowds expectantly heading into the stadium. All that fires me up.

One day Tania decided she would walk down with me. That lasted one game. For some reason it stressed me out. I don't know why, but it didn't feel right. I played really well that day, so it didn't have a negative impact. But I did make a conscious decision from then on to walk to the ground alone. Tania knows I'm nervous when I don't communicate well. She gives me space around games.

It's amazing that after 16 years in the competition, my personality still changes 24 hours before a game. It's not rational, it's not right; it's selfish, and it's hard on the family, but for some reason it happens. On the Thursday night I go to bed relaxed, but by 2 o'clock on Friday afternoon I'm edgy, and almost any sound from the kids makes me uptight.

A medium level of anxiety is a good thing. It sharpens you. The worst games I've played are the ones where I haven't been anxious. I have played well over 200 games, and there have been a couple of times when I've thought, *I don't know if I can get into this*. They have been my worst performances.

I've followed the career of cyclist Lance Armstrong and his amazing Tour de France achievements. Lance is so driven. He says, 'Blow the rest of the world. I want to achieve something – I'm *going to* achieve it.' He breaks his opponents. When he's riding, he assesses the situation, rides up to someone and says, 'Here I am, mate – I'm going to destroy you.' That is the zone he gets into. It must be exhausting, cranking himself up to that level all the time, but it's a measure of his competitiveness that he rarely lets that standard slip. I'd love to have a bit more of that in me. He got there by training harder than anyone else and bringing that mindset into every competition.

I was always taught that it is necessary for players to psych themselves up, get angry, hate the opposition, abuse them and treat them as the enemy – a big ask when I'm not really that sort of person. I get excited about playing footy because I love playing it; hurting others isn't part of the equation. People have sometimes questioned this attitude: 'How can you be a good player if you don't go into a game wanting to hurt people?'

A lot of people confuse competitiveness with aggression, thinking that aggression is necessary for competitiveness. In fact, many leaders make this mistake when assessing people. Yes, aggression can be a useful tool when used in the right way, but it isn't necessary. I believe I am in the top 1 per cent of the human race for competitiveness, yet I don't behave aggressively, or feel aggressive. It is important for leaders to realise that a person who doesn't demonstrate aggressive or domineering tendencies may be just as good a fighter as a person who struts around telling everyone how competitive they are.

I've found other useful strategies, not many of which involve whiteboards. I believe that there are dangers in over-analysing performance. Instinct should never be subdued by tactics. I have never minded doing the preparation. I've worked hard on my game: I spend a lot of time away from the club doing extra skills work, kicking the footy, stretching, running and doing weights. I like to think that no one has done more physical work than I have. But when it comes to an analysis of my game or the opposition's, I struggle. We are given tapes to take home and watch, and stat sheets to read, and often it's too much for me. I play better if I go into a game with hardly any information in my head and just strive for the ball than if I worry about one move or another.

This might not go down well with the tacticians of the sport, but a clear head is often the best weapon I take into a game.

I don't like a lot of clutter in my head about what we're going to do. Footy's not like gridiron. It's not even like soccer. In soccer you can get the ball in your back half with no one really challenging you. In footy, you're challenged the whole time. There are random events happening all the time, and that means things change all the time.

I'm an uncomplicated footballer. I play on instinct and flair. I've occasionally copped criticism from the media because I'm a free-flowing sort of player, but I think the positives of that style for me have easily outweighed the negatives. If I had played a more defensive role I would have had to be more structured, so I think I've been lucky to have played most of my footy in midfield/forward roles.

I like to have a broad outline. We're going to move the ball through the middle. We're going to kick long. We're going to handball off the ground. We're going to stand 30 metres out from goal. I think that sort of game plan and guidelines are essential. But I baulk when coaches try to say, 'Right, when the full-back kicks to position X, we're going to run back, handball and switch the positions.' It's just over-complicating the game and taking the flair away from the player. Guys who have been playing footy long enough know how to direct the ball towards the goal.

There is a fair bit of luck in footy, too. Why go right instead of left? Why does the ball come out and go your way? It always fascinates me that when three or four guys go up for a mark in a pack and everyone's crumbing the ball, it goes to one side. To the champions like Nathan Buckley and Michael Voss, it's obvious where the ball is going; for some reason, others find it impossible to read where the ball is going. This is what differentiates champions from the average player. Is it luck or skill?

To me, it's about watching the direction of the player's hands. It's like throwing against a brick wall: if the hands are flat and pointing that way, there's nowhere else the ball can go.

Those great days when throughout the game you know where the ball is going and that you're going to get it – I'd love a few more of those before I retire.

If someone walked up to me and asked me how to get into the zone, I would look at them blankly and say, 'You and me both!' I would probably add that on the days I have felt the greatest on the field I haven't taken a magic potion, but I have had perfect faith in my preparation and training. I have never performed at my optimum level if I have felt that my preparation had holes in it. Sometimes you can prepare perfectly and perform badly, but I don't know too many people who have prepared badly and performed at their peak.

Being in the zone is not about purely relaxing or calming yourself, it's about comfortably achieving your ultimate goal. In his book *Good Business: Leadership, Flow and the Making of Meaning*, Mihaly Csikszentmihalyi describes being in a state of flow (or what we call 'the zone') as having eight characteristics:

1   Goals are clear.
2   Skills and challenges are high and equal.
3   Control is no problem.
4   Feedback is immediate.
5   Concentration deepens.
6   In the present.
7   Sense of time is altered.
8   Loss of ego.

On reflection, I've definitely felt all these things, but I haven't consciously been trying to achieve them.

Chapter 16

2003–05: Highs and Lows

In late May 2003, I experienced a familiar feeling: the one where your heart sinks into your shoes. It was a feeling I'd become used to with football. It was an injury feeling. I thought I'd had everything a footballer can get, from my head to my feet. But I had never had deep vein thrombosis. I suppose I shouldn't have been too surprised.

Let me backtrack a few weeks.

I was virtually injury-free and feeling pretty good. I was 30, and because 2002 had been such a disappointing year due to the facial injury, I was conscious that I had to make the most of my football. I didn't know how long I would play for – everyone says 30 is the magical number in a footballer's career, so I went out of my way to try to play my best pre-season in a long time.

I didn't have the greatest of starts. I was disappointed with the first five or six games, except the game against Collingwood on 25 April, when I won my second Anzac Day Medal. In hindsight, I think I had over-trained, because I was always tired during the games: I was struggling to run and to 'get up'; I was too often feeling heavy and lethargic. I questioned my diet and so started a new one, which involved eating and drinking a lot more before a game in the hope that I would have more energy in the second half. I also took a lot of Musashi products – amino acids (which enhance your recovery, your strength, and your speed) and protein powders.

Then, a week after the Anzac Day game, I got a knee in the calf from Richmond's Mark Chaffey. Initially I thought the calf was just bruised, but I couldn't get rid of the pain. When I had an MRI scan at Epworth Hospital they told me I had a blood clot and that it was serious. The amount of blood that had bled into the calf had caused the circumference of my calf to increase by 3–4 centimetres. I couldn't walk on it. It was excruciatingly sore and my calf felt as though it was about to burst. The doctors considered draining the blood from it, to release the pressure, but decided that that was impractical.

I was warned to be careful because if blood clots are dislodged, they can move into your brain and cause a stroke. This was around the time when everyone was talking about deep vein thrombosis (DVT) from flying. Steve Waugh had suffered one, so it was in the news. The doctors said I didn't have DVT, but rather a blood clot closer to the surface. I went on TV and said it was a deep vein thrombosis that wasn't deep. After all the time I'd spent in medical rooms I should have known better. Later, I watched myself on TV and thought, *That is the most stupid thing I've ever said.* Our fitness coach, John Quinn, agreed with that assessment, saying it was one of the more stupid things he'd heard.

Of course what the media picked up on was that I had DVT, and it turned into a circus. There were cameras everywhere. The media knew that if I had DVT I would have to take blood-thinning medication, and would probably miss the rest of the year. I had a further calf scan, and surprisingly, was told that the clot had gone. Either the first assessment was wrong or this one was. It was too small an amount of time for it to have simply disappeared. We went with the report of no clot. I was relieved – these freak injuries were becoming ridiculous. I went from missing the rest of the season, having missed 10 weeks the year before because of my facial injury, to my leg being just fine.

We organised a press conference and everyone was expecting me to confirm that I had DVT. There was a sense of occasion about it: *Not another serious injury to James Hird*, they must have been thinking. *And suffering a condition that's in the news – send the cameras!*

You know it's something serious when it's not just the sports journalists who turn up but the news journalists as well. There was a distinct look of disappointment on their faces when I announced that there was nothing wrong. It went from a lead story – a footballer getting DVT, he could die – to 'Footballer fine and playing next week'. The sports journalists were all happy for me and congratulated me on the result, but the news hounds frustratingly folded up their gear with body language that said, *What a waste of bloody time*. I still missed a week, because of soreness, but after all the drama that tends to accompany my injuries, I was relieved that this one had been an anticlimax.

The paramount rule in football is to never take anything for granted. If you find yourself playing with a great group, and you're successful, don't imagine it will go on and on. Essendon learned this the hard way after 2000. The football landscape changes quickly. In 2000 and 2001 we had a great list. And then, because of salary-cap pressures, we lost several key players . . . and we were back in the pack.

The first key departure was Damien Hardwick, who moved to Port Adelaide at the end of the 2001 season. Damien was a hard backman, a core player who was part of our leadership team. Then, at the end of 2002, we lost our next group of leaders: Blake Caracella, who was traded to Brisbane (and later moved to Collingwood); Chris Heffernan, who went to Melbourne; and Justin Blumfield, who joined Richmond.

Over the past two or three years, Lloydy and Scotty Lucas and a few others had been leaders, but we really missed that group. None of those three – Blake, Chris or Justin – really went on to take the game by the scruff of the neck at other clubs. I believe that it might have been different for them if they'd stayed at our club. I think being traded kicked the wind out of them. When you put passion and love into a club and you are traded, something has to change. If it were me, some of my desire for the game would disappear, and I think that might have happened to those three.

Justin's now out of the game. Caracella won a premiership with Brisbane, but he hasn't played the football he was playing at Essendon, and Heff has returned from Melbourne to Essendon. He enjoyed his time at Melbourne and made some good friends, but, although he hasn't said this, I don't think Melbourne was ever home. He knows we care for him and we want him. I hope that although it was Essendon who traded him, the scars will heal. We didn't want to trade any of them. They are good players and good people, but the salary cap meant someone had to go. It's a reality of football. We didn't have the 10 per cent extra in our salary cap that Sydney and Brisbane have. That 10 per cent is the difference between keeping – or not keeping – those players.

The innocence of football is belted out of you when you are traded like that.

In my opinion, organisations underestimate the importance of passion. When players leave one club and go to another, the new club sometimes doesn't get the whole player. If the passion and fire are not ignited by the new club, that part of the player can be lost – and believe me, that part is important.

After the frustrations of 2002 – my injury in Perth and the fact that we didn't assert ourselves in the finals – I wanted 2003 to be a great year. On Anzac Day I was happy to show the football world I was still at the top of my game. In the traditional 'block-buster' we beat Collingwood, in front of the usual huge crowd. I was very happy with my game, picking up 27 possessions, kicking five goals and winning my second Anzac Day Medal, as well as earning some praise from Sheeds, who described me as the most courageous player he'd seen: 'He's had a cracked foot, head broken and been crook [with the flu] for the past two weeks. He's a superstar. I would have loved to have played with him.'

Again, Anzac Day was a memorable day for me.

I was as keen to perform well as I'd ever been. As I've said, I was aware – and the newspapers certainly made me aware – of the significance of turning 30, which I'd done in February.

Sheeds was also pondering my future. In a newspaper article he was quoted as saying: 'The remainder of Hird's career is an issue requiring adroit handling. I think, sooner or later, we'll have to move him back like we did with Mark Harvey [he reinvented himself as a half-back in 1993], who was either getting injured or injuring his teammates. Eventually it will happen.'

Sheeds then wondered whether I should have a year off, as Tim Watson had after he'd retired (prematurely) in 1991: 'Watson retired at around 31 years of age and I always felt that we should have given him a year off and not delisted him. I wonder whether that time is coming for Hird. Maybe, maybe not, but Watson was very good for us when he came back.'

I couldn't see myself walking away for a year and then coming back. Besides, I still wanted to play footy.

As for Sheeds', suggestion that I be played on the backline, I think he was turned off that plan when I played on Lance Whitnall one day and Lance got about 30 possessions in 15 minutes (or so it seemed). I don't think Sheeds has made that suggestion since. In the last six years I think I've played down back about three times, and it always seems to have been on Lance. I think he just licks his lips every time I walk over to him to pick him up, because he always says: 'You know you're no good down here.' He's probably right there.

Despite my high hope for the year, by midway through 2003 it didn't look like we would be making the finals. We'd have to win a lot of footy to get there. The critics weren't confident either, especially after the DVT scare. After that incident, I think most people in football believed I was finished – and not for the first time either. That might explain why, in two games (against Geelong and St Kilda), the opposition left me to do what I liked, which hadn't happened for years. It was very unusual. Normally I am heavily tagged, but in these games I wasn't manned up on. I had a lot of latitude, and I was able to get under their guard.

I really should be grateful that the Cats and the Saints left me alone, because those games set my season up. We started winning the games we needed to, and I found some very good form. I had a stretch of 11 games that were of a very high standard.

We beat Fremantle when they were flying, and we beat Brisbane in Melbourne, which we hadn't done in five years. It felt good. Finally my body was doing what I wanted it to after a couple of years of inconsistency. I was playing a lot in the midfield and Sheeds had faith in me to run my own show. He said to me, 'Wherever you think the ball's going to go, go and get it.'

We won nine of those last 12 games, putting ourselves into the finals, finishing 8th at the end of the home and away season. It wasn't a great finish for the team, but personally some of my footy that year was the best I've ever played, probably comparable to my form in 1996.

I finished the year equal first – with Scott Lucas – in our club best and fairest. It was my fourth best and fairest at Essendon, which meant I was now equal third with Simon Madden and Tim Watson for the most best-and-fairest awards at the club. I was three votes away from winning the Brownlow Medal. I made the All Australian team, too – on the bench, which Sheeds wasn't happy about. 'If he's on the bench,' he snarled, 'it must be the greatest team ever picked.'

It again made me wonder why you play terrific football one week and not-so-good football the next.

In the finals, we played Fremantle in Perth and were expected to lose. I kicked three goals and had 28 possessions and we beat them by 44 points, which was very satisfying; we hadn't won over there for a long time.

I was very happy with my own game, as were the football writers.

Reviewing the win over the Dockers in the *Herald Sun*, Mark Robinson wrote that I was playing arguably the best football of my career, including 1996:

Inspiring. Relentless . . . His past six weeks have been magnificent, even by his stellar standards. His Brownlow Medal rush is not a joke. Conceivably he could have five best on grounds . . . Only Voss has the all-round game to match Hird. Buckley is

263

probably more precise, McLeod more flamboyant, but when it comes to providing the command performance, in a cut-throat final, on foreign turf, Hird stands a fraction taller.

The next week we played Port Adelaide in the first semi-final. Unlike the week before, when I did know I'd play well, this week I didn't know it was not going to be my night. It was a long way from a perfect performance.

I was well beaten by Port defender Stuart Cochrane. That meant it was two years in a row we'd lost to Port in the same final, and two years in a row I'd played pretty poorly in that match. It was frustrating, but that's the way it goes. We lost by 39 points. It was a crushing way to end what had been a great second half of the year. I think the season had caught up with me.

There is no question they were a good team – they were a bit unlucky not to make the Grand Final that year – but I felt sick at the end of the game. I'd had a good year, but we'd struggled in the finals. Personally, I had one really good final and one poor one. I wish the papers hadn't pumped me up after the Fremantle game, saying how good I was, because I think that made me more of a target. Brendan Lade gave me a beauty 10 minutes into the game – a knee right in the back, which hurt for the rest of the game. And Stuart Cochrane followed me all day, almost into the bathroom. He didn't worry about getting the ball himself, he just ran wherever I ran. He played a great game.

I am good friends with their coach, Mark Williams, but that didn't stop Chocko using every tactic available to him. I'm pretty sure he fired up the runner who came over to me, tormenting me with words. That was taking it a bit far, I thought: I felt like smacking that runner.

It was a frustrating year from the team's point of view; a good year, but not a great year. We had a reasonably good side, but we just fell short in the finals. Whenever we were put under real pressure, we faltered. That had been the story since 2001 – we hadn't been able to get any continuity. Injuries and a lack of consistent form had plagued us.

We went to Cancun in Mexico for the end-of-season trip. It is always good to wind down with the boys for a few days after we've all put in so much focused and serious effort during the season. It was a fun and relaxing trip, and it was great to be able to let our hair down, to not worry about what we ate or who was watching us, or have to train . . . or, in fact, do anything.

And no Stuart bloody Cochrane following me around.

Sometimes newspapers run lists of the injuries which have befallen me. Almost every inch of my body is represented. But until May 2004, my eyes have been standout exceptions.

At AAMI Stadium, playing Adelaide, I was marking late in the first quarter when the Crows' Tyson Stenglein accidentally poked me in the eye. I had my shot at goal, missed, then left the field. At half-time I was taken to hospital by ambulance. It turned out that I'd bled into the anterior chamber of the eye. This was a worry if the bleeding seeped into the pupil: it can cause you to lose your eye. I had to keep my blood pressure down, which meant not moving around too much, and drops were put in my eye to freeze it, which meant I couldn't see. I was immobilised, confined to the house for 10 days.

I recovered from the poked eye, but if you're me, you never take being fit and able-bodied for granted. As a teammate once said, it wouldn't be wise to stand next to me if there's lightning around. Who knew what wild injury rides were around the corner?

I didn't have to wait long to find out.

Two hundred games. Fourteen years. Boy, I'd taken my time to get there.

My 200th game was due to occur in July 2004 against Richmond. At a media conference I paid tribute to Tania, 'for moral and all sorts of support'. 'Along with my kids, my mum and dad, and Sheeds, she has been the one who has been there,' I added.

I was asked whether or not my father would be at the game. 'I hope so,' I said. I didn't know. I hadn't spoken to him since he'd visited me in Perth in May 2002. Maybe the media were fishing for some explanation of my relationship with Dad (which neither of us had spoken about in any detail). I found the fact that I didn't know whether or not he was going to be at the game probably as sad as the fact that the journalists asked me about it.

But here I was, at my own good-news story media conference. I'd made it – 200 games for the Essendon Football Club. I was truly proud to have reached this milestone.

I wanted to mark it with a genuine gesture of thanks to some fantastic people at Essendon who had helped me in so many ways. I've never been one for big parties. I like talking to people one on one. So rather than a big 'do', I decided that at the end of my 200th game I'd have a get-together specifically to thank the people at the footy club who are important to me, particularly the trainers and staff. These are the unsung, the ordinary heroes. They aren't written about in the papers, they don't make any money from their efforts, and they don't receive a lot of recognition.

One of the people at the club who has done a lot for me is former head trainer John Kilby. To say John is a club stalwart would be to understate the matter: he's been at the club for more than 45 years. He virtually grew up there. He's sensational. Charlie Italia is another Bomber veteran. Every year since I started Charlie has massaged me before the game. Charlie's the bank manager who drove me to see Tania when I asked her out the first time. He was also the first person who knew I was going to ask her to marry me, because my money was in an account at his bank and when I asked to withdraw most of it, he wanted to ensure it wouldn't be spent frivolously. An engagement ring for Tania got his approval.

There's Gary, who rubs me during the week – he won't let anyone else touch me. And there's Colin Hooper, who every night at training, rain, hail or shine, kicks the footy at me. He's always telling the young kids, 'If you want to be like Hirdy you've got to do this and this.' Now you see all the young kids out with Hoops kicking a footy.

They're all great people, and I wanted to get them together and thank them. I wanted to especially thank the people who are not paid employees of the club, the people who do it for love. I bought 45 bottles of Penfolds 407, signed and wrote a little message on each one, and planned to give them out after the game and say a few words.

The day started well. I ran through the banner with Stephanie, Thomas and Alexander, which was a great thrill for me and for them.

And then things went sour. Twenty minutes into the second quarter I leapt for a high ball and was crunched between Tiger defenders Ray Hall and Joel Bowden, with Lloydy in there some-where, too. I think Ray Hall's knee got me right in the middle of the back.

It wasn't what they first feared – another punctured lung – but I'd broken a rib, which had caused some bruising and bleeding at the base of the lungs. X-rays revealed that the bleeding had stopped and there had been no damage to internal organs.

'If anybody gets it, it seems to be him,' Sheeds told reporters. 'It is quite amazing. He has had just about everything now. You just wonder how he got to 200 games, this bloke.'

The boys rallied and won the game by 78 points, with Lloydy kicking nine goals.

I was in hospital for two days, and missed the opportunity to give out the wine. I later gave it to them individually, but I'd lost the moment a bit.

My teammates were not deterred – they went out to celebrate my 200th anyway. The only technical hitch was that I wasn't there. It was a party without the host. They videotaped the night for me and Sean Wellman put together a very funny DVD of the day. I was paying for the night, so they were drinking free beer, a point they made quite frequently and clearly on the tape. Solly came into the hospital with a couple of beers, which I appreciated. I have loved everyone I've played footy with, but some you form a special bond with, and Solly's one of those. I find it interesting that I often form these bonds with people who are very different from me, as Solly is.

We went on to make the final eight and played Melbourne in the elimination final at the MCG – we won in the last minutes, after an off-the-ground snap from David Hille. I played against Troy Broadbridge, who tragically died in the Boxing Day tsunami later that year. Troy's first game of AFL football had been against Essendon, and so was his last. (We played Melbourne again in Round 1 of 2005 and they came out very ferociously and completely beat us up. There is no doubt they were playing for Troy and they did him proud that day. We were upset about losing, but Melbourne had a much better reason to win.)

We lost to Geelong the following week.

The 2004 season ended the same way the last two had: in the second week of the finals, with a less than inspiring performance. It occurred to me after this game that an era had ended. We needed to stop preparing for tomorrow, and start investing in the long-term future of the club. Premiership and 200-game players

Mark Mercuri, Joe Misiti and Sean Wellman all retired at the end of that year, leaving me as the only one left who had played in the 1991 Essendon under-19 team and the 1992 reserves premiership team. It was a sign to me that my time was nearly up and that I needed to sort out a succession plan.

Succession planning is crucial in all organisations. Leaders who like to see the organisation collapsing after they leave are not true (or good) leaders. Leadership is about the organisation you lead, not your own ego.

At the end of the 2004 season I went to Ireland to play an International Rules Test series. Unfortunately, we lost both games. We copped a fair amount of criticism over those losses, the charge being that we didn't treat the matches as seriously as we could have. One Irish commentator said we were the worst Australian team that had come to Ireland to play International Rules. On our results, we might have been, but I didn't take too much notice of the bagging. The series is about playing football, but it's also about experience, and we had a terrific experience.

I think we treated the 2000 and the 2004 tours the same. In all fairness, the players we had in 2000 were a lot better than those in 2004. Garry Lyon did a very good job as coach in 2004, but the Irish took it a lot more seriously than we did. I think Garry would be a very good AFL coach. Unfortunately, the International Rules squad comes ready-made: no coach can do a lot in two weeks.

There was a drama during the trip that I could have averted. But these things happen.

One night before the first game I picked up the phone.

An Irish voice said: 'Is that James Hird?'

'Yes.'

'Well, you'll die out on the ground tomorrow. We'll make sure that happens.'

I didn't think too much about it, but I did mention it to a couple of teammates. Before the second game I received another call.

'You better look over your shoulder on the way to the game. We're going to kill you.' He said something about being lucky to walk off Croke Park without a bullet in my head.

Mark McVeigh, my Essendon teammate, who was sent off in the first game after an altercation with an Irish opponent, also received threatening calls. We didn't take them seriously.

I could have and should have kept the rather disturbing calls to myself, but at a press conference just before the second game I heard myself telling the world. It just slipped out of my mouth – a bit like the umpires comment. I had been asked how I was finding Ireland. 'Oh, it's great, fantastic,' I replied. 'The people are great – except for the bloke who rings in the middle of the night telling me he wants to kill me.'

Garry Lyon, our coach, was sitting next to me. He leaned over and whispered: 'You know you've just created one of the biggest international incidents in Australian–Irish history.'

We suddenly had reporters from all around the world wanting to talk to us about how the Irish were trying to shoot Australians. Until then the Irish media hadn't been paying much attention to us. We had a training session an hour and a half later and that night there were 20 cameras filming us.

Irish team manager Pete McGrath and captain Padraic Joyce apologised and described the threats as disgraceful.

In the end I was glad to get out of Ireland; the media had made it bigger than it should have been.

* * *

As a parent, you sometimes feel you have no control over the most important things. It's scary. For all the injuries I've had, the hardest times in my life have been when my kids have been seriously ill. One of them came just after the Ireland matches.

After the two Tests, Tania met me in France and we had a two-week holiday. One night Tania's mum rang and said Tommy, who was three, was really pale and, she thought, anaemic. We didn't worry about it, but when we got back home he was still very pale. I was worried because I'd read on the plane about three-year-old boys whose weight remains below a certain level: was it cancer? We took him straight to Bruce Reid, our club doctor. He confirmed that Tommy was anaemic.

Given that his iron and B1 levels were good, there were two possibilities. One was TEC, which is a viral complaint and nothing serious; it eventually rights itself when the body produces haemoglobin again. The other was leukaemia. We went straight to a specialist. I was expecting the worst, but Tania, who is much more positive than me about these things, suggested that we should remain optimistic until there was reason to be otherwise.

Tom had to have blood taken every two weeks to ensure he didn't need a tranfusion and to see if the issue would right itself. He was so brave. He'd say, 'Come on, Mum and Dad, time for my needle.' They'd whack the needle in, and he wouldn't cry. Within two months the anaemia cleared up, and there have been no further complications. Just another thing to shake our perspective, a reminder of how difficult things *can* get and how lucky we are.

The years 2002, 2003 and 2004 were, needless to say, disappointing years for me. We might not have been the best team, but we could have done better than we did. We didn't grasp the opportunities we had. If the players were being honest with themselves, they'd say we weren't where we could have been. We wasted time in those years.

The 2005 season was the one we had to have. We finished 13th, the lowest finish since I'd been at the club, and the only time since I was captain that we didn't make the finals. To have that pattern broken under my watch was very disappointing for me. We tried to top up our list with guys from other clubs, but eventually we had to bite the bullet and admit that we deserved to finish where we did – we just didn't have the talent out on the park. We had young guys coming through, and no consistency in the second half of our games.

Essendon has done very well to play in the finals so often. But when you're rebuilding, you have to pay a price. I was hoping the price had now been paid. The fact that during my captaincy, the side had always made the finals, was something I'd been very proud of. It was upsetting to concede that record. Personally, my footy was all over the place. I didn't play at the level I require of myself.

In some ways 2005 was the most disappointing year I've had as a footballer. Physically I was all there, but mentally I lost my way a bit. I talk a lot about passion and gut feeling and instinct, but in 2005 I somehow forgot my own rules and tried to think about the way I was playing too much – I lost my instinct. I was also frustrated by the lack of ability in the team. I'd been part of a good team for 10 years at Essendon and this wasn't a good team. It was an up-and-coming team with flashes of brilliance, but not a group that was able to put it all together.

There was a big exit from the club at the end of the year. We delisted eight players: Damien Cupido, Mark Bullen, Ben Haynes, Justin Murphy, Mark Alvey, Sam Hunt, Paul Thomas and Ty Zantuck. We traded Ted Richards to Sydney and Matthew Allan and Justin Murphy retired. Basically, we decided to start again.

We made a decision to go back to Kevin Sheedy's plan and promote youth.

In 2005 we were only slightly above mediocrity, but not much. To blame the guys we cleared would be totally wrong. It wasn't about them; it was about having the space to give young blokes an opportunity. To do that you have to make room on the list. You can't say that Sheeds doesn't give players an opportunity. There might be one or two who can say that over the years, but not many. All players are given a go – but you're out if you're not good enough or if your attitude isn't what it should be.

The traditional line of thinking in sport is that inspiration comes from the senior members of the team. This is often true, but the older members of the team need inspiration too. A lot of my inspiration has been derived from the free-and-easy way the young guys play. For example, watching Andrew Lovett win the 2005 Anzac Day Medal was inspiring, because it reminded me what playing with no inhibitions can achieve.

Youth's innocence and simplicity should be a reminder to all of us that over-complicating life with agendas and rules can restrict us and prevent us reaching our true potential. I love playing in a young, free team unburdened by rules – provided that there is one spot left for the old guy!

Finally, how do you know if someone is up to the task if you don't give them the opportunity to try? Without taking a chance on young players, a football team can't regenerate; equally, society can't grow unless we let ourselves be inspired by new and fresh ideas.

I came out of season 2005 on the Sunday, had 'Mad Monday' with the boys – the annual letting down of the hair at season's end – and started training on Tuesday. I had one day off. I climbed back to being as fit as I'd ever been. This game is turning into a running game: if you can't run, you won't keep up. I got caught out a bit with that in 2005, so I wanted to improve.

I realised 2006 might be my last year. I was determined that if I had a bad year, it wouldn't be because I didn't work hard enough. It would be because I was no longer good enough, or because my body couldn't keep up. Older players tend to get complacent and lazy, and I was determined that that would not happen to me.

I had a great pre-season, most of it training by myself – I was ordered away from the club by Sheeds. I felt inspired, excited. And, at 33 years old, I felt I still had some great football left in me.

The clock was ticking. I would not take 2006 for granted.

Chapter 17

A Career off the Field

My grandfather, Allan T. Hird, can be gruff, but he is a genuine and loving man who has always cared about all aspects of my life. I have always been close to him.

There are people at Essendon who are still scared to speak about him – I think he went through a few people when he was president of the club, a position he held for five years. I suspect he was not particularly diplomatic and liked things to be done his way. His reputation still causes people to shudder.

Allan worked as a senior adviser in the Education Department in the 1980s. When we visited him in Melbourne as kids, he had his own driver, which really impressed me. I thought he must be important.

My grandfather has taught me a lot about footy and life. The biggest 'bee' in his bonnet was about paying too much attention to sport and not enough to study. It seemed to work.

After I finished Year 12 in 1990 I began a civil engineering course at RMIT in Melbourne. I was fairly apathetic about study; I would probably have given it up if it weren't for Mum, Dad and my grandfather. They were continually in my ear about it, especially after I failed numerous subjects in my first two years. After those first couple of years I worked out how to balance professional football and study, and I graduated with honours in 1996. But to me, uni was a means to an end, not a passion: never in my wildest dreams or nightmares did I imagine becoming a civil engineer. I hoped that having a degree would give me credibility, and would be a sign to future employers that I had some academic intelligence and the ability to follow things through.

I made great sacrifices to complete my study while playing football: the greatest were a social life and sleep. While most of the boys were out tearing up the town, I was seen (in my younger years) as something of a recluse because of my study commitments. The fact that I completed my degree still amazes me – I often wonder how I managed to pass subjects that relate to building roads, gravel composites and basic physics. But I did, and it has indeed given me extra self-confidence in situations where I might otherwise have doubted myself or felt intimidated. I can reach down into my bag, dust off my degree and feel at home amongst a very eclectic group of people.

My grandfather Allan cared about all aspects of my life. When I was living in Canberra, we would often visit him at his farm in Romsey or his house in Melbourne. If my footy was going well, he would ask about my studies – how were they were going? Was I studying hard enough? When my studies were going well, the questions would revolve around footy. In 1996 I finished my engineering degree and won the Brownlow Medal. It had clearly been a great year. His perspective was: 'Have you got a job yet? What are you doing about a job?'

He taught me on a different level from my parents. Like any other 19- or 20-year-old who has left home, there was a time when I was less than receptive to my parents' advice – but I would still listen to Allan. He could say things which, if my father had said them, would have led to an argument.

When I moved down south and my parents were still in Canberra, he would come to every AFL game I played in Melbourne and take my stats. Afterwards he'd ring me up and we'd talk about them.

He has a very strong personality and is always supportive. At one time I was playing for the Essendon reserves at the Junction Oval and Denis Pagan was coaching us. After every game, Denis would give each player a summary of how he'd played. It was really good to get some feedback. When my turn came, Denis told me that I had played okay, but I hadn't run hard enough – that I could have done a lot better. No sooner had he said that than over the back of all heads came my grandfather's voice: 'You must have been at a different bloody game than I was!' He wasn't backward in coming forward.

My grandfather is 86 now and lives in a home in Sunbury. He's suffering from dementia, but still seems to find some joy in life, and we still sometimes see glimmers of his old spark. I visit him as often as I can, and am really pleased that Stephanie, Tom and Alexander have had the chance to know him.

I was lucky to have a grandfather who gave me such attention and care. His expectations helped me to make sure that I worked on all aspects of my life. I have always believed strongly in having a career away from football: not just to get away from that often protected and isolated world, but to foster essential skills for the inevitable day when my boots are hung up.

There is big money in football. But the big money has a downside: it can insulate players against feeling the need to explore and invest in a career after football, and it can rob them of opportunities to become self-reliant. If you're 24 and making $250,000 a year, people do things for you. Things that maybe you should be doing for yourself. It's something I think all young players should be aware of.

I strongly believe that players benefit greatly from having a life outside football, whether it's a job, study or just other interests; having a balanced life actually strengthens your ability to focus and freshens your approach to your footy. I don't believe anyone should think about football 100 per cent of the time, and that's what will happen if you don't do anything else.

Throughout my time in footy I've always been one of the hardest trainers. I've put in as much work as the other players, if not more, and yet have also had other interests. Sometimes I have taken on too much. I look back on certain years and reflect that maybe it did affect my footy a little. But I still believe that overall, keeping balanced has made me a better footy player.

Some people seem to think that to be a 'professional' AFL player you have to spend 12 hours at the club every day. This would mean stretching out sessions or coming in four times a day. I don't believe that's what 'professionalism' is about, or that those sort of inefficiencies help anyone. To me, 'professional' means finding your optimal level of training, and your optimal lifestyle; together, these will make you the best player you can be. What is optimal will be different for every person, but it's certainly not optimal for anyone to spend six or eight hours a day, every day, on the sport. The meaning of 'optimal' includes efficiency – get in, do your work, do your recovery, see your physio and then get out and do something where your brain switches off from footy. As psychologists will tell you, if your brain's working on the same thing 24 hours a day, seven days a week, you're going to get mentally stale pretty quickly.

Of course it's important to get fit, stay fit and to get your skills right, but it is also crucial to stay mentally fresh, because it's a long season. We start training in November and the season finishes at the end of September, if we're successful. Someone who is mentally stale by June can't put in the work he needs to, and won't be playing as well as he can for the rest of the season.

The Players' Association, the AFL and the clubs try to encourage players to pursue other interests, such as university courses. The Players' Association has spent a lot of money on educating kids about job paths. I think the message is getting through, but it's getting through slowly.

The challenge is to stop players retiring from footy at 28 with no other life skills. This can lead to all sorts of problems, including drug use. Your life shouldn't be at its peak when you're 28; it should keep getting better. I'm not talking about finances either. I'm talking about keeping your brain working during and after you stop playing footy, and ensuring that your feelings of self-worth don't drop drastically when you stop. I worry about the guy who finishes playing at 28 and feels that there is nothing for him. His footy's gone, he can't get a job, he has no skills outside football. Most importantly he may not have developed the very important skill of being able to work hard in situations other than footy. Knuckling down and working hard at things, even if they're not always interesting, is part of life, and it is a vital lesson.

Players today are on good money, and only have to train a couple of times a day. If they want to, they can go and have coffee the rest of the time. Everything's done for them until they retire. You turn up at the club and everything's washed, your locker has been cleaned, your boots are cleaned and the fruit is all cut up. All you have to do is put on your gear and run out. Some players might say, 'It has to be – because if it's not, I won't perform at my optimum level.' As a result, when they do retire, they don't understand how the world operates. I don't think it would hurt them once in a while to tidy their own locker or pour their own drink.

Essendon encourages all their guys to get out and do something: a job or study. During pre-season, combining these is difficult because of the demands of training, but I think it imposes healthy levels of responsibility on players. I've had disagreements with a number of people at the club who have the attitude that 'We pay them a lot of money, so we're going to have them here at the club as long as we want.' My argument is 'Yes, you pay them a lot of money, but don't you want them performing at an optimum level?' There is certainly the expectation during working hours that the players work for the club full-time, so they have to do whatever the club says. I suppose that's true, but if the club wants the boys to play the best footy they can play, a balance must be found.

Marketing departments and sponsorship departments, are always going to be at odds with players, because marketing and sponsorship departments are trying to accumulate money. They have to find revenue for the club . . . and let's face it, a lot of that money goes to pay the players. But the players are saying, 'Hang on, you can't have us out at 11 o'clock the night before a game, because if we play terribly you're the one who's going to be kicking us up the backside!' I would further say that if we're doing sponsorship things all the time and training all the time, how can we develop ourselves so that after footy we're not used commodities that no one wants?

I've also had disagreements with the club about how many sponsor functions we do. When I was captain I had a reputation for saying we were doing too many. I suppose I did whinge a bit about them, and I think I annoyed the club occasionally, but I felt that every time we did sponsor functions the day before a game it had the potential to affect the way we played. And our core business is to win games of footy. If we don't win, few companies will sponsor us anyway. The club had a totally different view on that and I hope a rational model can be worked out. There's definitely work to be done there.

When I left school I didn't know what I wanted to do. Dad suggested engineering. He thought it would be a good base degree, and would give me opportunities to work outside, which I like. It did appeal to me. I wasn't passionate about anything in particular at school, except perhaps history, but given my English skills, I thought engineering was a safer option.

I had a terrible first two years at uni. I failed six of my 12 subjects the first year and five the next year, but then I warmed to it, and after six years I ended up with an honours degree. I met some really good people doing the course who gave me some help. We encouraged each other. One of the guys, Sean Pinan, ended up living with me, which was great, because anything I didn't understand I could ask him about. I hope I helped him too.

I wasn't treated any differently because of my football; I needed the help of my uni partners more than they needed mine. I certainly learned that there are situations in life where footy doesn't help.

In 1996 I was at my busiest: frantic football and full-on study. Some people say you can't do both, but I have always subscribed to the adage that 'Busy people get more done'. Certainly it was a juggle, and there were pressures, but I felt able to handle them. It was the year I enjoyed the most socially; it was also the year I studied the hardest and played my best footy. It all just seemed to click. My grandfather was very pleased.

Still, there was one problem. I didn't want to be a civil engineer. I'd finished the degree, but I felt like a guy who'd read a lot of books about engineering and yet didn't really understand the process. I know a lot of uni students feel that way: they come out of uni and don't understand how they are going to apply their knowledge. I was fascinated by how buildings are built, but the reality of being part of it didn't excite me. Tania was finishing her law degree at the same time. She had a path and would go on to do articles. I was looking for one: something where I could learn a process.

I was interested in trying a media career, because I had strong views on the game, and thought it would be exciting, and good experience, to articulate those on radio or TV. But my media career had some teething problems.

To tell the story, I have to go back to the beginning of that career. In 1994 I was living in a house in Parkville owned by Mum and Dad. They'd bought an investment house that I could live in, which was good of them. I lived with Alister Carr, who used to play for Essendon and was best man at my wedding, and a friend named John Garnaut, a mate from Canberra who was at uni in Melbourne. As a footballer you can't afford to be too wild, but we did have some big parties.

Uni social life doesn't help much with football. I went to some Thursday night balls when I had to play on a Saturday. One was the Law Ball, which I went to with Tania . . . and stayed until 3 in the morning. My manager at the time had organised for me to have my first interview with 3AW the next morning, doing some commentary on the finals. Unfortunately, I stayed at Tania's house and forgot all about it. He was expecting me to be at my house, and had to drive around Melbourne looking for me. Here was my big chance to get into the media and I arrived half an hour late to meet Shane Healy, the CEO of the station. I played the next day – and played okay. Back then, you could get away with that, but if one of the younger kids did that today, I'd be shocked at the lack of professionalism.

Now, back to the end of 1996 and of my studying. In 1997 I got a job with Ansett. It was the first time I felt excited about a job.

Ansett had a graduate program through which they recruited eight students to work in different parts of the company. I loved the idea that I would learn how to run a business. I hadn't come from a business family, so I lacked some knowledge in this area.

My first rotation was Airport Operations, which meant learning how to run an airport, from the ramp, which encompasses the cleaning of aeroplanes, the loading and unloading of bags, and all other tarmac-based airport operations, through to customer service and check-in. I then went to Ansett International for about six months. Rod Eddington took over Ansett when I was there. He later went to British Airways, where he was CEO from 2000 to 2005. It was interesting to learn from someone as senior and professional as Rod.

I enjoyed my time at Ansett, but the pressure of working there and playing football became too much. One Sunday night after I played Geelong, I flew to Japan to study Osaka Airport, got back in for Tuesday morning training, then went to Sydney on Wednesday morning; I was back by Wednesday afternoon for training, after which I flew to Sydney again. I was pushing myself too hard. It was no wonder I had injuries throughout that year.

I then realised I couldn't have a full-time job. Football had changed in the space of two years from a part-time obsession to a full-time commitment. Trying to fit too much in eventually wore me down. I always thought playing footy was hard, but it's easier than going to work. When guys complain about training being too hard, I think, *What would you prefer: to be sitting in an office, standing on a roof in 40-degree heat, or running around kicking a footy?*

I needed to rethink my career off the field. I was still under contract with Channel 9 when Channel 7 asked me whether I was interested in an internship. This meant that under the auspices of various senior people, I would learn the television business behind the scenes; I would also appear on air for them about football issues. It was fewer hours than I was doing at Ansett and would develop my media experience, so I accepted.

I worked my way through Channel 7's sales, sports and strategy departments, which was fantastic. I learned a hell of a lot about how TV stations are run. Channel 7 was great for me. Gordon Bennett, the head of sport, was very supportive, as were Susan Wood, the head of publicity, and Michael Harms, the head of sales. And Kerry Stokes, the owner of the network, would sometimes come and chat.

But it was difficult to develop any long-term mentoring relationships because I was continually moved around. I spent three years there and met a lot of good people. I now know how a sales department for a TV company is run, how the strategy side of the company operates and how the programming works.

There was one snag. The station wanted me to appear on a new show called *Live and Kicking*, which was supposed to challenge *The Footy Show*. It wouldn't go head to head, but would run on Wednesday, the night before *The Footy Show*. It was an attempt to trump them.

Harvey Silver, the original producer of *The Footy Show* and the person often credited with being the brains behind it, joined *Live and Kicking*. Jason Dunstall was the host, and the panellists included Doug Hawkins, another ex-Channel 9 employee, and Paul Couch from Geelong. I think Jason is a very good media talent and did a pretty good job – for a guy who was still playing footy at the time. To be hosting his own TV show without having had any media training was impressive.

It seemed like a good fit for me: I'd had some experience on *The Footy Show*, I was employed by Channel 7, it wasn't too time-consuming, and all I had to do was talk about football.

Or so I thought.

The show was disappointing, and not a success commercially. There had always been a nervousness at Channel 7 about how well *The Footy Show* had performed on Channel 9 even without the ability to use any footage from games. *Live and Kicking* was an attempt to try to build a show which was a similar mix of serious football talk and vaudeville, but with football footage thrown in. The trick was to get the mix right.

For me, what sounded like a good idea at the time went horribly wrong. As mentioned previously, I found myself doing things I felt uncomfortable about at the time (and regret now), such as dressing up in women's clothing, wearing funny suits and cracking gags. I was criticised for it, and fair enough. Untrained footy players doing vaudeville acts is not funny. I told the producers I wasn't comfortable doing those things, but they insisted. My discomfort became more and more obvious. I felt like a fraud.

I don't think Channel 7 realised how central Eddie, Sam and Trevor were to the success of *The Footy Show*. The ingredients, the mix and the tone all needed to be right, and *Live and Kicking* didn't seem able to achieve it.

In the show's second year I went part-time. Susan Wood, the network's publicity chief, was a big support for me. She could tell I was uncomfortable, and in the end she helped me to get off the program, for which I was grateful. I left *Live and Kicking* in 1998, when I was midway through my three-year contract with Channel 7. In 1999 Dermott Brereton took over the show.

Spending time in management at Channel 7 had fascinated me. If I were given the choice of working on-air or off-air, I would take the off-air role every time. Not because I get nervous or don't enjoy the bright lights, but because what you see on-air is just the tip of the iceberg. The strategy behind a successful TV station is incredible. It is like most other companies, but it just happens to be more high profile than your local widget factory.

In my view, the job of management is to create an environment that enables highly talented people to create or buy the best possible TV shows for a given budget. This environment must stimulate great ideas – the ones that in hindsight are brilliantly simple, but work. It is then up to a highly motivated programmer to put those shows into the best time slots. The environment has to encourage the salespeople to generate the greatest revenue possible from those shows. The station that does this the best wins the ratings and revenue war. The common theme, to me, is highly motivated and competent people. Like a footy team, the focus must be on the common goal and creating an environment that will get the most out of the best team.

In 2001 I didn't have a television contract. Late that year I received a call from Eddie McGuire. He wanted to know if I would be interested in returning to Channel 9. I felt lucky to be asked, and said yes. After all, not many of the players who went from Channel 9 to Channel 7 were able to go back the other way.

Channel 9 had got back the AFL football broadcast rights and there was a real vibe there. They were starting to sign people up. I joined a Channel 9 team again, doing pretty much whatever they wanted me to do on-air around football.

After I left Channnel 7 I still wanted to work in a profession. I didn't want to be just a footballer or a media contributor. I enjoyed my on-air media roles, but I wanted to be involved in the strategy side of a business. A friend of mine, David Evans, the managing director of stockbroking firm J.B. Were's retail division, called me one day in 2000. 'I know you're going to leave Channel 7,' he said. 'Do you want to have a crack at stockbroking?' I told him I knew nothing about stockbroking, but he said they would train me.

It was the beginning of a three-year stockbroking career.

In the mid 1990s I'd been a regular program commentator for radio 3AW. Rod Law was one of the producers there and we'd become very good friends. In December 2000, with Rod's encouragement, I joined Were's as a private client adviser specialising in sports and media. I was working alongside Rod, who had left the Seven Network in September 2000. Under the guidance of David Evans, our role would be to fill a gap in the marketplace for significant but short-term earners looking for long-term stability.

We soon developed a small client base, including a few Essendon footballers. I enjoyed it, but not the selling side. I liked the strategy aspect, thinking about which industries were going to be the best, where the best buys would arise, which companies would grow the best, where the best value was – helping people. I am not good at the hard sell when I don't fully believe in what I'm selling, and people could tell when that was the case. In the stockmarket, while there are a lot of stocks you can fully believe in, there are some that you can't be sure about. I would be on the phone and say, 'Everyone says it's good, but I have some doubts.' Giving out that kind of message too often became a problem.

In the beginning, I spoke to some teammates about stocks, but I turned out not to be much use to them because I was too defensive. They would ask about a stock, and if there was any chance of it going down I'd discourage them: I knew I had to see these guys every day for the next two years. They were prepared to take the risk, but I couldn't do it, so I ended up putting them in no-risk managed funds returning 7 per cent. It was like dealing with your family. The advice I gave them meant they wouldn't lose money – but they wouldn't make the big dollars either.

I was being too guarded. Most people put money into the stockmarket knowing there's a risk they might lose it; they are happy to take that risk. But I didn't want my teammates to be able to say, 'He's lost me money.' I didn't want to lose credibility among my teammates over a non-football issue. Neither did I want to go to training and talk about how their shares were going instead of tactics and footy.

In the end, Rod and I made a policy that we wouldn't advise family or really good friends.

The time commitment issue also arose. My football commitments, combined with work at Were's, were crunching me. We'd have a morning meeting at Were's at 7.30 am, and you were supposed to be at your desk from then until noon. After that you could take a couple of hours off, provided you returned for the last couple of hours of the market. My football commitments meant I was at Were's at exactly the wrong hours. I could get there at 11 am, but I had to leave again at 3 pm, so I'd miss the planning meeting as well as the opening of the market, after which discussion was needed. Clients would want to speak to you after closing, when I was always at training, off-line. Stockbroking is very much a personal-relationship job. You have to be accessible by phone to people 12 hours a day. At training, the minute you walk in, phones are switched off. If you walk in there at 1 pm and you leave at 7 pm, that's six hours your clients can't contact you – it's not the best thing for them.

It just wasn't working.

Rod Law and I were a good team and he would cover for me, but in the end, he was doing 90 per cent of the work and it wasn't fair on him. I also felt that most people at Were's were thinking, *What's his value? He's just swanning in and spending an hour or two and then swanning out*. It wasn't said to me, but I got that feeling. David Evans made it quite clear to me that that wasn't the case. Were's were very good to offer me a job, but in my assessment, I couldn't deliver what they wanted.

In 2000, at the Sydney Olympics, I briefly met Ben Crowe, a sports marketer. I didn't know it that night, but Ben would change my professional life. I had been feeling that I needed change, both in my career outside football and in my management. I needed to look at my career in a broader way. I was being managed by Ricky Nixon's Flying Start agency, which had quite a few of the top AFL players on its list, including Wayne Carey and Anthony Koutoufides. In 1995 Flying Start set up Club 10, where 10 of the game's top players, which then included Gary Ablett, Wayne Carey, Gavin Wanganeen, Garry Lyon, Stuart Loewe, Glen Jakovich, Tony Modra, Gavin Brown, Jason Dunstall and me, were marketed as such.

After weeks of agonising, I decided to change my management group and make a break with Ricky. At the suggestion of Rod Law, I approached Ben. He agreed to manage me, and he has since the end of 2000. It is the best move I've made outside of football. Ben has taught me a great deal about ensuring direction in my life, understanding the business of sport and marketing; and has become a good friend as well.

In 2004 Ben invited me to become an equity partner in his business, Gemba (formerly CroweLovett). It had been set up by Ben and former Melbourne footballer Glenn Lovett as a management consultancy firm specialising in sports media and entertainment.

Before I met him, Ben had spent five years in Hong Kong as director of sports marketing for Nike Asia Pacific, and had also been marketing manager for the Hong Kong Jockey Club. At Nike International, he worked with some of the world's biggest athletes – including Michael Jordan, Tiger Woods, Cathy Freeman, Steve Moneghetti, Pete Sampras, Andre Agassi and Shane Warne. He and his wife Sally wanted to move back to Australia to raise their two children (they now have three), so they came back to Melbourne and he set up his own company.

The company is a consultancy, created to help other companies do things better in the entertainment and advertising industry. Companies that operate in highly creative fields (music, film and sport, for instance) struggle with how to get big without losing the intuitive 'just do it' spirit that made them great in the first place. This yin and yang relationship between analysis and creativity is a balancing act: 49 per cent process and 51 per cent gut instinct, in my view. Consultancies that have empathy for this must be pretty rare, because Gemba has grown a lot in four years: we now have 21 staff and clients all over the world, including Manchester United, Foster's, Toyota, Coca-Cola and Quiksilver.

At the end of December 2005, Glenn Lovett left the company. The partners then were Ben, Rob Mills, the former marketing director of Adidas Australia, who obviously has some pretty good sports marketing knowledge, and me. I'm as full-time as footy allows. If I'm not at the footy club, I'm at work. I love it.

We help companies who operate in or sponsor sport with their business planning and strategies, and we're an eclectic mix of highly intelligent consultants and creative marketing die-hards. It's a challenging but very rewarding job, and with Ben's guidance I'm making good headway in the field. It's almost a university of life, because while you help companies do things better, you also learn, about business strategy and about people and relationships. It's the greatest environment for learning in, and our huge results with clients prove to me that our formula works.

In some ways my name has helped in the business, although in others it hinders, too. It certainly opens doors. But some people have preconceived ideas about footballers. They see us as having limited knowledge of the world outside football. So while my name sometimes gets me in the door more easily, the first few meetings are often harder than they are for other people. Still, provided I deliver, I do pretty well.

Ben is, in my opinion, the best sports marketer in Australia by a mile. His 17 years of working all over the world have given him great insights. His ability to capture people's imagination and take them on a journey is exceptional, as good as I've seen in business anywhere. He's also been a strong personal support, and is a fun person to be around.

In 1995 I wrote a regular column for *The Age* on the world of AFL football. In 1997, Steve Harris, now the CEO of the Melbourne Football Club and then publisher of the *Herald Sun*, rang and asked whether I'd like to join the *Herald Sun* as a columnist. I wasn't unhappy at *The Age*, and they had been good to me, but Steve said he'd double the pay. I said yes.

Writing about football while still being a player is an interesting and occasionally difficult experience. I haven't always been comfortable making comments and judgments. As a player, I have always been anxious about whether what I write in my column will affect my performance – or help the opposition. And of course I don't want to bag the industry I'm a part of and work in every day. So in a way it's a compromised position.

It's not worth it for me to go out and absolutely can an opponent or the AFL. The AFL is my boss, when it comes down to it. I've written strong columns on Telstra Dome – how the surface wasn't great, how all the players would slip on it, that there needed to be something done because players were at risk of injury – and it caused me grief. It's the same with *The Footy Show*. I'm not going to delve into the weaknesses of another footy club.

I have a great deal of respect for a lot of journalists. They have to write every day, whether there's a story or not. Now and again they write absolute crap, but I feel for them; they have to fill the paper. The coverage of football has just exploded in recent years. It used to be match reports, injuries and controversial comments. Now it's everything – from football club politics to player misdemeanours, intelligent analysis of the game, and even poetic, almost romantic interpretations of the game by writers such as Martin Flanagan. I like Martin's work, and I know most players do too, because it comes from a different perspective.

There is also room for the ones who like to be controversial, such as Patrick Smith of *The Australian*. Patrick writes strongly and without fear. He cops a hiding from players, but everyone reads what he writes and talks about it. Caroline Wilson at *The Age* is similar. Her articles are not going to win her too many friends either.

The current media saturation of the game has positive and negative effects. There is no doubt that the media environment has played a huge role in there being so much more money in the game. This increase in funding has benefited everyone, from grass-roots footballers to superstars, and to the football-mad supporter too. On the negative side, the average football follower has lost some access to the game. Playing in super-stadiums rather than suburban grounds, and scheduling games to suit TV, has led to everything having a more corporate feel. And come July–August, the blanket coverage can be too much.

For the players, the doubling of salaries in the last five years is counterbalanced by greatly reduced privacy. It may not always feel like a change for the better. For one thing, the increase in media attention means there are more reports on your playing. It's interesting reading match reports, especially of games you've played in. Some reporters seem to have no idea what happened. I find it hard to read these reports because they rarely catch the ebbs and flows and the overall context. What also strikes me about them is that you are either a hero or a villain – there's not a lot in between. Obviously, 'James Hird was okay today' doesn't make much of a headline. We all take what's written in the media with a grain of salt. I would say 85 per cent of the journos are on the mark and do a very good job; 15 per cent either sensationalise things or just keep pushing their own agendas.

I do quite a lot of public speaking. I try to say what is in my head and not dress it up too much. I don't want to preach to people or obviously teach them lessons.

I've worked in a few businesses, so I can see how footy relates to business. A footy club is a microcosm of life. I like to use life examples and footy examples. I have lots of stories about real-life footy situations that are not common knowledge, and people find them fascinating. They are not about the day Matthew Lloyd kicked 10 goals; everyone knows that kind of story. I tell stories that surprise people. The one I love telling most relates to when leaders show compassion and care. For example, when Sheeds turned up at Stephanie's hospital bed on the night before our preliminary final, he showed little interest in whether I played the next day or not; his only concern was for my daughter.

Business audiences are interested in how my experience as the captain of a football team might relate to their worlds. There are 42 players at the club. As captain, I could not treat player 1 the same as player 42, because they are different people, with different needs and different strengths and weaknesses. Everyone understands that. The question is how do you manage different people efficiently? There is so much competition in business these days that if your people aren't happy, and don't feel cared about individually, they won't work 100 per cent for you – and you won't have them for very long.

I have also been able to attach my name to some products, but I've only endorsed products I believe are good, like those of Zegna and Nike. I've been with Nike for seven years now. I wear their clothes and boots, attend functions, and I've been in commercials for them. Before them, I was sponsored by Reebok for five years. However, after I broke my foot I couldn't find a Reebok boot which suited my foot, so they decided they didn't want to sponsor me anymore, which was fair enough. A friend of mine knew a rep at Nike, Paul Crowe, who gave me a pair of boots. I signed with them soon after. I can understand that boot companies wouldn't like anyone breaking a foot in their boots. Nike took a risk when no one else would and it's been a good relationship.

I've had associations with Weet-Bix (Sanitarium), which I've eaten all my life. It's all Mum and Dad would give me, so that was a no-brainer. I did the ads with Brett Lee, one of the Australian cricket team's fast bowlers, and George Gregan, the captain of the Australian rugby union side. I'd played cricket with George as a kid in Canberra, and he used to be a gun fast bowler.

My sponsorships and endorsements started more modestly. My first was from Essendon Mazda, and it was in my second year of playing. There was no money involved; they just lent me a car for a while. It mightn't sound like a big deal now, but I was driving a brown 1987 Mazda 626 at the time, so I was very happy to be able to at least temporarily upgrade to a blue MX6. For a 20-year-old, it felt like a pretty good deal.

An early TV ad I remember doing – but I don't expect anyone to remember seeing it! – was one that appeared on late-night television in 1997. It was for windscreen wipers. My partner in this venture was Kangaroos captain Wayne Carey. Wayne and I had to stand in the MCG car park, with the stadium in the background, holding up some windscreen wipers. I'm not sure I was ever up late enough to see the ad. But some of those windscreen wipers would have come in handy on the family Holden that day when we drove down to the MCG in the rain, with Dad and his towel acting as a human windscreen wiper!

I was part of the 'Oh what a feeling' Toyota ads when they did a series on great moments of football. The strategy for this ad campaign was written by Ben Crowe and Glenn Lovett, and the ads were conceived by Mojo, and they have been very successful, mostly because they are so simple and funny. And they are talked about. There are plans for more 'great moment' ads. For my ad, they chose the game just after the umpires saga – where I kicked what turned out to be the winning goal against the Eagles and then spontaneously hugged an Essendon supporter sitting in the front row. Instead of Telstra Dome, where the game had actually taken place, we re-created the goal on a windswept oval in Heidelberg, and this time, when I kicked it through I ran up and hugged a slightly startled groundsman.

They were very funny ads. Wayne Harmes recreated his lunge into a wet forward pocket in the 1979 Grand Final, which in real life led to a classic goal for Ken Sheldon. It became known as 'Harmes's punch'. For the 'lunge', they used a wet bit of plastic which Wayne slid across.

Dermott Brereton's ad was special. It recreated the moments after Dermie was pole-axed by Geelong's Mark Yeates in the 1989 Grand Final (two broken ribs were the result): he vomited, but played on. In the re-creation, one of the guys whacked

Dermott with a piece of 'wood', and slow-mo was used to dramatic effect. There is a little bit of ham in all of us, but more in Dermott than most.

I have learned a lot in my footy career that I have taken into my business life. But I have also learned a lot from business which I have used in football. The most important thing has been perspective: there is life outside footy. I treasure my footy world at Essendon, but playing the game is only one part of life. This is an important message for footy players to understand.

BEN CROWE ON JAMES

James Hird is smart, a footy legend, a successful businessman, a great family man and, allegedly, a good-looking bloke. This makes him an all-round absolute pain in the arse as a client, a business partner and a friend. The good news is that he can't sing or surf, and he has big ears. That's probably the extent to which I can bag him! When we first started working together I used to joke that it felt as if he was managing me sometimes, such was his ability to ring me for advice but end up advising me on issues of life and business.

One of the first things I noticed about James was that he licked his hands before a key play. The only other athlete I have ever seen do this was Michael Jordan. It's purely an instinctive thing, but whenever Jordan did it, I used to watch intently to see what happened next. Sometimes – though not always – Jordan produced what can only be described as pure instinctive magic. Same for James.

From where I sit, intuition is one of his greatest assets. The other 'values' which best sum him up are passion, respect and empathy; courage is up there as well.

His intuitive mind is one of the best I have ever seen, both on the field and in life. I took my three young boys to watch James's last game as captain in 2005. In the dying minutes, for some reason I told Sam, my five-year-old, to only watch James, and watch him carefully as the boundary umpire prepared to throw the ball in. Unbeknownst to me, I had inadvertently also alerted the nine or 10 elderly MCC members standing alongside us in the Members' Stand, who also decided to only watch James. He sprinted in from 30 metres away, read the play off the Melbourne ruckman, blind turned around two opponents and snapped a freakish left-foot goal from the boundary line to put the Bombers within range of victory. Little Sam wasn't terribly impressed, but the elderly Melbourne supporters around me just stared at each other in silent amazement . . . and then all stared at me. I remember feeling a funny kind of power and pride, as if I had predicted it!

It's this freedom to be 'in command but out of control' (to borrow a concept from Malcolm Gladwell's book Blink*) that makes James so entertaining to both watch and converse with. It also makes him look as if he's in slow motion on the football field. He has a ridiculous sense of space and great peripheral vision; in my opinion these come from the trust he has in his intuitive and instinctive mind. He's been labelled courageous, but I think his greatest courage is his courage to follow his heart and his intuition. It's almost as if they have predetermined things for him. Clearly they have rarely let him down.*

Away from football, there is a lot that the world can learn from James Hird the person. Of all the senses we use in life, James seems to listen and feel his way through life more than relying on the more traditional ways of seeing the world. There is a lesson in that for the rest of us. One thing he has is an abundancy of empathy. Together with this great belief in 'hard listening', he has this 'seek first to understand' approach, and an ability to read the play with people in seconds, size up the situation or a person's feelings, and respond or act accordingly. This is amazingly powerful, and one of his greatest strengths.

His intellect is also remarkable. One of the wonderful things about being around James's transition from footy to business is watching how surprised very senior corporate people are by his business mind. Because of the star-lover syndrome, we tend to label our celebrities as 'unreal' – but not intelligent. We get caught up in the smell of liniment and never really think of them as smart. I have witnessed James speak to PricewaterhouseCoopers' top Australian clients without any notes and hold them completely captivated with anecdotes on leadership, business and life; he'll have them in the palm of his hand before they realise it.

He is also a great storyteller, which is one of the skills great leaders need. I have watched him pop into the Quiksilver CEO's office to say gidday and fall into an impromptu workshop, pulling in other senior executives to listen and discuss his stories and views on youth culture and fashion. He starts purely from his own knowledge as an ambassador for Zegna and Nike, but then produces the kind of insight that most of us marketers would take years of experience to capture.

In many ways James is also a very simple man, who loves to break things down and make them easy for himself (and others) to understand. The great paradox is that as business and life become more complex and technology-driven, there is a greater need than ever to keep things simple for the world to understand. In this way he is already a great businessman or brand manager, because he appreciates the art of simple, consistent communication in a world of confusion and clutter.

One of his most brilliant (and, I'll admit, frustrating) traits as a client and now a peer is his killer ability to ask, 'Why?' Asking why repeatedly forces you to justify your position and deepen your perspective – and can completely unravel my seemingly perfect arguments. I have seen him do this many times, always with a smile on his face, but always with a laser-like intention to get to the truth of an issue. As we grow into adults, many of us become a little institutionalised in our thinking, and in corporate culture we are almost taught not to ask why – that asking why too much is a sign of disrespect. James will never become a corporate yes-man, and in an increasingly politically correct world, the rest of us can learn from that.

People ask what James is like, as if he has only one personality trait or emotion. We expect our public figures to always be happy to meet us, as if we are the first person to ever come up to them in public. Like all of us, James can be all of funny, grumpy, serious, carefree and private in one day and at any moment. There are myths that James is arrogant, because he used to zone out in public and go into a trance-like state, looking through people. This was more a defence mechanism, not unlike the way Japanese commuters on the Tokyo subway go into an imaginary 'happy place' to get through a long crowded journey. It was just shyness, and over the years he has replaced it with a smile, which he has learned takes only a second but can last a lifetime for the recipient.

One of the reasons Australia has so much respect for James Hird is that James Hird has so much respect for others. Especially those he loves – his mum, his wife and his family. He has incredible respect for Margaret and Tania, and you can see it in his body language when he is with them. You instinctively know these are important people, simply by the way he stands proud around them; I have seen him do the same thing with friends or colleagues he wants to include in a conversation. Somehow his body language commands others to respect his mates or those he cares about. It reminds me that no matter how famous you are, the basics of respect are still paramount. He has good solid people around him, such as Tania and Rod Law, to keep him grounded, in case he ever needs a reminder that he puts his pants on one leg at a time – just like the rest of us.

James believes that no matter if you're three or 73, you should never stop learning. He is desperate to learn – about life, about business, about himself. He reminds me of John Travolta in Phenomenon; it's almost a craving for knowledge. He loves the consulting environment because it involves a constant search for knowledge and improvement. He hates over-thinking, and detests the MBA culture that is seeping into the corporate world, over-complicating decision-making by using analysis rather than insight. He loves deep analytical thinking, but he loves even more the emotional gut instinct that goes with intuitive decision-making. There is no better example of this balance than James.

James will be fine after football, but the rest of us won't be – we will miss watching him. James will be okay because he seems focused on making changes and experiencing the most out of life. He has taught himself that change is good, and he seems happy if that means walking a path that no one else has walked in terms of the way he shows up as a person.

Finally, in discussing this book before he started it, we joked that he should one day write a book to dispel all the myths about the billion-dollar self-help industry and the authors trying to tell people what the meaning of life is. He quipped that he'd love to write a book with only one page in it, in which he declared that the answer to the meaning of life is that, wait for it . . . there is no answer. That is the answer: if we enjoy the experience, live life for the moment, use our intuition, let go and feel our way and stay curious, rather than trying to control all the outcomes, we'll appreciate the journey and enjoy the ride so much more. Brilliant! And simple!

Enjoy the ride, Jimmy.

Chapter 18

Changes in the Game

Change is no longer shocking. Some changes in football happen slowly; others occur overnight. When you watch replays of games from 15 or 20 years ago you can see how the style has changed. That has been a slow change. Almost imperceptible. You notice that no one uses the 'torpedo' anymore. You notice that players have stopped kicking to packs or even to two-man contests. You notice that the game is getting faster, slicker, more ruthless; mistakes glare like neon signs now. There is nothing forgiving about football today.

In the 16 years I've played, the game has changed enormously, on and off the field. In 1991, football was a much simpler game in almost every way. The zone kick-out had been implemented by Robert Walls, but there was still a lot of man-to-man, one-on-one play. In 1991 Kevin Sheedy played an extra man on Tony Lockett, one behind him and one in front, and it was huge news. Today, the strategies Sheeds talked about and put into practice are commonplace.

Twenty years ago you got the ball and kicked it to a contest. You had no problem booting it 40 metres to a guy one-on-one or two-on-two. Now, until you get to the last kick in the forward line, you avoid contests. It's a shame and has removed the spectacular mark, the one-on-one contest, the physicality. The players are fitter, can jump higher and are probably stronger than they have ever been, because their athleticism and training standards have lifted. But the contests have diminished enormously, except at the stoppages, which are becoming a blight on the game. There used to be three or four players in that competition. Now there are eight or 10. It used to be a lot easier to get the ball. Now, if you don't have a dominant ruckman, it's pot luck. And it's harder to watch the game as a spectacle when there are crowds of 15 to 20 players surrounding the ball.

Today's game is lightning quick and much harder-running. You run harder and longer than you used to, and there are no places to hide. They used to 'rest' a ruckman or rover in the forward pocket, but there's not a lot of solace to be found there anymore. If you need a rest, the bench is the only place.

This brings us to one of the major revolutions in football in my time: player rotations. It used to be that players named on the bench spent most of the day there. Kevin Sheedy can take most of the credit for the idea of rotating players off the bench. The best player on the ground – someone like champion West Coast on-baller Chris Judd or Ben Cousins – doesn't play 120 minutes anymore; he'll be used in bursts. This has only been an accepted tactic for the past two years or so, and the Eagles are very good at it. It rests their best players – they play for 20 minutes in the first quarter, then go off for five minutes. They end up with much more petrol in the tank. On-ballers rarely stay on for the whole game.

Another dramatic change has occurred in the field positions. When I started, players lined up where they were named on the field, give or take. Forwards were forwards, defenders were defenders, and the only real leeway was in the roles of the centremen, wingmen or on-ballers, who moved around from half-forward to half-back. Now, the concept of selected positions has been rendered almost irrelevant. There are still full-forwards and full-backs, and maybe centre-half-forwards and centre-half-backs, but everyone else moves around the ground according to the game plan. The result of this is that games sometimes lose the spectacle element of old. When you have 36 players up one end of the field, for instance. If players are not confined to specific positions, and the field is not sliced up the way it is in netball, there is no way of avoiding this. This game, like all games, needs to evolve naturally. If people ask me what position I play, I can't answer. My position is probably what the footy cards of the 1960s and '70s would've called a 'utility'.

As I've mentioned, the increase in the pace of the game has required us all to be much fitter. It is now a game based on pace. If you can't run and run for a long time, you have no place in it. Similarly, a poor pre-season won't give you the motor to keep going during what is a very long season. You need to be fresh right to the end of the season, which means you have to work hard at the beginning of it. I've always ensured that I have a good fitness base to cope with this. The new rules introduced in 2006 – being able to kick the ball out without waiting for the flags, and having less time to hold the ball before getting rid of it – give an advantage to the running teams over the taller, slower teams. Anyone who can't run in this game is in a lot of trouble. You can almost sacrifice a little skill for the ability to run. Coaches hate players who kick the ball away and turn it over, but they also hate guys who can't keep up.

I am not an advocate of getting rid of the requirement that full-backs wait until the flags have been waved to signal a point. I don't believe that it adds to the game. The change will speed the game up, but to what advantage? I think accountable play will be reduced, and there will be more loose players because there will be no time to man up.

I like contests in footy, and this rule will further reduce the number of contests; there has already been a huge decline over the past few years.

There are now rules for everything. Before the 2006 season, the AFL brought in the so-called Matthew Lloyd rule. Lloydy was known to take his time kicking for goal. He had his routine fixed: he'd adjust his shorts, pull up his socks and throw grass into the air to gauge the wind direction. This took an average of 45 seconds. The new rule allows a player kicking for goal 30 seconds before the umpire calls play on. I can't see the point. What difference does taking 45 seconds instead of 30 make? If Lloydy takes 45 seconds and has eight set shots at goal, that's a total difference of two minutes. How often is he going to have eight set shots for goal in a game? Probably once every five weeks. Let's say he has five shots for goal, which is probably accurate on average: that constitutes a bit over one minute. I would have thought that accuracy in goal-kicking, and spectator excitement due to anticipation, would do more for the game than speeding it up by a minute.

Some rules need review. The main one, in my opinion, is holding the ball. I think the umpires are far too hot on this rule. The players who make the game great are the ones who go for and win the ball, and you should give them a bit of leeway. They get penalised too easily, and that's frustrating to watch. Often a player just trying to get the ball is interpreted as diving on the ball. So there's one player, on his hands and knees, showing courage and fighting desperately for the ball; the other player, who just holds the first player's jumper, and shows no skill at all, is the one who's awarded the free kick. It seems to me a total misunderstanding of what the game is about. It penalises the hard worker.

Often, problems can be sorted out organically, rather than by rule changes. I think the potential blight of flooding – the defensive tactic of putting your whole team onto the forward line so the opposition can't score – sorted itself out. It was only a couple of years ago that everyone said flooding was going to ruin the game, but teams found a way around it.

There are those who say that because Sydney won the flag in 2005, and Sydney used that tactic, football will go that way and become a defensive, strategic game. I don't think this dour type of play is sustainable over the long term, and I would be surprised if that type of play will win the premiership in 2006.

Training and preparation have changed a lot, too. Clubs are now training smart. We used to train three days a week, from 5 pm to 8.30 or 9 pm, and were flogged every session. There would be weights and maybe a team meeting – an intense three contacts with the club per week. Now it's every day, but the sessions are shorter. The number of meetings has doubled, and the player commitments expected by the AFL have increased. Players are required to do 24 hours of commitments for the AFL annually; it doesn't sound much, but it adds up. It takes a lot longer than those 24 hours to do it, because they're spread over the whole year in bits and pieces, and they don't include travel time. Playing AFL football today is a whole lifestyle. You have to live and breathe it.

Some people believe players should not drink alcohol during the season, but I disagree. I suppose I would, being a great lover of wine. I find a glass of wine at night relaxes me (although

Changes in the Game

not the night before a match). It has a positive not a negative effect. I guess this one comes down to the individual, as do so many issues relating to preparation and training. Each person's body is different, so I don't think there should be blanket rules.

Another major change relates to drugs. Random drug-testing does have an impact on your life as a player. Your club now has to know where you are, 24 hours a day, seven days a week, because the AFL might pick you for a random drug test. I get tested two or three times a year. I don't mind at all, because I strongly believe it is good for the game. If random testing is the way to eradicate drugs from the AFL, it's fine by me.

Another area of change is the explosion of media interest in players. As I've mentioned earlier, players are now under intense scrutiny all the time; a little less so in the off-season, perhaps, but a footballer doing anything tends to be news in sports-crazy Melbourne.

Sometimes players have brought the trouble and pain on themselves. Each incident must be treated individually, but the one that surfaces too often is players drinking and then driving. The reality is that most AFL players are under 25, have quite a bit of time on their hands, and want to go out and socialise. That's natural. But like every other member of the community, players must be responsible on this critical issue. Any drink-driving incidents will receive a lot of publicity. There is nothing surer. Whether players should be role models, or are comfortable being role models, is a separate issue; the reality is that what they do becomes news very quickly.

There was a well-publicised case of Jay Schulz, of the Richmond Football Club, drink-driving in 2005. This one had extra ramifications because the Tigers were being sponsored by the Transport Accident Commission – to the tune of $600,000 – and the TAC then withdrew its sponsorship. It was a huge burden for a young man (and, of course, the club), and the wrath of the media and the general public rained down on him. I wrote a column about it for the *Herald Sun* – and received a letter from his mother asking me to give him a break. It's always great to hear from a supportive family.

Players, like other people, have to work out for themselves what consitutes good behaviour. The club, the player's parents and family will all offer advice – and so will a lot of other people, even if not asked! – but in the end it's up to the individual.

As we grow older, like it or not, we all become role models. Role models to the youth of the world. I am a role model not only because I am a footballer, but because I am 33 years old and should be able to teach people younger than me what is acceptable and what is not. My greatest obligation is to my kids, and I am conscious of how I behave, not because I am associated with the Essendon Football Club, but because my kids look to me to see how to behave in certain situations. I do not want my kids to have to look elsewhere for their role models; I want them to look up to me. Unfortunately, some people don't have strong family role models and instead look to people who have a high profile as leaders. This is where our responsibilities as footballers arise. People in a position of power have a choice: they can be a positive influence on the community or a negative one. For society's and our own betterment, it is important that we make the right choice.

Footballers have problems, like anyone else in the community. We do our job closely observed by media, the public, friends and family. Our job is done in public, and each week we are marked for our efforts by the media and then by hundreds of thousands of football followers.

I am happy to say that there is now more awareness and understanding of players' lives and problems off the field, and some of
this can be credited to the brave stance of people such as Wayne
Schwass and Nathan Thompson. In February 2006, Wayne, the
former Kangaroos and Swans star, spoke of his nine-year battle
with depression. Nathan, a Kangaroos player, had spoken two
years earlier of his battle with depression. Depression in men, not
just footballers, is prevalent and growing, and is finally being
discussed. Steve Rogers, the former rugby league player for
Cronulla, took his own life in February 2006, and he suffered
depression as well. I was a rugby league follower in Canberra and
Steve was one of the greats. It shocked me and shocked Australia,
but it helped lift the veil from what was once a secret illness.

There is a link between football and depression, as Wayne and
Nathan have shown. Football players are put under huge pressure
and undergo huge highs and huge lows. There is little consistency.
From one week to the next you can go from the greatest to the
worst and back again. It is not only the media; it is also the fans,
the coaches, your teammates and your friends. Any Melbourne-
based player with any sort of profile is asked about footy every
day. If you are not playing well, you can be made to feel as though
you're no good and that you're not working hard enough. You
can easily become down on yourself, particularly if you're not
thick-skinned or your inner confidence isn't strong.

When I'm struggling with injuries, I get upset. Things seem
harder than they really are. To the public, it's almost as though if
you don't look upset about being injured, you don't care. People
want to see you upset, and everyone has an opinion – most of
them not positive. It's easy to see how depression and footy can
almost go hand in hand, given the attention players receive and
the fact that many of them lack other jobs or hobbies to balance
their lives.

Personally, I've never felt depressed in the clinical sense. Sure, I've been down and self-absorbed at times, but I have a really good support network around me, so whenever I take things out of context I have people to help me. They bring me some perspective, a reality check and a cup of tea.

I have had a little experience with the illness. Two past players, good friends at Essendon, suffer depression and have asked for my help. It's difficult helping them in a sporting environment where you're trying to get the most out of them and need them to follow the rather regimented rules of the club. Do you apply the same rules to someone you know to be struggling with this illness? Is it more important to have a go at them because they're late to training or to let it go? It's a delicate balance, and it's one I, as captain of the club and a friend to these two guys, have had to try to deal with.

The challenge is to try to understand why people behave the way they do, rather than seeing their behaviour in isolation. Here is an example. Wayne Schwass said that one of his strategies to hide from depression was to drink himself into oblivion. It made him feel better. So if I know a player has gone out and got drunk three days before a game when he shouldn't have, I would be disappointed in him because he's let the team down. But I'll also have to remember that someone in a rational state of mind wouldn't do that. His driving force is probably not to have fun, but a result of something being significantly wrong. He is probably crying out for help or trying to rid himself of the demons in his head. Failing to understand this only compounds the problem. But it's really hard to know how to deal with that in a club culture where everyone has to be equal. At Essendon we haven't solved that dilemma yet; I don't think the rest of the football community has either.

I was able to help one of those teammates of mine quite significantly; the second one was predominantly helped by others at the

310

club. I firmly believe that we need to be proactive about these things at the footy club, and make it an environment where people feel comfortable enough to talk about their problems.

One of the major changes to the football landscape in my time has been the demise of the Fitzroy Football Club, and the talk of mergers between clubs, which was pretty strong around the mid 1990s. It has largely subsided now, because huge television deals have meant more money for the clubs, and the AFL has committed to there being 16 clubs in the competition. Clubs who have gone through precarious times – North Melbourne/Kangaroos, Richmond, Bulldogs, Melbourne – are now no longer under threat of being merged.

Fitzroy's last game was a sad occasion. It's disappointing to see such great history removed from the competition. For the club's supporters, it must have been terrible. It would surely be hard to transfer your passion to another club. If Essendon folded, I could not follow another club with the same passion, even if I had been a supporter and not a player. Certainly, some Fitzroy supporters went for Brisbane, and others followed when the Lions won their premierships. But do they barrack for Brisbane with the same passion as they barracked for Fitzroy? I find it hard to believe that they do.

In 1996 the plans for the Melbourne–Hawthorn merger became quite advanced. I thought it would be a disaster. Who would people barrack for? It's like Essendon merging with Carlton. What fascinated me about Hawthorn's situation was the fact that they had won a Grand Final as recently as 1991. Not only that, but they'd come out of one of the most successful eras in football history. How can a club go from triumph to merger talks in such a short time?

Yet another major change since my career began has been the abandonment of the suburban grounds and the move by clubs to share the MCG and Colonial Stadium/Telstra Dome.

This too is sad, but it is an understandable progression. I treasure the memories of playing at some of the grounds that are now used only for training. I didn't get to play senior football at Windy Hill – the club's move to the MCG coincided almost exactly with the start of my senior career at Essendon, but I was able to run out there with the reserves a few times.

I played at Kardinia Park (now Skilled Stadium), Princes Park (Optus Oval), Western Oval (Whitten Oval) and Victoria Park in Collingwood (I never played at Moorabbin). In a lot of ways these grounds hold the best memories, because the crowds are so close – the way they should be. I was brought up loving the suburban ground, where you can smell all the smells, be close to the action, and where a lady can almost hit you over the head with an umbrella. I still love it.

There are compromises to be made at the old grounds, of course, as the facilities are not state of the art. Smelling the smells of a real ground takes on a whole new meaning when you're getting changed at Victoria Park, where I played reserves footy. In the Collingwood change rooms the showers were cold and the ground was so muddy that you were dirty before you ran out – and you stank. Essendon's 'away' change rooms weren't flash either.

At all of those grounds you had to do the warm-up in the changing rooms, which was very inefficient, given that you could barely fit all the players in. Another thing was that people could and did spit on you through the cages of the races and that was a very big downside. I'm glad we aren't spat on anymore, and I am pleased we have warm showers nowadays, but at the same time I'm thankful that I can think back and remember playing on those old grounds. Even playing on the bogs at Geelong, Footscray and

Carlton was a special experience. We played reserves games before the senior game, where the ground was just shocking. You knew you had to take your time changing direction in those bogs because of the mud.

I'm glad I caught the tail end of that era and had a chance to experience it. Today's players are used to playing on the MCG, Telstra Dome, AAMI Stadium, Subiaco, the SCG, Telstra Stadium in Sydney and the 'Gabba in Brisbane. They're all different from each other, but they're all huge stadiums. The differences between them aren't as great as those between the suburban grounds. At Windy Hill the ground was a funny shape; at Princes Park, if you were playing at centre-half-forward you knew the ball would go over your head because it was that size of ground; and Western Oval was bloody long. You worked out how to play grounds differently, far more so than is necessary today.

I have spent an inordinate amount of time rhapsodising over the MCG – it is far and away the best stadium in the country and whoever designed and built it got it completely right. On the other hand, and in order to tell the whole picture, it's time to record my thoughts on Telstra Dome (formerly Colonial Stadium).

I've been pretty critical of the surface of Telstra Dome, which has caused me some grief, because it became Essendon's home ground after the club stopped playing at Windy Hill in 1991. I'm sticking to my guns, though: my knees aren't great, and I've had bad foot problems, and I always pull up ridiculously sore after playing there. I think the surface of the ground was the last thing anyone thought about.

It just doesn't work. When you watch cricket being played at Telstra Dome, the cricketers slip over, and when you watch footy being played there, the footy players slip over. It's slippery because the surface is kept very wet in an attempt to prevent it becoming too hard – but it is already hard. Penetrometer readings are taken continuously and we are told that the reading at Telstra is not as hard as at the MCG. But honestly, we all play in both places, and everyone says Telstra is harder. I've stopped complaining because I was called into a few meetings with the management of the stadium and the club, and it was made clear to me that no one was going to do anything about it. Continuing to complain would just make me a whinger.

The thing that most frustrated me was the people telling me I was wrong – the AFL, the people in charge of the stadium, Channel 7, the club – were all satisfied with the penetrometer information. I know which ground is harder and which ground hurts more, because I run up and down it. There were times when the joins on the grass were so uneven you had to do a high-jump to get over them. It was ridiculous. I don't think it can be fixed. I understand that there is only 30 centimetres between the grass base and the concrete base, so it's no wonder there's not a lot of give. That surface is not ideal for footy, soccer, rugby or cricket, but it's bloody good for a concert. The Telstra Dome faces the wrong way, too, but if the roof is closed (which it usually is), that doesn't make any difference.

I know I keep harping on about it, but let's not kid ourselves: the MCG is the place, the benchmark, and the way it should be.

Chapter 19

Setting Yourself Up:
Football, Money and Fame

October 1997, Paris. Oh no, it's 9 pm, and we were due at the restaurant at 7 pm. I can't believe it . . . Lindsay Fox, the legendary Australian trucking tycoon, has booked us into the best restaurant in town – and is paying for our meal – and we've over-slept because of jetlag. I wake Tania and we get dressed (quickly), then dash to the restaurant. I hope we can talk our way in. I explain that we are guests of Lindsay Fox, and it does the trick.

'*Excusez-moi, monsieur, bien sur* – why didn't you say?' the maitre d' says with a smile. 'Any friend of Monsieur Fox is a friend of ours . . . Here, please sit, this is your table.'

The whole experience was quite an eye-opener, particularly some of the food. Then the roof opened, and to top things off, the Arab sheikh over in the corner ordered a $5000 bottle of Romanée Conti. Quite a night. There were moments when I wasn't sure whether I was awake or dreaming!

That's the upside of fame. The privileges that come your way. But it definitely has its downsides, because you never know when you'll find yourself in trouble. The stakes are raised because you're well known, and they are even higher when you're with a group of other well-known people (in this case Essendon footballers).

In 2002, for example, we were in Sydney for Mark McVeigh's twenty-first birthday party on a boat on Sydney Harbour. It was a terrific party. At 1 in the morning, after the celebrations on the boat had finished, we were walking back to the hotel – Paul Barnard, Solly, Jason Johnson, Lloydy and me, with our partners – when about six blokes jumped out of nowhere and assaulted Jason Johnson. Before we knew it, Jason had been punched in the jaw and put on the ground, and another teammate was being punched. Paul and Solly, who are pretty strong guys and know how to look after themselves in a fight, stepped in and put the aggressors down. Later we learned that one of our group had spoken to the girlfriend of one of the aggressors. The police came and listened to our story, which they were good about, and we went on our way. The matter was ended.

It was pretty full-on, and quite a revelation for me – I'd never really been in a pub fight before, and fighting just does not sit right with me. I don't believe it's in my teammates' personality either.

The incident underlined how easy it is to find yourself in a news story (even though we didn't, luckily). We hadn't done anything to bring on the incident, but if it had happened in Melbourne we would have been in the paper, associated with a brawl, and having to explain ourselves. Not pleasant.

All that is certainly a downside of being well known. One of the aspects of retirement I'm looking forward to is the spotlight coming off me a bit. I won't miss walking along the street and being recognised. It's not something I've longed for. It's not that

I mind saying hello to people, and I'm grateful that people have over the years been friendly and respectful to me, but I'm not naturally drawn to being the centre of attention, which I suppose is a strange thing to say for someone who does his job in front of crowds of up to 80,000 people.

Sometimes it's a hassle being recognised, but generally speaking, I am treated with friendliness and respect. Sure, I get, 'Hirdy, you're a poof!' now and then, and sometimes I'm asked for autographs in inappropriate situations (like in the middle of my grandmother's funeral), but mostly people have been very good to me. Judging by the newspapers, it sounds as if Ian Thorpe has it twice as bad as me. You just have to deal with it and move on. It can be hard when you have your children with you and someone's yelling out of the car, 'You're a wanker!' It can also be scary. I remember in November 2005, when Tania and I were walking back from dinner in Chapel Street, South Yarra, a group of four or five people, who'd obviously been drinking, began following and taunting us. It wouldn't have taken much for something bad to have happened.

I also get quite a lot of friendly feedback. Interestingly, more people have been on side with me since I made those the comments about umpires.

Football has been good to me financially. When I was starting out with Ainslie in Canberra, I didn't realise how much advantage it could bring. I've been given not just a sound financial base to build from, but also a profile that has allowed me to pursue other opportunities. I've also been lucky in that I have received sound financial advice from good people, and I've tried to spend my money wisely.

Football at the elite level can now bring riches. That wasn't the case for the stars of the game when I started. The current generation is fortunate that a lot of money now flows into the game – a lot through media and sponsorship deals – and they can, if they are guided soundly, set themselves up well.

I did an interview on 3AW once with the late David Hookes. 'Sometimes,' I said, 'you almost feel guilty being paid each week.'

'You could always give it back,' Hookes said. I just laughed.

In my first year at Essendon, in 1991, I wouldn't have had much to give back. In that year, I was earning $100 a week living allowance and $15 a game for playing in the under-19s (in the reserves you got $150). The $100 went straight to the lady I was living with and covered my living expenses. I was injured for the first half of that year, so I didn't have any money. I didn't have a car, so I caught buses and trains. I had a couple of thousand dollars in a Commonwealth Bank savings account, which I'd had since the age of five, and I lived off that.

In 1992 I was paid about $1000 for each senior game, and I played about five games. In 1993 I was on a similar contract – probably around $1500 a game. I played 16 games that year, so I earned about $25,000. Finally, I could buy a car! I found the brown 1987 Mazda 626 I mentioned earlier, and it became my pride and joy. (Until the boys at the club saw it, that is – they had a few unfavourable things to say about it, particularly about its colour!) Still, I drove it for years and the trusty old thing is still used as a spare car by anyone in my family who needs it.

In 1994 I had the same contract as before. That year I won the club best and fairest. I thought it might jack up my price a little, but it didn't. Instead, Roger Hampson, the club's chief executive officer, offered me a contract that was less than I'd been given the year before. I sought advice from our footy manager, Danny Corcoran, who put me in touch with an accountant called John Riordon. John helped organise a base payment of $50,000 plus $1500 a game. That arrangement stayed in place until my Brownlow victory at the end of 1996.

For a while I was out of contract, and Melbourne Football Club president Joe Gutnick was in the paper saying he wanted me. He claimed on the radio that he had a shopping trolley, a heap of money, and was looking for players; my name was mentioned. Danny Corcoran had just gone to Melbourne, and Essendon knew he was a great friend of mine, so that put a bit of pressure on them. I was never tempted to leave, though. When the new Essendon CEO, Peter Jackson, arrived, he didn't want to lose me. He offered me $150,000 in 1998, $195,000 in 1999 and $200,000 in 2000. I thought that was pretty good money, especially considering that injuries were keeping me off the field.

When I had just started working with Ansett I flew to Sydney with a couple of Ansett executives, who were both probably being paid $250,000–$300,000 per year. On the plane, as I was sandwiched between these two, my bosses, we picked up the *Herald Sun* and there was an article saying, 'Hird demands $1.2 million over three years'. John Riordon, my accountant, had leaked it to the paper – that was the way it used to work back then. These guys looked at me as if to say: 'You're kidding me. We work 18-hour days, we're never home, we travel all around the world, we're highly intelligent, we've been in the game 25 years . . . And you're a 25-year-old asking for this amount?'

In 2000 I signed a lucrative five-year contract. Five-year deals are extremely rare, almost non-existent, these days. The club got its money's worth out of me, though, because I played the majority of games in those years, and won a best and fairest and a couple of All Australian selections. At the end of 2005, I told the club I would take a significant pay cut.

I've never sensed open resentment from teammates about my contracts. It's natural for some people to say, 'You've got the talent, great – you've earned it', and for others to get bitter when they see you on a large contract and they know they do the same training and work the same hours. They're still good people.

There was one player who clearly felt aggrieved about all this. Just after I won the Brownlow Medal in 1996 this player went in to negotiate his contract. He said to the footy manager at the time, 'What do you mean I can't have X increase? James Hird wouldn't have won his Brownlow without me, and in fact his Brownlow should have been awarded to me because I did all the hard work for him and got him the ball all the time.' I remember laughing my head off when I heard that. This guy wasn't a bad player, but he was struggling to get a game, week in, week out. That sort of resentment is bound to happen.

Football has resulted in some security for my family. John Riordon's mantra was 'Property, property, property', so in 1996 I bought a house in East Melbourne, a great part of town, not least because of its proximity to my favourite ground, the MCG. It was a two-storey Victorian terrace, which I rented out for the first few years because I was living in an apartment in the city and I didn't need a house of that size. When Tania and I were married, we totally gutted and renovated it – we moved in three weeks before Stephanie was born.

We didn't use an architect, because we had firm ideas on what we wanted, and as a result we produced our dream home. It was our first family home, and it will always be special. We lived in it for six years, until 2005. That's still my favourite part of Melbourne, and if I ever find a house with enough of a back garden for the kids I'll be back there in a flash. I used to love walking to the MCG from home, it was a very special thing to do. I was really quite sad to move.

In 1997, Tania found a bargain house – it was way above what we could afford, but had huge potential and lots of land. I thought I could meet the repayments with my footy money, so we

320

bought it and rented it out. After another extensive renovation, we're happily living there now.

The truth is that you don't play football for the money. The money is a happy by-product. You play for the love of the game. And if that sounds like a cliché, ask any footballer in the few months after his retirement whether it's the money or the camaraderie and brotherhood he misses most. I bet I know which it is.

Chapter 20

The Swan Song

It did feel slightly strange. On 24 September 2005, Grand Final day, I was sitting in a lounge-room in an apartment in Coolum, on Queensland's Sunshine Coast, watching the footy with my family, just like millions of other Australians. I sat there with my son Tommy, sort of barracking along, watching the Sydney Swans beat the Eagles and take their first flag in 72 years, and the red and white paper raining down on coach Paul Roos. The Swans' victory means the AFL has taken a big step towards making our code a truly national one. Flags have also gone to the Eagles in Perth, to Adelaide, Port Adelaide and Brisbane. It can only be good for the future of the game that the team in the country's biggest potential market has won.

But on that day, with the barbecue going and a beer in my hand, it was also a game of footy I could enjoy with my family. Except, of course, I would have preferred to be out playing on the

MCG. Watching Grand Finals is fine until someone wins; that's when I really want to be there. That's the moment that doesn't feel good when you're watching rather than participating.

As a family we usually go to Queensland at that time if we're not in the finals, so it was a hint of what the future will be like post 2007. This next year, 2007, will definitely be my last year with the Bombers, and it raises a lot of questions.

Life without football. What will it be like? How will it feel? I know some things for sure: I will miss the players as friends and colleagues, I will miss Sheeds, I will miss the fantastic support staff. I will miss the fans, those wonderful Essendon supporters with red-and-black blood. I will miss arriving at the club and seeing the same faces and saying hello to people I've greeted for so many years. I will miss the big Anzac Day games. I will miss the friendship of players from other clubs.

I'm not sure whether or not I will miss the anxiety and nerves that always accompany the couple of days before a game, the sleepless nights when I don't even know why I can't sleep. I certainly won't miss the broken ribs, throbbing feet, punctured lungs, fractured eye sockets and smashed head, or the dark feelings when I've realised that a season has slipped away because my knee or foot have forced me from the field.

I will miss a lot about the game. But what I'll miss most of all are two feelings. The first is coming off the ground knowing I have played well, knowing I've given my all, and we've won. That feeling is such a reward. And equally, I'll miss sitting with my boots off in the change room next to another player and chatting about the game, what went right, what went wrong, little moments out there – and then my kids coming in, happy to see me, and saying, 'Dad, you kicked a goal!'

I haven't found this in any other part of my life – a situation where I am physically and emotionally spent, with mates all around, and a really strong sense of camaraderie. It's a very special feeling, and I've experienced it since I was seven years old. From age seven to age 33, that feeling hasn't changed. You walk off the ground and the reason for the euphoria you feel isn't that you're being paid a lot of money or because you're playing in front of a huge crowd of people; it's the satisfaction of playing the game with some mates. That, to me, is what playing football is all about.

It's been a joy and an honour to play for Essendon for so long. I'm proud that I won four club best-and-fairest awards, and was named All Australian five times (I was captain in 2001). In 1997 I was named on the half-forward flank for Essendon's 'Team of the Century'. Of those I played with, Gavin Wanganeen was in the back pocket, Michael Long was on the wing, Terry Daniher took the other half-forward flank, Simon Madden was in the ruck and Tim Watson was ruck-rover. Mark Thompson was on the bench.

In 2002 the club named me as number 3 on a list of its 25 best-ever players, which was another huge honour. Above me were only the legendary full-forward John Coleman at number 2 and the great Dick Reynolds at number 1. Needless to say, I was in pretty impressive company. Of the contemporary players, Simon Madden was named number 5, Tim Watson number 6, Mark Harvey number 18, Gavin Wanganeen number 19, Matthew Lloyd number 22 and Michael Long number 23.

How do you express how much all that means to you? The Essendon footy club has been such a huge part of my life, so the honour is incredible. That wasn't part of the dream I had as a child. I don't know how you can have a dream like that. (Similarly, I'd never dreamt of winning a Brownlow.) For me, being named on the list meant I had been accepted as a player who can do things, make things happen and change the course of the game – and that there is a lot of respect for me. Being placed third? Apart from Coleman and Reynolds, you could argue that the rest of the top 10 could be placed in any order.

The extraordinary feeling you get being part of a football club is the strongest memory I'll take away when I retire. You become extremely close to the players as a group, and feel a real loyalty towards them. In a good playing group – and I am lucky to have been part of many in the years I've been at Essendon – you're akin to close brothers, or best mates. When you read comments about players playing for each other or for the coach, believe them, because they are true. I really enjoy going down to the club and catching up with the boys. Perhaps someone will tell a story that's ridiculously funny, or an 18-year-old guy will give it to me and bring me down to earth. You can be 18 or 33 – there are no barriers. Football is a great leveller. Those from the best schools and those who are worth the most money mix with those from the worst schools and those with the least, and everyone is equal. Lindsay Fox is as passionate about footy as the bloke with no teeth sitting in the outer watching St Kilda. There's no difference – it's all about passion.

And that's what I will miss. I'm going to feel a huge jolt when I stop. I've been playing, watching, analysing, breathing the game since I was about five years old, badgering Dad to come and have a kick while he was trying to watch the replay. Here I am now, so many years later, facing a new life.

I was always aware that my retirement day would arrive, and I wanted to be ready for it. But I'm not sure you can ever really be ready. A lot of players finish their careers because of injury, which almost happened to me on a couple of occasions. Many leave at a time of their choosing. In making my decision to play through to the end of 2007, I'm hoping that I fit into the latter camp. I've had too many interruptions and setbacks in my career to plan anything with too much confidence. You become philosophical:

whatever happens, happens. That doesn't mean you don't hope for it to end in a particular way.

To many former players, coaching is a way to stay in the game, but I have never wanted to coach. There are elements of coaching that excite me: for example; achieving with a group of people where the goal is pretty obvious and everyone is highly motivated. It would be rewarding and stimulating to have the opportunity to build a really good team around you, to be surrounded by people who inspire you and whom you inspire, and being able to guide young men towards success.

Unfortunately, there is so much more to a coach's involvement in footy than there used to be, and so much more stress. You see coaches getting eaten up by the media – they get trashed. I can handle criticism, but I think I'd have a very hard time with the media if I were a coach. If things didn't go well, I'd probably say some things I would later regret. I remember watching Bomber Thompson making a spirited, angry defence of Brad Ottens, who was struggling with form, and asking the media to leave Brad alone. I respect Bomber for that.

Some journalists get upset when coaches and players don't bare their soul and tell them everything. But it's drummed into players and coaches that your first obligation is to the other players and coaches. You're encouraged to keep things in-house, to keep the media out. Secrets must remain just that. You tell what needs to be told and no more. That's a fair enough approach, I would have thought, given the potential for headlines.

This is not being disrespectful to the men and women who cover football. I've had a very good run in the media and have been very well looked after by a lot of journalists. I've rarely had bad things written or said about me. There are two or three journalists who don't like me, what I stand for, or the way I play football. You probably know who they are. But 90 per cent have a fair bit of respect for me and for what I do.

The other reason I'm not looking for a coaching career is that by the end of 2007 I will have been at Essendon for 17 years, and there are other parts of life I want to experience. I'm planning for that to involve travelling to Europe with my family, and showing Stephanie, Tommy and Alexander different cultures. I would love to spend a year living in another country – perhaps France, with some time in Italy and Germany. Tania and I have spoken about it at great length. I'd like to not plan it too much, but when I say that to Tania, she is aghast – it's a little hard to embark on a journey like that with three kids and not do some planning!

I'm looking forward to a life that is not as rigid as it has been: juggling footy and a career outside the game has meant constant organisation, planning, structure and control. With footy there are permanent guidelines. They are there out of necessity, of course – you know the ramifications of staying out too late or having that extra glass of wine or not looking after your body. When I retire from footy, and those guidelines are no longer there, it may cause me to lack a little focus, but it could also be a relief.

I'd like to indulge some of my passions. I enjoy learning about wine, for instance. My parents always had a bottle of wine with dinner, so it's been a natural progression. Dad would give me a taste every now and then from when I was about 13 – I didn't like it much, but because Dad said I could have a sip and it seemed to be something special, I always had a taste. My interest in wine probably stemmed from his. Certainly, my interest grew when he took me to northern Victoria and bought a few bottles. Another one of those generational things.

Tania's stepfather Bill has a huge interest in wine and is very knowledgeable on the subject. While in Europe, Bill bought a lot of French and German wine and takes pride in his cellar, which he is very generous in sharing. He has taught me a great deal.

I also read a lot about wine. One of the Essendon board members and friends, Alex Epis, has a vineyard at Macedon, north-west of Melbourne, which we've visited a few times – his pinot noir and chardonnay are excellent and show what putting your passion before making money can do in the wine industry. I'm fascinated by grape-growing and winemaking. Some people try to make it appear quite complicated, but it's agriculture; it's knowing why a grape grows better in one place than another. I have always had a romantic idea to one day grow my own grapes, but when you look at how hard these blokes have to work, it loses some of its appeal. Growing wine to make money is a mistake, because not too many people do.

My decision to play on in 2007 has surprised most people. I think people outside Essendon and my family believed that I would be just as happy pursuing other opportunities. But to me my life has and always will include football, and the only way for me to truly enjoy it right now is to play it.

In 2006 I retired inside my head at least a dozen times. By the end of that season, which was certainly not one of Essendon's better ones, I had used all sorts of reasons to convince myself it was the right thing to do, and I had tried to retire many times. I listened to the journalists who'd say that you don't want to outstay your welcome, and I started to believe the doomsayers who said I was too old. But every time I did 'retire' I felt sick in the stomach. Thankfully, everyone close to me believed I could still play. Tania was convinced I was still a valuable player and was leaving the game with good football left in me. Matthew Lloyd and my teammates were certain that I was good for the team and believed that with me in the side for 2007, we would have a real chance of achieving greatness. Sheeds told me that I'd be making a mistake and would be being 'soft' and 'taking the easy life' if I retired in 2006. My mum (as only mothers can do) wanted the best for her son. My partners at Gemba stated their disappointment that I wouldn't be able to work full-time in 2007, but believed that I should follow my passion and didn't stand in my way.

Most importantly, I believe I still have what it takes to contribute to the Essendon Football Club on the field, and I still love playing the game. I am not under any illusions that the 2007 season will be easy, but as long as my contribution is positive I want to delay my retirement another year.

There is so much to do after football. I'm looking forward to kicking the footy with the kids in a local park, surfing with Tania, travelling as a family, watching our kids grow up and generally feeling at ease with who I am. I hope I do well in my business life and that Gemba is a huge success. I hope my future includes a strong involvement with the Essendon Football Club – and I hope to watch them win a few more premierships. I hope everyone I played with at Essendon goes on to have happy and fulfilling lives, and that I can keep in touch with many of them. I hope I can say, at the end of my career, that I was able to get every drop out of my talent and my body. I hope the AFL thrives, that no clubs are forced to merge, and that the game keeps growing and holds off challenges from other codes and sports as the dominant sport in the country.

I hope my contribution to the game is seen as a positive one, and is inspirational for young players coming through, just as people like Tim Watson and Terry Daniher were inspirational for me. I hope all those kids with posters of their heroes on their walls enjoy the game, in whatever way, as much as I have.

That's the dream I have now.

AMILIA AND KATHERINE HIRD ON JAMES

*A*fter school each afternoon, Jim was our chaperone, making sure we got home safely. He could do what he wanted between intersections, but he had to wait and cross each road safely with us.

His last day of Year 6 was no exception. He finished muck-up day and was waiting at the school gates to walk us home. He said goodbye to some mates and we started walking home, the three of us.

When we were about 100 metres down the road, we noticed Jim's bottom lip start to quiver and his eyes become glassy. Jim began to cry, and we gathered around to see if we could help with anything. Was he in trouble? No, he had shaving cream on his favourite Lightning Bolt tank top and couldn't bear the thought of facing our parents with ruined clothes.

We took great pleasure in telling him that the shaving cream was just soap, and there was nothing to be worried about. The crying subsided and he quickly brushed us off and ran ahead to the next corner.

You won't get too many words out of Jim. He's usually listening, not talking. He's got the huge Hird ears and he uses them well more often than not.

He also doesn't open up often. He will give each of us a call every now and again to talk through something that bothers him. Once you've heard what he has to say, you have to be quick with your response. As quickly as he has blurted out his issue, he has heard your response and is off the phone and back in control. He doesn't like things to be over-analysed or over-discussed. He'll always give a brief but considered response when one of us goes to him with a question, and that's what he likes in return. And always has.

We continued to live in Canberra for the first few years when Jim was playing at Essendon, and we had no idea about the status of football players in Melbourne. We found out one day when we went to a large extended family reunion (Jim didn't come, using the standard 'I'm training' excuse). We were standing with a group of people, when one very distant cousin, whom we had never met, boasted to the group that he was related to James Hird. We just looked at each other. It was a bizarre moment. That combined with seeing the pile of fan mail back at his flat made us realise the impact he was having in Melbourne.

We really missed Jim when he left home; while he had almost made it through his teenage years before he left, we missed out on having him around all the time for ours. The house was a lot quieter when he left – and the need to be constantly aware that a ball might hit you in the face was gone.

We felt his absence most when Mum and Dad separated. It was a difficult time for all of us in different ways. Throughout that time we provided each other with the kind of support that you only share with people you have spent so much time with. We were fortunate to grow up in a loving family and to be taught how important we were to each other.

When Jim's team won the under-9s Grand Final, Dad explained to the three of us what a special occasion it was, as some people never get the chance to play in a premiership team. It's clear to us that Jim has taken this advice to heart. He appreciates every success and uses the strength and confidence each one gives him to launch himself at his next objective.

None of us is a natural extrovert, so it's been interesting seeing how Jim handles the spotlight – with great composure and dignity, it turns out. Which is what we've always seen, and have come to expect.

He has always made it a priority to involve us in his good times, whether it's out on the ground with him after the 2000 Grand Final or sitting at the end of his hospital bed after his 200th game. One of the better times was seeing him tower over the crowds with his platform shoes, cloak and mask as Darth Vader at Tommy's Star Wars fourth birthday party. There's always been plenty to celebrate with Jim, and we know there always will be.

Acknowledgments

The decision to write this book was a tough one.

Thank you firstly to Ben Crowe, my friend and business partner, who, along with Tom Gilliatt, my publisher at Pan Macmillan, excited me about the possibility of writing a book that dealt with more than just football.

Peter Wilmoth's ability to extract the real James Hird was first class. The endless hours of questions and interviews seemed to take no time at all with Peter's professional and thoughtful approach.

Tania is often credited with being my wife but she is so much more. Her knowledge of the English language and her ability to mould and edit the book is a result of her expertise and intimate knowledge of our lives. I thank her for taking the book from being a manuscript with potential to something I am very proud of.

Thank you to everyone who contributed to *Reading the Play* via a tribute. You obviously spent a great deal of time and effort to write them.

My life is one of chaos and without the team at Gemba, who organise the chaos, I could not even nearly achieve what I do. A special thanks to Sheree, Fran and Nikki, who I know will be glad that this book is finally in print.

The football world has been great to me and I will never forget what Essendon and football in general has done to enrich my life. I have been fortunate to meet many very special people at Essendon, and I thank all of them. A special thanks to Ady, who I promised would get a mention in the book.

Finally, thank you to everyone who has supported me in my life. It has been a great ride and I look forward to the next chapter.

James Hird
Melbourne, August 2006

Index

Index

Index

Hird, Margaret (mother) 5, 6, 7, 10,
11–13, 14, 19–20, 30, 32, 39, 55,
82, 85, 101, 115, 133, 170, 252,
266, 276, 282, 300, 327
tribute to James 24–30
Hird, Stephanie (child) 2, 83, 85–6, 94,
101, 116, 130–4, 136, 138, 140,
155, 180, 216, 239, 242–3, 244,
267, 277, 293, 320, 327
Hird, Tania (née Poynton) 2, 63,
74–87, 99, 101, 104, 105, 110,
111, 116, 130–4, 136, 138, 140,
141, 142, 154, 155, 163, 170, 180,
185, 217, 242–3, 252–3, 266, 267,
271, 282, 300, 315, 317, 320, 327,
328
tribute to James 89–96
Hird, Thomas 2, 83, 85, 86, 101, 181,
244, 245, 267, 271, 277, 322, 327
Hobart 162
holidays in Europe
1995 63, 77–9
1997 76–7
1999 111
Hookes, David 92, 318
Hooper, Colin 205, 267
Howard, John 196
Hunt, Rex 60
Hunt, Sam 272

Ibiza 140–1
Icke, Stephen 103
injuries 89, 97–116, 170, 179, 323
ankle fracture 107
ankle ligament, torn 149
broken foot 108–14, 117–18
broken ribs 40–1, 106, 267
deep vein thrombosis 257–9
eye 265
face and skull fracture 97–102, 261
groin strain 150–7
hamstring 47, 49, 106–7, 107, 108,
128
knee 34–7, 106
major 1993–2004 114–15
medial ligament 40
mental effect of 102–3, 105, 109–10,
115–16, 152–4, 156, 309
punctured lung 41, 58, 106
shin splints 22, 28–9, 106

instinct 2–4, 65, 182, 272, 297–8, 301
International Rules 133, 140, 144–5,
269
Ireland 92, 133, 140, 144–5, 269–70
Italia, Charlie 266

Jackson, Peter 188, 201, 319
Jackson, Phil 227
Jackson, Wayne 168
Jakovich, Glen 103, 289
Jarman, Andrew 39
J.B. Were 286, 288
Jeans, Allan 'Yabbie' 17, 227
Johns, Andrew 141
Johnson, Brad 144
Johnson, Jason 126, 128, 316
Johnson, Mark 126, 251
Jordan, Michael 227, 290, 297
Joyce, Padraic 270
Judd, Chris 208, 219, 303
Judkins, Noel 174, 195

Kangaroos 41, 58, 67, 102, 109, 122,
127, 129, 137, 147–8, 165, 166,
174, 192, 295, 309, 311
Keilor Park 35
Keiwa Valley 15
Kelly, Paul 64
Kennett, Jeff 121, 122, 236
Kernahan, Stephen 'Kicks' 51
Kickett, Dale 166
Kickett, Derek 50, 59
Kilby, John 266
King, Billie Jean 248
King, Steven 133
Koutoufides, Anthony 148, 289
Krakouer, Jimmy 192

Lade, Brendan 264
Lalich, Judd 103
Lane, Tim 104
Langford, Chris 17, 46, 227
Law, Rod 101, 104, 133, 200, 287,
288, 289, 300
tribute to James 215–20
Laycock, Jason 229
leadership 8, 52, 59, 89, 124–5, 128,
155–6, 158, 174–7, 181–2, 196,
221–32, 269
Lee, Brett 294

339

Index